A guide to the
World Bank

JAN 0 9 2012

The World Bank

D0746023

A guide to
The World Bank

THIRD EDITION

THE WORLD BANK
Washington, D.C.

© 2011 The International Bank for Reconstruction and Development / The World Bank
1818 H Street NW
Washington DC 20433
Telephone: 202-473-1000
Internet: www.worldbank.org

1 2 3 4 14 13 12 11

This volume is a product of the staff of the International Bank for Reconstruction and Development / The World Bank. The findings, interpretations, and conclusions expressed in this volume do not necessarily reflect the views of the Executive Directors of The World Bank or the governments they represent.

The World Bank does not guarantee the accuracy of the data included in this work. The boundaries, colors, denominations, and other information shown on any map in this work do not imply any judgement on the part of The World Bank concerning the legal status of any territory or the endorsement or acceptance of such boundaries.

ISBN: 978-0-8213-8545-6
eISBN: 978-0-8213-8657-6
DOI: 10.1596/978-0-8213-8545-6

Library of Congress Cataloging-in-Publication Data
A guide to the World Bank. — 3rd ed.
    p. cm.
Includes bibliographical references and index.
    ISBN 978-0-8213-8545-6 — ISBN 978-0-8213-8657-6 (electronic)
    1. World Bank Group. 2. Developing countries—Economic conditions. 3. Economic assistance. 4. Economic development. I. World Bank.
HG3881.5.W57G853 2011
332.1'532—dc23
                                                                2011023128

Cover design: Bill Pragluski, Critical Stages LLC (http://www.criticalstages.com)
Cover photos (clockwise from lower left): Curt Carnemark, Arne Hoel, Dana Smillie

Interior photos: Curt Carnemark (page xviii); IFC (page xx); Laura McDaniel (page 6); Dana Smillie (page 50); Yuri Mechitov (page 158); Scott Wallace (page 202)

CONTENTS

APPENDIXES

Boxes

Figures

Maps

Tables

PREFACE

Since the second edition of this book was published in 2007, the global landscape has undergone a major transformation. The global economic crisis of 2008–09—arguably the deepest and most complex since the Great Depression—stalled or reversed years of hard-won development progress, with millions pushed back into extreme poverty. In 2010 and 2011, the world faced a number of historic development challenges—from natural disasters to food and fuel price spikes, and political upheaval in the Middle East and North Africa. Challenges have become increasingly global, and the rise of emerging economies will inevitably have major implications for the global economic and geopolitical landscape. This will require robust multilateral institutions that can legitimately convene all powers, old and new, to reach effective solutions.

As a premier development institution with global membership, the World Bank Group (WBG)—with its experience, financial resources, convening power, legitimacy, global reach, and knowledge and expertise—is well placed to help developing countries both adapt to this new landscape and take advantage of emerging opportunities. To step up to the challenge, we are advancing multiple reforms to promote inclusiveness, innovation, efficiency, effectiveness, and accountability. We are expanding cooperation with the UN, the IMF, other multilateral development banks, donors, civil society, the private sector, and foundations. But the effort must go further to realize a World Bank Group that represents the international economic realities of the 21st century, recognizes the role and responsibility of growing stakeholders, and provides a larger voice for developing countries.

This new, updated third edition of *A Guide to the World Bank* provides readers with an accessible and straightforward overview of the Bank Group's history, organization, mission, and work. It highlights the numerous activities and organizational challenges faced by the institution, and explains how the Bank Group is reforming itself to meet the needs of a multipolar world. The book then chronicles the Bank Group's work in such areas as climate change, financial and food crises, conflict prevention and fragile states, combating corruption, and education. For those wishing to delve further into areas of particular interest, the book guides readers to sources containing more detailed information, including websites, electronic products, and even mobile phone applications. For the first time, this *Guide* is published with a companion *World Bank at a Glance* app (http://bit.ly/WBguideapp), which puts a wealth of information about the Bank Group at readers' fingertips while also keeping them up-to-date on Bank Group activities.

My hope is that this third edition of the *Guide* continues to help build a better understanding of the World Bank Group and its important work—to assist developing countries and their people to overcome poverty and establish a sustainable path for development.

Caroline Anstey
Vice President
External Affairs
The World Bank

ACKNOWLEDGMENTS

The first edition of *A Guide to the World Bank*—published in 2003—was conceived and edited by Paul McClure. The second edition, published in 2007, and this third edition were both produced by a team led by Stephen McGroarty.

The book benefited greatly from the advice and feedback of the following people: Issam Abousleiman, Muhamad Al Arif, Kaisa Antikainen, Ana Elisa Luna Barros, Jose Manuel Bassat, Geetanjali Chopra, Valery Ciancio, Benjamin Crow, Kristen Day, Cevdet Denizer, Heather Dittbrenner, Dina Elnaggar, Richard Fix, Melissa Fossberg, Angela Furtado, Hannah George, Nadine Ghannam, Ashfaque Hai, Declan Heery, Farah Hussain, Colleen Keenan, Kamran Khan, Jung Lim Kim, Andrew Kircher, Michael McDowell, Brenda Mejia, Xenia Morales, Roger Morier, Miguel Navarro-Martin, Frauke Nitschke, Greta Ober-Beauchesne, Tara O'Connell, Francine Peltz, Merrell Tuck-Primdahl, Joseph Rebello, Giorgio Saavedra, Caroline Sadacca, Mallory Lee Saleson, Estela T. Sanidad, Adam Shayne, Jeannette Marie Smith, Peter Stephens, Miriam Van Dyck, Zing Venner, Venu Venugopal, Alejandra Viveros, and Alejandro Yepes.

A special thanks to Dana Lane who was indispensable in researching, fact checking, and writing. Many people in the World Bank's Office of the Publisher contributed to or provided assistance to this project. Cindy Fisher expertly managed the design and editorial production of the book, and Denise Bergeron adeptly coordinated the printing process. Thanks also go to Jose de Buerba and Mario Trubiano for the book's promotion and marketing and to Carlos Rossel and Santiago Pombo for their continuous support and guidance.

ABBREVIATIONS

AIDS	acquired immune deficiency syndrome
AMC	Asset Management Company
ARD	Agriculture and Rural Development (Department)
CAS	Country Assistance Strategy
CASM	Community and Small-Scale Mining (Initiative)
CFO	chief financial officer
CGAP	Consultative Group to Assist the Poor
CGIAR	Consultative Group on International Agricultural Research
CIEPLAN	Corporación de Investigaciones Económicas para Latinoamérica, or Corporation for Latin American Studies
CommDev	Sustainable Community Development Fund
CommNet	Communications Network
CSO	civil society organization
DAC	Development Assistance Committee (OECD)
DEC	Development Economics (Vice Presidency)
DIFC	Dubai International Financial Centre
DIME	Development Impact Evaluation (Initiative)
DRF	Debt Reduction Facility
EFA	Education for All
EITI	Extractive Industries Transparency Initiative
ESMAP	Energy Sector Management Assistance Program
FDI	foreign direct investment
FPD	Financial and Private Sector Development (Vice Presidency)
GAFSP	Global Agriculture and Food Security Program
GAVI	formerly Global Alliance for Vaccines and Immunisation
GDLN	Global Development Learning Network
GEF	Global Environment Facility
GGFR	Global Gas Flaring Reduction (Partnership)
GICT	Global Information and Communications Technology (Division)
GRPPs	global and regional partnership programs
HIPC	Heavily Indebted Poor Countries (Initiative)
HIV	human immunodeficiency virus
HR	human resources

IBRD	International Bank for Reconstruction and Development
ICSID	International Centre for Settlement of Investment Disputes
ICT	information and communication technologies
IDA	International Development Association
IDA16	16th replenishment of IDA
IEG	Independent Evaluation Group
IFC	International Finance Corporation
IFCOE	Infrastructure Finance Centre of Excellence
IJS	Internal Justice System
IMF	International Monetary Fund
IMT	Information Management and Technology (Unit)
INT	World Bank Integrity Vice Presidency
JPPAD	Junior Professionals Program for Afro-Descendants
KNA	Knowledge Networks Agency
MDG	Millennium Development Goal
MDRI	Multilateral Debt Relief Initiative
MIGA	Multilateral Investment Guarantee Agency
NGO	nongovernmental organization
OECD	Organisation for Economic Co-operation and Development
OPCS	Operations Policy and Country Services
P4R	Program for Results
PIC	Public Information Center
PPAR	Project Performance Assessment Report
PPIAF	Public-Private Infrastructure Advisory Facility
PREM	Poverty Reduction and Economic Management (Network)
PRI	political risk insurance
PRSP	Poverty Reduction Strategy Paper
SA	Staff Association
SDN	Sustainable Development Network
SMEs	small and medium enterprises
StAR	Stolen Assets Recovery (Initiative)
UN	United Nations
UNAIDS	Joint United Nations Programme on HIV/AIDS
UNDG	United Nations Development Group
VPU	vice presidential unit

WAVES	Wealth Accounting and Valuation of Ecosystem Services
WBI	World Bank Institute
Y2Y	Youth to Youth (Community)

All dollar amounts are U.S. dollars unless otherwise indicated.

The livelihoods of the poorest are critically associated
with access to water services. Properly managed
water resources are a critical component of
growth, poverty reduction, and equity.

The World Bank Group Mission

To fight poverty with passion and professionalism for lasting results. To help people help themselves and their environment by providing resources, sharing knowledge, building capacity, and forging partnerships in the public and private sectors.

International Bank for Reconstruction and Development
International Development Association

To promote sustainable private sector investment in developing countries, helping to reduce poverty and improve people's lives.

International Finance Corporation

To promote foreign direct investment into developing countries to help support economic growth, reduce poverty, and improve people's lives.

Multilateral Investment Guarantee Agency

More than 1.4 billion people worldwide lack access to
electricity. The World Bank supports developing-
country efforts to provide cleaner, more
stable energy sources to households
and businesses.

Introduction

Conceived in 1944 to reconstruct war-torn Europe, the World Bank Group has evolved into one of the world's largest sources of development assistance, with a mission of fighting poverty with passion by helping people help themselves.

New World, New World Bank Group

Much of the news from the developing world is good:

- During the past 40 years, life expectancy has risen by 20 years—about as much as was achieved in all of human history before the mid-20th century.
- During the past 30 years, adult illiteracy has been nearly halved to 25 percent.
- During the past 20 years, the absolute number of people living on less than $1.25 a day has begun to fall for the first time, even as the world's population has grown by 1.6 billion people.
- During the past decade, growth in the developing world has outpaced that in developed countries, helping to provide the jobs and boost revenues that poor countries' governments need to provide essential services.

Moreover, in our fast-evolving, multipolar world economy, some developing countries have become economic powers, and others are rapidly becoming additional poles of growth. These countries have increasingly provided the demand that is driving the global economy. As important importers of capital goods and services, developing countries have accounted for more than half the increase in world import demand since 2000. Millions of people in transition and developing countries are joining the world economy as their incomes and living standards rise.

The developing world, however, confronts new and difficult challenges. A devastating global economic crisis has interrupted growth and slowed the rate of poverty reduction, and recovery remains uncertain and uneven; pandemics have threatened the lives of millions; food insecurity has undermined the well-being of many; armed struggle has destroyed lives and dimmed the future in conflict-affected regions; and the need to mitigate the effects of climate change—particularly in developing countries—is more urgent than ever before.

In the face of such obstacles, the challenge of reducing poverty is both enormous and complex. But with the world's population growing by an estimated 2.5 billion people over the next 40 years, and with the vast majority

Box 1 The Five World Bank Group Institutions

The World Bank Group consists of the following five institutions:

- *The International Bank for Reconstruction and Development (IBRD)* lends to governments of middle-income and creditworthy low-income countries.

- *The International Development Association (IDA)* provides interest-free loans—called *credits*—and grants to governments of the poorest countries.

- *The International Finance Corporation (IFC)* provides loans, equity, and technical assistance to stimulate private sector investment in developing countries.

- *The Multilateral Investment Guarantee Agency (MIGA)* provides guarantees against losses caused by noncommercial risks to investors in developing countries.

- *The International Centre for Settlement of Investment Disputes (ICSID)* provides international facilities for conciliation and arbitration of investment disputes.

Even though the World Bank Group consists of five institutions, only IBRD and IDA constitute the World Bank.

Box 2 Millennium Development Goals

- Eradicate extreme poverty and hunger
- Achieve universal primary education
- Promote gender equality and empower women
- Reduce child mortality
- Improve maternal health
- Combat HIV/AIDS, malaria, and other diseases
- Ensure environmental sustainability
- Develop a global partnership for development

---

of those people residing in developing countries, it is a challenge that must be met.

Role of the World Bank Group

The World Bank Group, also referred to as the *Bank Group*, is one of the world's largest sources of funding and knowledge for developing countries. Its main focus is on working with the poorest people and the poorest countries. Through its five institutions (box 1), the Bank Group uses financial resources and its extensive experience to partner with developing countries to reduce poverty, increase economic growth, and improve the quality of life.

The Bank Group is managed by its member countries (borrowers, lenders, and donors), whose representatives maintain offices at the Bank Group's headquarters in Washington, D.C. Many developing countries use Bank Group assistance ranging from loans and grants to technical assistance and policy advice. The Bank Group works in partnership with a wide range of actors, including government agencies, civil society organizations, other aid agencies, and the private sector.

The Millennium Development Goals

Along with other development institutions, in 2000 the Bank endorsed the Millennium Development Goals (MDGs), which commit the international community to promoting human development as the key to sustaining social and economic progress in all countries. These goals, which call for eliminating poverty and achieving sustained development (box 2), are used to set the Bank Group's priorities and provide targets and yardsticks for measuring results. They are the Bank Group's road map for development (see chapter 2 for more detail).

With the deadline for the MDGs fast approaching, a new cloud of uncertainty shadows developing countries' efforts. The world experienced a historic financial and economic crisis, which began in the richest economies of the world and threatened to slow progress in the poorest. Lessons from past crises show that the harm to human development during bad times cuts far deeper than the gains during upswings. Under these conditions, protecting the gains to date and pressing ahead with actions for further progress to achieve the MDGs are especially important.

The World Bank Group has stepped up to the challenge posed by the crisis. It has taken numerous initiatives to limit the slide in global economic growth and avert the collapse of the banking and private sectors in many countries. The Bank Group has also provided financing to governments and to the private sector, thereby softening the impact of the crisis on the poor. Efforts to strengthen social safety nets have also been scaled up.

World Bank Reforms

Although its fundamental mission of reducing poverty and improving lives has not changed, the Bank is adjusting its approaches and policies in response to the needs of developing countries in the new economic context. Rising to the challenges of development now requires institutions that are not only close to the people in developing countries but also able to mobilize key actors—whether governments, the private sector, or civil society—to address global threats together. It requires institutions that are innovative, adaptable, and able to seize new opportunities. To step up to the challenge, the Bank Group is sharpening its focus on strategic priorities, reforming its business model, and improving its governance.

These reforms, which promote inclusiveness, innovation, efficiency, effectiveness, and accountability, fall into five areas:

- *Reforming the lending model.* The Bank is modernizing its financial services and lending model to provide more tailored responses to borrowers' needs. The approach calls for closer attention to results and for streamlined processes, improved supervision, and higher-risk investments.
- *Increasing voice and participation.* The Bank is seeking to elevate the influence and representation of developing and transition countries in the Bank Group, with an additional seat on the Board of Executive Directors for Sub-Saharan Africa and an increase in the voting power of developing countries.

- *Promoting accountability and good governance.* Governance and anticorruption are key concerns of Bank operations across sectors and countries. The Bank's focus on governance and anticorruption is based on the mandate to reduce poverty: a capable and accountable state creates opportunities for the poor.
- *Increasing transparency, accountability, and access to information.* The Bank's Access to Information Policy offers opportunities for the Bank to share its global knowledge and experience with a wide audience and to enhance the quality of its operations by providing more information about projects and programs than ever before.
- *Modernizing the organization.* The Bank is undergoing a series of reforms to make it a better development partner. First, it is modernizing its lending and knowledge products and services to better serve its clients and better support their efforts to reduce poverty. Second, the Bank is improving the way the institution shares and accesses knowledge and expertise from inside and outside the institution. Third, it is modernizing the processes and systems underpinning the Bank's work.

For more information on World Bank reforms, visit http://www.worldbank. org/worldbankreform/.

Purpose of the Guide

This guide introduces the reader to the conceptual work of the World Bank Group. Its goal is to serve as a starting point for more in-depth inquiries into subjects of particular interest. It provides a glimpse into the wide array of activities in which the Bank Group institutions are involved, and it directs the reader toward other resources and websites that have more detailed information.

The following chapters explain how the World Bank Group is organized, how it operates, and how its work focuses on countries, regions, and specific topics in development. Appendixes provide further information on Bank Group contacts, on the organization's history, and on country membership and voting shares in the institutions.

We welcome comments on this publication as well as on the many projects and activities of the Bank Group institutions. To provide comments, write us at books@worldbank.org.

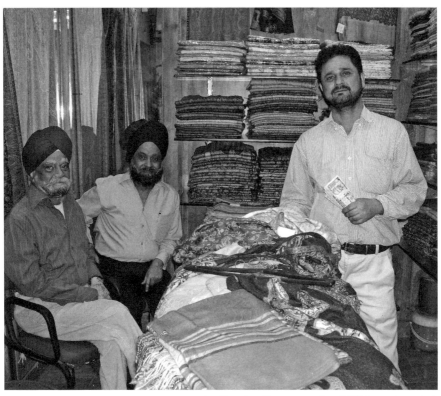

Small and medium enterprises (SMEs) are the growth
engines of developing economies. IFC fosters SME
development through investments in financial
institutions that provide financing to SMEs.

1 How the World Bank Group Is Organized

This chapter explains how the World Bank Group is governed and how it is organized to do its work. It provides detailed information on the five World Bank Group institutions and other major organizational units. The final section explains the World Bank Group's relationship with the International Monetary Fund and the United Nations.

Governance of the World Bank Group

Each of the five institutions of the World Bank Group has its own Articles of Agreement or an equivalent founding document. These documents legally define the institution's purpose, organization, and operations, including the mechanisms by which it is owned and governed. By signing these documents and meeting the requirements set forth in them, a country can become a member of the Bank Group institutions.

Ownership by Member Countries

Each Bank Group institution is owned by its member countries (which are its shareholders). The number of member countries varies by institution, from 187 in the International Bank for Reconstruction and Development (IBRD) to 146 in the International Centre for Settlement of Investment Disputes (ICSID), as of April 2011. Chapter 3 explains the requirements for membership and the country classifications that the Bank Group uses. In practice, member countries govern the Bank Group through its institutions' Boards of Governors and the Boards of Directors. These bodies make all major policy decisions for the organization (figure 1.1).

Boards of Governors

The World Bank Group operates under the authority of its Boards of Governors. Each of the member countries of the Bank Group institutions

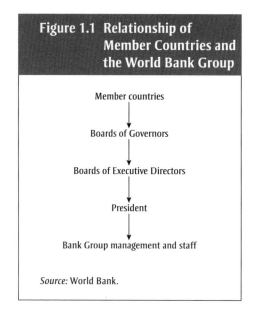

Figure 1.1 Relationship of Member Countries and the World Bank Group

Member countries

↓

Boards of Governors

↓

Boards of Executive Directors

↓

President

↓

Bank Group management and staff

Source: World Bank.

appoints a governor and an alternate governor, who are usually government officials at the ministerial level or the head of the country's central bank. If a member of IBRD is also a member of the International Development Association (IDA) or International Finance Corporation (IFC), the appointed governor and alternate governor serve ex officio on the IDA and IFC Boards of Governors. Their term of office is five years, and it may be renewed.

Multilateral Investment Guarantee Agency (MIGA) governors are appointed separately to its Council of Governors. ICSID has an Administrative Council rather than a Board of Governors. Unless a government makes a contrary designation, its appointed governor for IBRD sits ex officio on ICSID's Administrative Council.

The governors admit or suspend members, review financial statements and budgets, make formal arrangements to cooperate with other international organizations, and exercise other powers that they have not delegated. Once a year, the Boards of Governors of the Bank Group (including ICSID's Administrative Council) and the International Monetary Fund (IMF) meet in a joint session known as the *Annual Meetings* (more information on these meetings appears in the final section of this chapter). Because the governors meet only annually, they delegate many specific duties to the executive directors.

Boards of Directors

General operations of IBRD are delegated to a smaller group of representatives, the Board of Executive Directors. These same individuals serve ex officio on IDA's Board of Executive Directors and on IFC's Board of Directors under the Articles of Agreement for those two institutions. Members of MIGA's Board of Directors are elected separately, but it is customary for the directors of MIGA to be the same individuals as the executive directors of IBRD. Unlike the other four institutions, ICSID does not have a board.

The president of the Bank Group serves as the chair of all four boards (and as the chair of ICSID's Administrative Council), but he or she has no voting power.

IBRD has 25 executive directors. The five largest shareholders—the United States, Japan, Germany, France, and the United Kingdom—each appoint one executive director. The other countries are grouped into constituencies, each of which elects an executive director as its representative.

The members themselves decide how they will be grouped. Some countries—China, the Russian Federation, and Saudi Arabia—form single-country constituencies. Multicountry constituencies more or less represent geographic regions, with some political and cultural factors determining exactly how they are constituted.

The executive directors are based at Bank Group headquarters in Washington, D.C. They are responsible for making policy decisions affecting the Bank Group's operations and for approving all lending proposals made by the president. The executive directors function in continuous session and meet as often as Bank Group business requires, although their regular meetings occur twice a week. Each executive director also serves on one or more standing committees: the Audit Committee, the Budget Committee, the Committee on Development Effectiveness, Human Resources, and the Committee on Governance and Executive Directors' Administrative Matters.

The boards normally make decisions by consensus; however, the relative voting power of individual executive directors is based on the shares held by the countries they represent (figure 1.2). For more on the constituencies, voting power, and elections of the executive directors, see appendix E.

World Bank Group President and Managing Directors

The World Bank Group president is selected by the executive directors. The president serves a term of five years, which may be renewed. There is no mandatory retirement age. In addition to chairing the meetings of the Boards of Directors, the president is responsible for the overall management of the Bank.

The executive vice presidents of IFC and MIGA report directly to the World Bank Group president, and as mentioned previously, the president serves as chair of ICSID's Administrative Council. (ICSID operates as a secretariat whose secretary-general is selected by the Administrative Council every six years.) Within IBRD and IDA, most organizational units report to the president and, through the president, to the executive directors. The

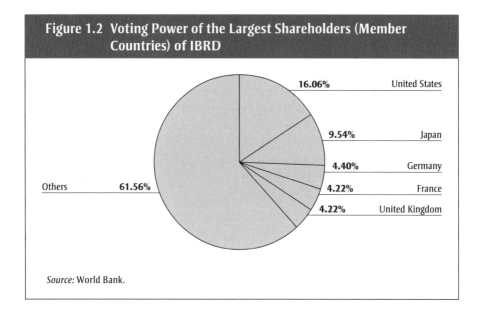

Figure 1.2 Voting Power of the Largest Shareholders (Member Countries) of IBRD

16.06% United States

9.54% Japan

4.40% Germany

4.22% France

4.22% United Kingdom

Others 61.56%

Source: World Bank.

two exceptions are the Independent Evaluation Group and the Inspection Panel, which report directly to the executive directors. In addition, the president delegates some of his or her oversight responsibility to three managing directors, each of whom oversees several organizational units.

For more information about the World Bank Group president, see box 1.1 and visit http://www.worldbank.org/president/. For information about previous presidents of the Bank Group, go to http://www.worldbank.org/archives/ and click "History." See also appendix C.

The Five World Bank Group Institutions

Although the institutions that make up the World Bank Group specialize in different aspects of development, they work collaboratively toward the overarching goal of poverty reduction. The terms *World Bank* and *Bank* refer only to IBRD and IDA, whereas the terms *World Bank Group* and *Bank Group* include all five institutions (box 1.2).

The World Bank: IBRD and IDA

Through its loans, risk management, and other financial services; policy advice; and technical assistance, the World Bank supports a broad range of programs aimed at reducing poverty and improving living standards

Box 1.1 World Bank Group President Robert B. Zoellick

 Robert B. Zoellick, a U.S. national, is the World Bank Group's 11th president. Before joining the Bank Group, Mr. Zoellick served as international Vice Chairman of the Goldman Sachs Group and as Managing Director and Chairman of Goldman Sachs's Board of International Advisors. Previously, he served as Deputy Secretary of the U.S. State Department and was the 13th U.S. Trade Representative in the U.S. cabinet.

Mr. Zoellick has also served as Deputy Assistant Secretary for financial institutions policy and Counselor to the Secretary at the U.S. Treasury Department. He was also Undersecretary of State for Economic and Agricultural Affairs at the U.S. State Department. In the private sector, Mr. Zoellick was Executive Vice President of Fannie Mae, the large U.S. housing finance corporation.

Mr. Zoellick graduated Phi Beta Kappa from Swarthmore College in 1975. He earned a JD magna cum laude from the Harvard Law School and an MPP from the Harvard Kennedy School of Government in 1981.

Box 1.2 Origin of the Term *World Bank*

The term *World Bank* was first used in reference to IBRD in an article in the *Economist* on July 22, 1944, in a report on the Bretton Woods Conference. The first meeting of the Boards of Governors of IBRD and the IMF, which was held in Savannah, Georgia, in March 1946, was officially called the "World Fund and Bank Inaugural Meeting," and several news accounts of this conference, including one in the *Washington Post*, used the term World Bank. What began as a nickname became official shorthand for IBRD and IDA in 1975.

in the developing world. It divides its work between IBRD, which works with middle-income and creditworthy poorer countries, and IDA, which focuses exclusively on the world's poorest countries. Developing countries use IBRD's and IDA's financial resources, skilled staff members, and extensive knowledge base to achieve stable, sustainable, and equitable growth.

IBRD and IDA share staff and headquarters, report to the same senior management, and use the same standards when evaluating projects. Some countries borrow from both institutions. For all its clients, the Bank emphasizes

- investing in people, particularly through basic health and education;
- focusing on social development, inclusion, governance, and institution building as key elements of poverty reduction;
- strengthening governments' ability to deliver quality services efficiently and transparently;
- protecting the environment;
- supporting and encouraging private business development; and
- promoting reforms to create a stable macroeconomic environment conducive to investment and long-term planning.

Bank programs—which give high priority to sustainable social and human development and to strengthened economic management—place an emphasis on inclusion, governance, and institution building. In addition, within the international community, the Bank has helped build consensus around the idea that developing countries must take the lead in creating their own strategies for poverty reduction. It also plays a key role in collaborating with countries to implement the Millennium Development Goals (MDGs), which the United Nations (UN) and the broader international community seek to achieve by 2015.

In conjunction with the International Finance Corporation, the Bank is also working with its member countries to strengthen and sustain the fundamental conditions for attracting and retaining private investment. With Bank support—both lending and advice—governments are reforming their overall economies and strengthening their financial systems. Investments in human resources, infrastructure, and environmental protection also help enhance the attractiveness and productivity of private investment.

The International Bank for Reconstruction and Development

IBRD is the original institution of the World Bank Group. When it was established in 1944 (box 1.3), its first task was to help Europe recover from World War II.

Box 1.3 IBRD Basic Facts

Year established: 1944
Number of member countries: 187
Cumulative lending: $523.6 billion[a]
Fiscal 2010 lending: $44.2 billion for 164
operations in 42 countries
Web: http://www.worldbank.org/

Source: World Bank Annual Report 2010.
a. Effective fiscal 2005, includes guarantees.

Today, IBRD plays an important role in improving living standards by providing its borrowing member countries—middle-income and creditworthy poorer countries—with loans, guarantees, risk management, and other financial services, as well as analytical and advisory services. It provides these client countries with risk management tools and access to capital on favorable terms in larger volumes, with longer maturities, and in a more sustainable manner than the market in several important ways:

- By supporting long-term human and social development needs that private creditors do not finance
- By preserving borrowers' financial strength through support during crisis periods, which is when poor people are most adversely affected
- By using the leverage of financing to promote key policy and institutional reforms (such as safety net or anticorruption reforms)
- By creating a favorable investment climate to catalyze the provision of private capital
- By providing financial support (in the form of grants made available from IBRD's net income) in areas critical to the well-being of poor people in all countries

IBRD is structured like a cooperative that is owned and operated for the benefit of its 187 member countries. Shareholders of IBRD are sovereign governments, and its borrowing members, through their representatives on the Board of Executive Directors, have a voice in setting its policies and approving each project and loan. IBRD finances its activities primarily by issuing AAA-rated bonds to institutional and retail investors in global capital markets. IBRD's financial objective is not to maximize profit, but to earn adequate income to ensure its financial strength and to sustain its development activities. Although IBRD earns a small margin on this lending, the greater proportion of its income comes from investing its own capital. This capital consists of reserves built up over the years and money paid in from the Bank's 187 member country shareholders. IBRD's income also pays for World Bank operating expenses and has contributed to IDA, debt relief, and other development causes.

IBRD products and services

IBRD's loans, guarantees, risk management products, and analytic and advisory services may be packaged together or offered as stand-alone services. Also, unlike commercial banks, IBRD is driven by development impact rather than by profit maximization. IBRD borrowers are typically middle-income countries that have some access to private capital markets. Some countries eligible for IDA lending because of low per capita incomes are also eligible for some IBRD borrowing because of their creditworthiness. These countries are known as "blend" borrowers (table 1.1). Hundreds of millions of the developing world's poor, defined as those who live on less than $2 a day, live not in the world's very poorest countries, but in middle-income countries, which are defined as those with an annual gross national income per capita between $996 and $12,195 (as of April 2011). (For more on country classifications, see *World Development Indicators*, http://publications.worldbank.org/ecommerce/.)

Countries are considered to have graduated from IBRD borrowing when their per capita income exceeds the level that the Bank classifies as middle income. For more information, including a list of IBRD graduates, see chapter 3 and box 3.2.

Even though IBRD does not maximize profits, it has earned a positive operating income each year since 1948. This income funds development activities and ensures financial strength, enabling low-cost borrowing in capital markets and good terms for borrowing clients. Additional information on IBRD loans appears in chapter 2.

IBRD and the financial crisis

IBRD was able to respond with strength and speed when the 2008–09 financial crisis first hit, and when its clients needed it most. IBRD played a key role in contributing to opportunities to boost global growth and economic recovery in several countries. It delivered record new commitments

Table 1.1 Country Eligibility for Borrowing from the World Bank, as of July 1, 2010

Income group and country	2009 GNI per capita[a]	Income group and country	2009 GNI per capita[a]
COUNTRIES ELIGIBLE FOR IBRD FUNDS ONLY			
Per capita income of more than $6,885			
Korea, Republic of	19,840	Mexico	8,960
Trinidad and Tobago	16,560	Palau	8,940
Croatia	13,810	Turkey	8,730
Equatorial Guinea	12,420	Seychelles	8,480
Poland	12,260	Brazil	8,070
Antigua and Barbuda	12,130	Romania	8,040
Libya	12,020	Lebanon	7,970
Venezuela, RB	10,200	Argentina	7,600
St. Kitts and Nevis	10,150	Gabon	7,370
Chile	9,460	Mauritius	7,240
Uruguay	9,400	Malaysia	7,230
Russian Federation	9,380		
Per capita income of $1,165–$6,885			
Kazakhstan	6,740	Tunisia	3,720
Panama	6,740	China	3,620
Montenegro	6,550	Turkmenistan	3,420
Botswana	6,320	El Salvador	3,370
Costa Rica	6,260	Marshall Islands	3,060
Serbia	5,990	Ukraine	2,800
Bulgaria	5,770	Morocco	2,790
South Africa	5,770	Guatemala	2,630
Belarus	5,540	Syrian Arab Republic	2,410
Jamaica	5,010	Swaziland	2,350
Colombia	4,950	Paraguay	2,280
Iran, Islamic Rep.	4,540	Indonesia	2,230
Dominican Republic	4,530	Micronesia, Fed. Sts.	2,220
Algeria	4,420	Iraq	2,210
Macedonia, FYR	4,400	Egypt, Arab Rep.	2,070
Namibia	4,310	Philippines	1,790
Peru	4,160	Belize	—
Albania	3,950	Suriname	—
Fiji	3,950		
Ecuador	3,940		
Thailand	3,760		
Jordan	3,740		

(continued)

Table 1.1 *continued*

Income group and country	2009 GNI per capita[a]	Income group and country	2009 GNI per capita[a]
COUNTRIES ELIGIBLE FOR A BLEND OF IBRD AND IDA FUNDS[b]			
Per capita income of $1,165–$6,885			
Grenada	5,580	Armenia	3,100
St. Lucia	5,190	Cape Verde	3,010
St. Vincent and the Grenadines	5,130	Georgia	2,530
Dominica	4,900	Bolivia	1,630
Azerbaijan	4,850	Papua New Guinea	1,180
Bosnia and Herzegovina	4,700	India	1,170
Per capita income of $1,165 or less			
Uzbekistan	1,100	Vietnam	1,010
Pakistan	1,020		
Per capita income of $995 or less			
Zimbabwe[c]	—		
COUNTRIES ELIGIBLE FOR IDA FUNDS ONLY[c]			
Per capita income of $1,165–$6,885			
Maldives	3,870	Congo, Rep.	1,830
Angola	3,490	Honduras	1,820
Tonga	3,260	Moldova	1,590
Kosovo	3,200	Mongolia	1,590
Samoa	2,840	Djibouti	1,280
Vanuatu	2,660	Sudan[c]	1,230
Bhutan	2,020	Cameroon	1,170
Sri Lanka	1,990	Guyana	—
Kiribati	1,890	Timor-Leste	—
Per capita income of $1,165 or less			
Nigeria	1,140	Senegal	1,040
São Tomé and Principe	1,140	Lesotho	1,020
Côte d'Ivoire	1,060	Nicaragua	1,010
Yemen, Rep.	1,060		
Per capita income of $995 or less			
Zambia	970	Ghana	700
Mauritania	960	Tajikistan	700
Solomon Islands	920	Mali	680
Lao PDR	880	Cambodia	650
Comoros	870	Chad	620
Kyrgyz Republic	870	Bangladesh	590
Kenya	770	Burkina Faso	510
Benin	750	Guinea-Bissau	510

(continued)

Income group and country	2009 GNI per capita[a]	Income group and country	2009 GNI per capita[a]
Tanzania	500	Ethiopia	330
Rwanda	460	Malawi	280
Uganda	460	Congo, Dem. Rep.	160
Central African Republic	450	Liberia	160
Gambia, The	440	Burundi	150
Mozambique	440	Afghanistan	—
Nepal	440	Madagascar	—
Togo	440	Eritrea	—
Guinea[c]	370	Haiti	—
Niger	340	Myanmar[c]	—
Sierra Leone	340	Somalia[c]	—

Source: World Bank.

Note: On December 22, 2009, Vietnam was reclassified from an IDA-only borrower to blend status. On May 1, 2010, Guinea went from nonaccrual status to IDA. —= not available.

a. World Bank Atlas methodology; 2009 per capita GNI (gross national income, formerly GNP) figures are in U.S. dollars.

b. Countries are eligible for IDA on the basis of (a) relative poverty and (b) lack of creditworthiness. The operational cutoff for IDA eligibility for fiscal 2011 is a 2009 GNI per capita of $1,165 using Atlas methodology. To receive IDA resources, countries must also meet tests of performance. An exception has been made for small island economies. In exceptional circumstances, IDA extends eligibility temporarily to countries that are above the operational cutoff and are undertaking major adjustment efforts but are not creditworthy for IBRD lending.

c. Loans or credits in nonaccrual status as of June 30, 2010. General information on countries with loan or credits in nonaccrual status is available from the Credit Risk Department in Finance.

of almost $33 billion in fiscal 2009, almost tripling the previous year's level, followed by another record $44.2 billion in fiscal 2010, putting it on track to deliver on the commitments it made to the Group of 20 in spring of 2009.

This support includes safety nets for the poor, infrastructure to create jobs and build a foundation for recovery, agriculture to support small farmers, and microfinance to help small and microenterprises.

The International Development Association

After the rebuilding of Europe following World War II, the Bank turned its attention to the newly independent developing countries. It became clear that the poorest developing countries could not afford to borrow capital for development on the terms offered by the Bank; hence, a group of Bank member countries decided to found IDA as an institution that could lend to

Box 1.4 IDA Basic Facts

Year established: 1960
Number of member countries: 170
Cumulative commitments: $221.9 billion[a]
Fiscal 2010 commitments: $14.5 billion for 190 new operations in 66 countries
Web: http://www.worldbank.org/ida/

Source: World Bank Annual Report 2010.
a. Effective fiscal 2005, includes guarantees.

very poor developing nations on easier terms. To imbue IDA with the discipline of a bank, these countries agreed that IDA should be part of the World Bank. IDA began operating in 1960 (box 1.4).

IDA partners with the world's poorest countries to reduce poverty by providing credits and grants. Credits are loans at zero or low interest with a 10-year grace period before repayment of principal begins and with maturities of 20 to 40 years. These credits are often referred to as *concessional lending*. IDA credits help build the human capital, policies, institutions, and physical infrastructure that these countries urgently need to achieve faster, environmentally sustainable growth. IDA-financed operations address primary education, basic health services, clean water and sanitation, environmental safeguards, business climate improvements, infrastructure, and institutional reforms. These projects pave the way toward economic growth, job creation, higher incomes, and better living conditions.

IDA is funded largely by contributions from the governments of its high-income member countries (table 1.2). Representatives of donor countries meet every three years to replenish IDA funds. Since 1960, IDA has lent $222 billion. Annual lending figures have increased steadily and have averaged about $14 billion over the past two years. Additional funds come from World Bank Group transfers and from borrowers' repayments of earlier IDA credits, including voluntary and contractual acceleration of credit repayments from eligible IDA graduates.

Donor contributions to the 16th replenishment of IDA, known as *IDA16*, amounted to $49.3 billion, an 18 percent increase over the previous replenishment. These resources will finance IDA's commitments over the three-year period ending June 30, 2014. This strong outcome was the result of a

Table 1.2 Cumulative IDA Subscriptions and Contributions, as of December 31, 2010

Member	$ millions	Percentage of total
Argentina	69.80	0.03
Australia	3,300.26	1.63
Austria	1,936.65	0.96
Barbados	1.67	0.00
Belgium	3,527.99	1.75
Bosnia and Herzegovina	2.51	0.00
Botswana	1.63	0.00
Brazil	819.24	0.41
Canada	9,027.24	4.47
China	75.31	0.04
Colombia	24.95	0.01
Croatia	5.81	0.00
Cyprus	7.10	0.00
Czech Republic	93.25	0.05
Denmark	3,017.96	1.49
Egypt, Arab Rep.	9.11	0.00
Estonia	4.10	0.00
Finland	1,294.68	0.64
France	14,403.04	7.13
Germany	21,992.23	10.88
Greece	209.25	0.10
Hungary	105.24	0.05
Iceland	49.15	0.02
Ireland	500.65	0.25
Israel	70.95	0.04
Italy	8,621.07	4.27
Japan	40,278.56	19.94
Korea, Rep.	1,179.63	0.58
Kuwait	868.24	0.43
Latvia	0.92	0.00
Luxembourg	219.27	0.11
Macedonia, FYR	1.10	0.00
Mexico	168.39	0.08
Netherlands	7,197.59	3.56
New Zealand	273.22	0.14
Norway	3,186.11	1.58
Oman	1.39	0.00

(continued)

Table 1.2 *continued*

Member	$ millions	Percentage of total
Poland	89.08	0.04
Portugal	289.47	0.14
Russian Federation	407.10	0.20
Saudi Arabia	2,348.52	1.16
Serbia	7.01	0.00
Singapore	60.73	0.03
Slovak Republic	21.72	0.01
Slovenia	29.45	0.01
South Africa	175.58	0.09
Spain	3,164.60	1.57
Sweden	6,325.51	3.13
Switzerland	3,225.41	1.60
Turkey	155.73	0.08
United Arab Emirates	5.58	0.00
United Kingdom	20,058.71	9.93
United States	42,870.14	21.22
Total donors	201,779.60	99.87
Total nondonors	264.91	0.13
Grand Total	**202,044.49**	**100.00**

Source: World Bank.
Note: Numbers may not add up to totals due to rounding.

global coalition of traditional and new donors, borrowing countries, and the World Bank Group, involving the continuing support of traditional donors, IDA graduates agreeing to accelerate their credit repayments to IDA, economically more advanced IDA countries contributing through differentiated borrowing terms, a number of new donors joining, and several existing donors increasing their contributions.

Fifty-two donor countries pledged to contribute to IDA16, including traditional donors and emerging donors. IDA's largest direct contributions continue to come from the Group of Seven and other Organisation for Economic Co-operation and Development (OECD) countries. However, emerging donors play an increasingly important role, with IDA graduates such as China, the Arab Republic of Egypt, the Republic of Korea, the Philippines, and Turkey now joining as donors.

IDA lends to countries that lack the financial ability to borrow from IBRD and that in fiscal year 2011 had an annual per capita income of less than $1,165. Together these countries are home to around 2.5 billion people, half the total population of the developing world. An estimated 1.5 billion people there survive on incomes of $2 or less a day. Blend borrower countries, such as India, Uzbekistan, and Vietnam, are eligible for IDA loans because of their low per capita incomes while also being eligible for IBRD loans because they are financially creditworthy. Seventy-nine countries are currently eligible to borrow from IDA.

IDA eligibility is a transitional arrangement that gives the poorest countries access to substantial resources before they are capable of obtaining the financing they need from commercial markets. As their economies grow, countries graduate from IDA eligibility. The repayments, or *reflows*, that they make on IDA loans are used to help finance new IDA loans to the remaining poor countries. Some 35 countries have graduated from IDA since its founding. Examples include, in addition to the countries listed previously, Albania, Botswana, Chile, Costa Rica, Morocco, and Thailand. Eight countries subsequently "reverse graduated," however, and once again became IDA eligible.

IDA and the financial crisis

In addition to significantly scaling up commitments, IDA allowed for increased front-loading to support countries affected by the 2008–09 financial crisis. Through the IDA Financial Crisis Response Fast-Track Facility (FTF), IDA facilitated the country-level retention of canceled resources due to project restructuring and streamlined procedures. By October 2009, new IDA commitments under the FTF amounted to about US$1.5 billion for operations in 11 countries in Africa, East Asia and the Pacific, and Europe and Central Asia, and accounted for 7 percent of total commitments in FY09. Following calls from the G-20 leaders to consider how IDA could further help low-income countries affected by the crisis, a pilot Crisis Response Window (CRW) was established in December 2009. By March 2011, 75 IDA operations had been approved with at least partial financing by the pilot CRW, and about US$1.45 billion in commitments from CRW resources, with 22 percent being channeled as fast disbursing support.

The International Finance Corporation

IFC's three businesses—investment services, advisory services, and asset management—foster sustainable economic growth in developing countries by financing private sector investment, mobilizing capital in the international financial markets, providing advisory services to businesses and governments, and channeling finance to the poor. IFC helps companies and financial institutions in emerging markets create jobs, generate tax revenues, improve corporate governance and environmental performance, and contribute to their local communities. The goal is to improve lives, especially for the people who most need the benefits of growth.

Since its founding in 1956 (box 1.5), IFC has committed more than $100 billion of its own funds for private sector investment in the developing world, and it has mobilized additional billions from others. With funding support from donors, it has provided more than $1.7 billion in advisory services since 2001.

Direct lending to businesses is the fundamental contrast between IFC and the World Bank: under their Articles of Agreement, IBRD and IDA can lend only to the governments of member countries. IFC was founded specifically to address this limitation of World Bank lending.

IFC provides equity finance, long-term loans, syndicated loans, loan guarantees, structured finance and risk management products, and advisory services to its clients. It seeks to reach businesses in regions and countries that otherwise would have limited access to capital. It provides financing in markets deemed too risky by commercial investors in the absence of IFC participation.

IFC also supports the projects it finances by providing advice to businesses and governments on access to finance, corporate governance, environmental and social sustainability, the investment climate, and infrastructure. Much of the advisory work is funded by IFC's donor partners, through trust funds, or through facilities with a regional or thematic focus.

Box 1.5 IFC Basic Facts

Year established: 1956

Number of member countries: 182

Cumulative active portfolio: $132.3 billion (including syndications and guarantees)

Fiscal 2010 commitments: $12.7 billion for 528 projects in 103 countries

Web: http://www.ifc.org

Source: IFC.

To maximize its effect on development, IFC emphasizes five strategic priorities: strengthening the focus on frontier markets; building long-term client relationships in emerging markets; addressing climate change and ensuring environmental and social sustainability; addressing constraints to private sector growth in infrastructure, health, education, and the food supply chain; and developing domestic financial markets.

Project financing

IFC offers an array of financial products and services to companies in its developing member countries:

- Loans for IFC's account
- Equity investments
- Syndications
- Structured and securitized finance
- Trade finance

- Quasi-equity finance
- Equity and debt funds
- Intermediary services
- Risk management products
- Local currency finance
- Subnational finance

It can also combine its financial products and services with advice tailored to the needs of each client. The bulk of the funding, as well as leadership and management responsibility, however, lies with the private sector owners. IFC charges market rates for its products and does not accept government guarantees. Therefore, it carefully reviews the likelihood of success for each enterprise. To be eligible for IFC financing, projects must be profitable for investors, must benefit the economy of the host country, and must comply with IFC's environmental and social standards.

IFC finances projects in all types of industries and sectors, including manufacturing, infrastructure, tourism, health, education, and financial services. Financial services projects are the largest component of IFC's portfolio, and they cover the full range of financial institutions, including banks, leasing companies, stock markets, credit-rating agencies, and venture capital funds. IFC does not lend directly to microenterprises, to small and medium-size enterprises, or to individual entrepreneurs; however, many of its investment clients are financial intermediaries that on-lend to smaller businesses.

Even though IFC is primarily a financier of private sector projects, it may provide financing for a company with some government ownership, provided there is private sector participation and the venture is run on a commercial basis.

To ensure participation by investors and lenders from the private sector, IFC limits the total amount of own-account debt and equity financing it will provide for any single project. For new projects, the maximum amount is 25 percent of the total estimated project costs or, on an exceptional basis, up to 35 percent for small projects. For expansion projects, IFC may provide up to 50 percent of the total project costs, provided that its investments do not exceed 25 percent of the total capitalization of the project company. IFC investments typically range from $1 million to $100 million.

Resource mobilization

Through its syndicated loan (or *B-loan*) program, IFC offers commercial banks and other financial institutions the chance to lend to IFC-financed projects that they might not otherwise consider. These loans are a key part of IFC's efforts to mobilize additional private sector financing in developing countries and to broaden its development effects. Through this mechanism, financial institutions share fully in the commercial credit risk of projects, whereas IFC remains the lender of record.

Participants in IFC's B-loans share the advantages that IFC derives as a multilateral development institution, including preferred creditor access to foreign exchange in the event of a foreign currency crisis in a particular country. Where applicable, these participant banks are also exempted from the mandatory country-risk provisioning requirements that regulatory authorities may impose if these banks lend directly to projects in developing countries.

Advisory services

IFC supports private sector development both by investing and by providing advisory services that build businesses. Its advisory services are organized into five business lines: access to finance, corporate advice, environmental and social sustainability, investment climate, and infrastructure.

Much of IFC's advisory services work is conducted through facilities managed by IFC but funded through partnerships with donor governments and other multilateral institutions. Some facilities operate within specific regions, and others are concerned with such cross-cutting themes as carbon finance, cleaner technologies, social responsibility, sustainable investing, investment climate, and gender.

Asset management

A new line of business for IFC is asset management, part of a financial intermediation model in development that allows long-term investors to take advantage of growth opportunities in Africa and other less developed regions. The objective is to increase the supply of long-term equity capital to developing and frontier markets in a way that enhances IFC's development goals and generates profits for investors.

The Multilateral Investment Guarantee Agency

By providing political risk insurance (PRI), or guarantees, to investors and lenders against losses caused by noncommercial risks, MIGA promotes foreign direct investment (FDI) in emerging economies and thereby contributes to economic growth, poverty reduction, and the improvement of living standards.

Projects financed by MIGA create jobs; provide water, electricity, and other basic infrastructure; strengthen financial systems; generate tax revenues; transfer skills and technological know-how; and allow countries to tap natural resources in an environmentally sustainable way. MIGA helps investors and lenders by insuring projects against losses related to currency inconvertibility and transfer restriction, expropriation, war and civil disturbance (including terrorism), breach of contract, and failure to honor sovereign financial obligations.

MIGA insures cross-border investments made by investors from a MIGA member country into a developing country that is also a member of MIGA. Its operational strategy, which is designed to attract investors and private insurers into difficult operating environments, focuses on four priorities where it can make the greatest difference:

- *Investments in IDA-eligible countries.* These markets typically have the most need and stand to benefit the most from foreign investment, but they are not well served by the private insurance market.
- *Investments in conflict-affected countries.* Although these countries tend to attract considerable donor goodwill once conflict ends, aid flows eventually decline. With many investors wary of potential risks, PRI is essential to bring in investment.
- *Investments in complex projects, mostly in infrastructure and the extractive industries.* Given that 1.6 billion people still do not have electricity and 2.3 billion depend on traditional biomass fuels, investments in these sectors are critical for the world's poorest nations.

■ *Support for South-South investments.* Investments between developing countries are contributing an ever-increasing proportion of FDI flows. But private insurers or national export credit agencies in these countries, if they exist at all, are often not sufficiently developed and lack the ability and capacity to provide PRI.

Development effects and priorities

Since its creation in 1988, MIGA has provided more than $22 billion in guarantees (PRI) for more than 600 projects in more than 100 developing countries (box 1.6). MIGA is committed to promoting socially, economically, and environmentally sustainable projects that are, above all, developmentally responsible. Projects that MIGA supports have widespread benefits, such as generating jobs and taxes and transferring skills and know-how. In addition, local communities often receive significant secondary benefits through improved infrastructure. Projects encourage similar local investments and spur the growth of local businesses. MIGA ensures that projects are aligned with World Bank Group Country Assistance Strategies and integrate the best environmental, social, and governance practices. (More information about Country Assistance Strategies is provided in chapter 2.)

MIGA helps countries define and implement strategies to promote investment through technical assistance services managed by the Foreign Investment Advisory Services of the World Bank Group. Through this vehicle, MIGA's technical assistance is facilitating new investments in some of the most challenging business environments in the world. As part of its

---

Box 1.6 MIGA Basic Facts

Year established: 1988
Number of member countries: 175
Cumulative guarantees issued: $22.4 billion[a]
Fiscal 2010 guarantees issued: $1.5 billion for 19 projects in developing countries
Web: http://www.miga.org/

Source: MIGA.
a. Includes funds leveraged through the Cooperative Underwriting Program.

mandate to support FDI in emerging markets, MIGA also shares knowledge on political risk and FDI through its website (http://www.miga.org/) and through the Political Risk Insurance Center (http://www.pri-center.com/), which is a free service providing in-depth analysis on political risk environments and management issues affecting 160 countries.

The agency uses its legal services to protect the investments it supports and to remove possible obstacles to future investment by working with governments and investors to resolve any differences.

Added value

MIGA gives private investors the confidence they need to make sustainable investments in developing countries. As part of the World Bank Group, MIGA brings security and credibility to an investment, acting as a potent deterrent against government actions that may adversely affect investments. If disputes do arise, the agency's leverage with host governments frequently enables it to resolve differences to the mutual satisfaction of all parties.

MIGA is a leader in assessing and managing political risks, developing new products and services, and finding innovative ways to meet clients' needs. The agency can also enable complex transactions to go ahead by offering innovative coverage of the nontraditional subsovereign risks. MIGA complements the activities of other investment insurers and works with partners through its coinsurance and reinsurance programs. By doing so, it expands the capacity of the PRI industry and encourages private sector insurers to enter into transactions they would not otherwise have undertaken. MIGA's guarantees can be used on a stand-alone basis or in conjunction with other World Bank instruments, which offer an additional set of benefits.

The International Centre for Settlement of Investment Disputes

ICSID encourages foreign investment by providing international facilities for the conciliation and arbitration of investment disputes, thereby fostering an atmosphere of mutual confidence between states and foreign investors (box 1.7). Many international agreements concerning investment refer to ICSID's arbitration facilities. ICSID also carries out research and publishing in arbitration law and foreign investment law.

ICSID was established under the Convention on the Settlement of Investment Disputes between States and Nationals of Other States. The ICSID convention came into force in 1966. ICSID has an Administrative Council and a Secretariat. The Administrative Council is chaired by the

Box 1.7 ICSID Basic Facts

Year established: 1966
Number of member countries: 147
Total cases registered: 319
Fiscal 2010 cases registered: 27
Web: http://www.worldbank.org/icsid/

Source: ICSID.

World Bank's president and consists of one representative of each state that has ratified the ICSID convention. Annual meetings of the Administrative Council are held in conjunction with the joint Annual Meetings of the Bank Group and the IMF.

Although ICSID is an autonomous international organization, it has close links with the World Bank, and all ICSID members are also members of the Bank. Unless a government makes a contrary designation, its governor for the Bank sits ex officio on ICSID's Administrative Council. The expenses of the ICSID Secretariat are financed through the Bank's budget, although the parties involved bear the costs of individual proceedings.

ICSID provides three types of services:

■ *Facilities for the conciliation and arbitration of disputes between member countries and investors who qualify as nationals of other member countries.* Recourse to ICSID conciliation and arbitration is entirely voluntary; however, after the parties have consented to arbitration under the ICSID convention, neither can unilaterally withdraw its consent. Moreover, the ICSID convention requires all ICSID contracting states, whether they are parties to the dispute or not, to recognize and enforce ICSID arbitral awards.

■ *Certain types of proceedings between states and foreign nationals that fall outside the scope of the ICSID convention.* These proceedings include conciliation and arbitration proceedings when either the state party or the home state of the foreign national is not a member of ICSID. "Additional facility" conciliation and arbitration are also available for cases in which the dispute is not an investment dispute, provided that it relates to a transaction that has features that distinguish it from an ordinary commercial transaction. The additional facility rules further allow ICSID to administer a type of proceeding not provided for in the ICSID convention, namely, fact-finding proceedings, to which any states or foreign nationals may have recourse if they wish to institute an inquiry to examine and report on facts.

■ *Appointment of arbitrators for ad hoc (that is, noninstitutional) arbitration proceedings.* These appointments are most commonly made in the context of arrangements for arbitration under the arbitration rules of the UN Commission on International Trade Law, which are specially designed for ad hoc proceedings.

Organizing Principles within the World Bank Group

This section explains the basic principles on which the World Bank Group organizes its work and lists the major organizational units. Later chapters focus on the substance of what the Bank Group does.

Vice Presidential Units

The vice presidential unit (VPU) is the main organizational unit of the World Bank (IBRD and IDA). Such units are commonly referred to as *vice presidencies.* With a few exceptions that report directly to the president, each of these units reports to a managing director or to the Bank Group's chief financial officer (CFO). In general, each vice presidency corresponds to a world region, a thematic network, or a central function (figure 1.3). The network vice presidencies cut across the regional vice presidencies in the form of a matrix. This arrangement helps ensure an appropriate mix of experience and expertise. Consequently, a staff member may work for a network vice presidency but could be deployed to support work in a specific region or country.

The organizational structures of the other World Bank Group institutions have varying degrees of similarity to the organization of IBRD and IDA, reflecting the unique aspects of each institution's mission. Figures 1.4 and 1.5 show the organization of IFC and MIGA, respectively.

The following subsections provide additional information about the different types of VPUs and other major units within the Bank. For additional information, see http://www.worldbank.org/about/ and click "Organization."

Regional Vice Presidencies and Country Offices

Bank Group institutions have long organized much of their work around major world regions and have carried it out through offices in member

Figure 1.3 World Bank Organizational Structure, 2011

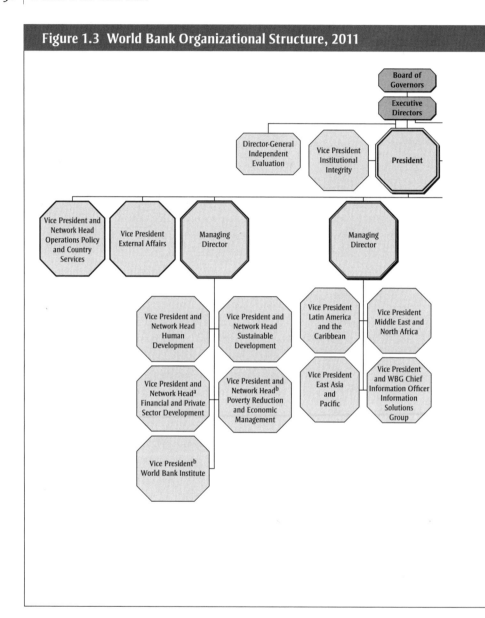

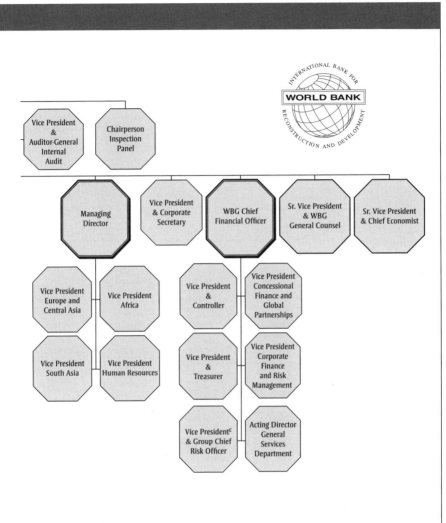

Source: World Bank.
a. Reports to IFC executive vice president on IFC business.
b. Dotted line to senior vice president and chief economist.
c. Dotted line to president.

Figure 1.4 IFC Organizational Structure, 2011

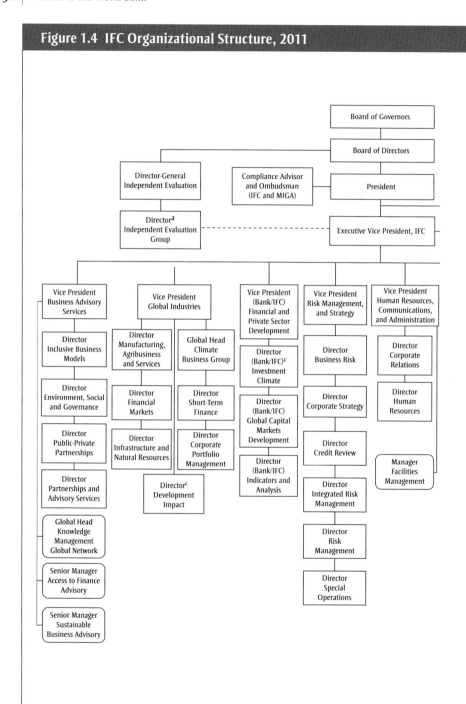

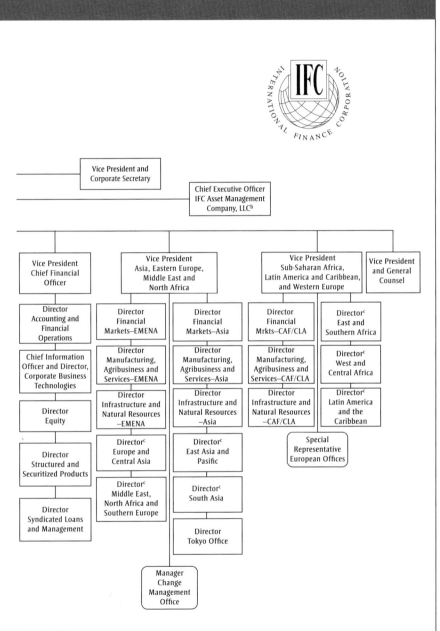

Source: IFC.

a. Reports to director-general, Independent Evaluation, and, for administrative purposes, the executive vice president.

b. The executive vice president is chairperson of the IFC AMC Board of Directors. AMC is a wholly owned subsidiary of IFC.

c. Dotted line to vice president, Business Advisory Services, on advisory business activities.

Figure 1.5 MIGA Organizational Structure, 2011

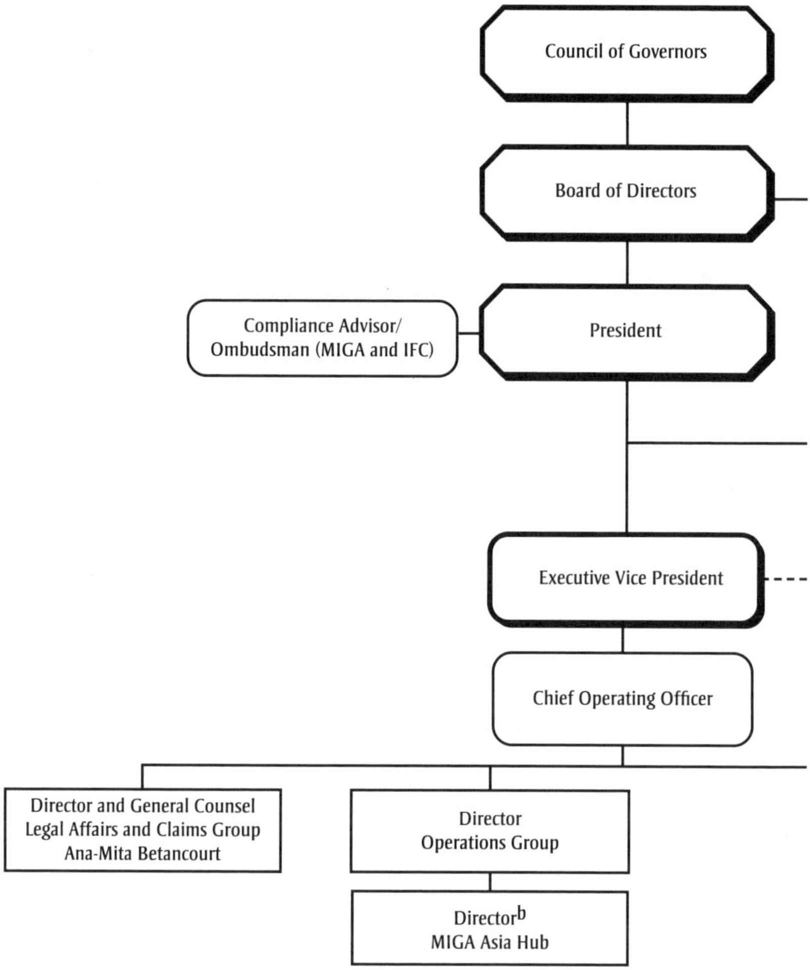

```
                          ┌──────────────────────┐
                          │ Council of Governors │
                          └──────────────────────┘
                                     │
                          ┌──────────────────────┐
                          │  Board of Directors  │
                          └──────────────────────┘
                                     │
┌──────────────────────┐  ┌──────────────────────┐
│ Compliance Advisor/  │──│      President       │
│ Ombudsman (MIGA and  │  └──────────────────────┘
│ IFC)                 │             │
└──────────────────────┘             │
                                     │
                          ┌──────────────────────┐
                          │ Executive Vice       │----
                          │ President            │
                          └──────────────────────┘
                                     │
                          ┌──────────────────────┐
                          │ Chief Operating      │
                          │ Officer              │
                          └──────────────────────┘
                                     │
     ┌───────────────────────────────────────────────┐
┌─────────────────────────┐    ┌──────────────────────┐
│ Director and General    │    │     Director         │
│ Counsel Legal Affairs   │    │  Operations Group    │
│ and Claims Group        │    └──────────────────────┘
│ Ana-Mita Betancourt     │               │
└─────────────────────────┘    ┌──────────────────────┐
                               │    Director[b]        │
                               │   MIGA Asia Hub       │
                               └──────────────────────┘
```

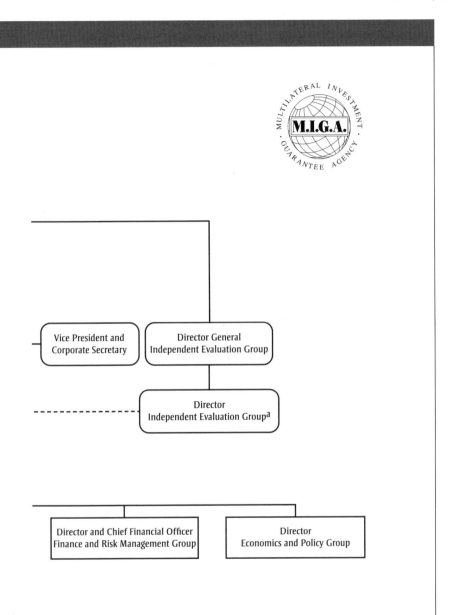

Source: MIGA.
a. Reports operationally to the Independent Evaluation Group and administratively to the executive vice president.
b. Reports operationally to the MIGA Operations Group and administratively to the chief operating officer.

countries. In recent years, decentralization has been a top priority, with the goal being to bring a higher proportion of Bank Group staff members closer to their clients. IBRD and IDA, for example, have relocated two-thirds of their country directors from Bank headquarters in Washington, D.C., to the field since the mid-1990s. The percentage of staff members who work in the field has also increased significantly. Similarly, more than 50 percent of IFC staff members are located in country offices worldwide.

Although all Bank Group institutions share an emphasis on countries and regions and are structured accordingly, precisely how each institution is structured varies. The following paragraphs give a brief overview of these organizational units. Chapter 3 summarizes the substance of Bank Group work in the regions, along with the countries covered.

The World Bank has six regional vice presidencies: Africa, East Asia and the Pacific, Europe and Central Asia, Latin America and the Caribbean, the Middle East and North Africa, and South Asia. The Bank operates offices in more than 100 member countries (see map 1.1). As part of their work, country offices coordinate and partner with member governments, representatives of civil society, and other international donor agencies operating in the country. In addition, many country offices serve as Public Information Centers (PICs) for the World Bank Group.

IFC defines its regions somewhat differently from the Bank. It assigns directors to the following seven regions: Central and Eastern Europe, East Asia and the Pacific, Latin America and the Caribbean, the Middle East and North Africa, South Asia, Southern Europe and Central Asia, and Sub-Saharan Africa. A few countries are assigned to regions different from those they are assigned to within the Bank. The regional departments are grouped into two vice presidencies, one covering Asia and Latin America and the other covering Europe, Africa, and the Middle East. IFC maintains its own network of more than 70 offices in member countries, which in some cases share quarters with a World Bank office.

MIGA has representatives resident in Africa, Asia, and Europe.

Network Vice Presidencies and Sectors

IBRD and IDA have created thematic networks to develop connections among communities of staff members who work in the same fields of development and to link these staff members more effectively with partners outside the Bank. The networks help draw out lessons learned across countries

Map 1.1 Offices of the World Bank Group

The World Bank Group operates out of more than 150 offices worldwide and regions, and they help bring global best practices to bear in meeting country-specific needs.

Each of the thematic networks covers several related sectors of development. In organizational terms, a subunit is generally dedicated to each sector. Each sector has its own board, with representatives drawn from the regions as well as from the network itself. The sector boards are accountable to a network council. Sector boards also identify themes—topics in development that are narrower than the work of the sector itself—on which a small number of staff members will focus, often in partnership with other organizations.

IFC and MIGA are organized along similar lines, with work divided among sectors (known as *industry departments* within IFC) and subsectors. A central function of this arrangement is to create coherent sector strategies for all the Bank Group's work in a given aspect of development. Networks and sectors have also created advisory services or "help desks" to field queries from Bank Group staff members—and, in most cases, from members of the general public—in their areas of expertise.

The sectoral programs correspond broadly to the sections in chapter 4, which provides information on many sector programs within the World Bank and within the corresponding industry departments or other units of IFC. Within the Bank, the thematic networks and the sectors they cover are as follows:

- *Financial and Private Sector Development Network.* Key areas include financial systems; capital markets; financial inclusion; investment climate; competitive industries; and innovation, technology, and entrepreneurship.
- *Human Development Network.* The sectors covered by this network are education; health, nutrition, and population; social protection and labor; children and youth; HIV/AIDS; and development dialogue.
- *Operations Policy and Country Services.* The sectors are country services, fragile and conflict situations, operational services, results and delivery management, procurement, financial management, safeguards, investment lending, development policy operations, guarantees, aid effectiveness, and technical assistance.
- *Poverty Reduction and Economic Management (PREM) Network.* The PREM Network sectors are poverty reduction, economic policy and debt, gender and development, and public sector governance.
- *Sustainable Development Network.* The sectors covered by this network are water and sanitation; energy; environment; agriculture and rural development; urban development; transport; infrastructure; information

and communication technologies; social development; and oil, gas, mining, and chemicals.

IFC industry departments and subsectors include the following:

- *Agribusiness.* The subsectors include animal production, aquaculture, beverages, dairy, fats and oils, fruits and vegetables, grains, and processed food, among others.
- *Global Financial Markets.* The subsectors include advisory services, carbon finance, consumer finance, sustainability and climate change finance, global trade liquidity, housing finance, insurance, Islamic finance, leasing, microfinance, small and medium-size enterprise banking, and trade finance.
- *Global Manufacturing and Services.* The subsectors include construction materials; energy-efficient machinery; forest products; life sciences; tourism, retail, and property development; fibers; and electronics, machinery, and appliances.
- *Health and Education.* The subsectors for health are facilities, pharmaceuticals, e-health, insurance, ancillary services, and education and training. The subsectors for education are primary and secondary education, tertiary education, and e-learning.
- *Infrastructure.* The subsectors are airlines, airports, buses, logistics, ports, port services, power generation, railways, shipping, toll services, and water and gas.
- *Private Equity and Investment Funds.* The department selects and structures new funds, leverages and shares the experience gained from its portfolio, and adapts best industry practices to the constraints of the different markets in which it operates.

In addition, the Global Information and Communication Technologies Department; the Oil, Gas, Mining, and Chemicals Department; and the Subnational Finance Department are joint World Bank–IFC departments. Sectors within MIGA include the following:

- Agribusiness, Manufacturing, and Services
- Banking and Financial Markets
- Infrastructure
- Oil, Gas, and Mining

Other organizational units have adopted certain features of a network. They include the Information Solutions Network, which comprises all staff members working in the field of information technology; the Communications Network (CommNet), an association of professionals across Bank Group headquarters and country offices who handle communications, issues management, and constituency relations; and the Administrative and Client Support Network, which comprises all staff members in office support positions.

Other Major World Bank Group Units and Activities

The rest of this section describes some of the other major units of the World Bank Group. These units may be VPUs, offices, or departments. In some cases, a single unit handles particular functions for all Bank Group organizations; in other cases, each organization has separate units that perform the same functions. This list is not comprehensive. For more information about World Bank Group organizational units, go to the institutions' websites: http://www.worldbank.org/about/ (click on "Organization"), http://www.ifc.org/, http://www.miga.org/, and http://www.worldbank.org/icsid/.

Corporate Secretariat

This unit supports the Boards of Governors and Executive Directors of the World Bank Group in carrying out their fiduciary and governance responsibilities. The Corporate Secretariat maintains relations across all the World Bank Group institutions (IBRD, IDA, IFC, MIGA, and ICSID) and serves as the key interlocutor among the Boards of Governors, the Boards of Directors, the president and senior management, operational management, and staff.

Development Economics

The World Bank's chief economist and senior vice president heads this main research and knowledge-generation VPU. Development Economics (known as DEC) provides data, analyses of macroeconomic and development prospects, research findings, analytical tools, and policy advice in support of Bank operations, as well as advice to clients. More information on Bank Group research and data is presented in chapter 2. DEC produces the annual *World Development Report*, prepared each year by a team comprising Bank staff members and experts from outside the Bank Group.

Ethics and Business Conduct

The Office of Ethics and Business Conduct promotes the development and application of high ethical standards by staff members in the performance of their duties. The office has four strategic business lines to ensure that staff members are aware of and uphold their ethical and business conduct obligations to the Bank Group. Those obligations include providing training, outreach, and communication on business conduct; managing programs to promote transparency and trust, including conflict of interest and financial disclosure; responding to and investigating certain allegations of staff misconduct; and tracking trends and providing insights to senior management. The office is accessible to all staff members, their families, and World Bank Group clients and vendors. It can be contacted anonymously through the Ethics HelpLine (ethics_helpline@worldbank.org) anytime, anywhere.

The office publishes the World Bank Group Code of Conduct and an annual report with aggregate data and generic descriptions of cases. To ensure the independence of the office's activities, the chief ethics officer reports directly to the president of the World Bank Group.

External Affairs

The External Affairs Vice Presidency at the World Bank manages strategic communications, issues management, and constituency relations; relations with the public, the media and other organizations, governments of donor countries, and the local Washington, D.C., community; arranges speaking engagements for Bank representatives; produces and disseminates publications; coordinates the Bank's worldwide network of PICs; and maintains the Bank's external website. Its overall mandate is to increase understanding and support for the Bank Group's mission at both the global and the country levels and to leverage the Bank Group's development impact through effective communications, representation, and issues management.

IFC and MIGA also maintain corporate relations functions.

Financial Management

The Bank Group's CFO is responsible for the finance and risk management functions for the World Bank Group. Key responsibilities include setting sound financial risk management policies; overseeing financial reporting, accounting, and related financial control functions; representing the Bank

Group on financial reporting, accounting, and external auditing matters; ensuring the overall integrity of financial transactions; effectively managing corporate resources; and mobilizing and managing concessional and grant financing in support of the Bank Group's country and global development efforts. For IBRD and IDA, these functions are performed by the following four vice presidencies, which report directly to the Bank Group CFO:

- *Concessional Finance and Global Partnerships.* This VPU oversees the mobilization of funds for IDA and key environmental and debt relief initiatives; manages trust funds and development grants; and is responsible for interaction with bilateral partners, multilateral development banks, and foundations.
- *Controllers.* This VPU oversees financial reporting, accounting, and related financial control functions; represents the Bank Group on global financial reporting, accounting, and external auditing matters; ensures the integrity of financial transactions; supports an appropriate fiduciary control framework; and administers disbursements for Bank lending operations.
- *Corporate Finance and Risk Management.* This VPU designs IBRD's financial policies and strategy, manages IBRD's financial risks, and supports decision making on the allocation of capital, administrative resources, and net income.
- *Treasury.* This VPU oversees asset management, bond and investment products, financing and risk management, debt management, and advisory services.

In addition to the four VPUs, the vice president and Bank Group chief risk officer also reports to the Bank Group CFO with a "dotted line" to the president. The Bank Group chief risk officer is responsible for developing the Bank group's framework for risk oversight, assessment, coordination, and reporting across IBRD, IDA, IFC, and MIGA. The Bank Group chief risk officer also works closely with the executive vice presidents of IFC and MIGA and with the other members of the Bank Group Risk Council.

The Bank Group's CFO is also responsible for signing off on the financial policies of the finance and risk management functions within IFC and MIGA.

IFC groups the following departments under its Risk Management vice presidency: business risk, accounting and financial operations, corporate business informatics, credit review, integrated risk management, special operations, and regional risk.

In MIGA, the following units report directly to the executive vice president: operations, legal affairs and claims, finance and risk management, and economics and policy.

General Services

This unit is responsible for the design and maintenance of office space; procurement of goods and services; translation and interpretation; security; travel and shipping support; printing and graphic design; and mail, messenger, and food services. IFC and MIGA handle some of these responsibilities through their own offices for facilities management and administration.

Human Resources

The World Bank and IFC each have human resource (HR) vice presidencies that work in close partnership with their respective business units and senior management, at headquarters and in country offices. Collectively, their role is to develop and implement HR policies and strategies that enable the Bank Group to attract and retain a diverse, high-quality, mobile, and productive workforce to deliver on its mission. HR work covers a wide range of issues, from global HR strategies, policies, and programs that support the business objectives at the corporate level to strategic staffing, decentralization, organizational development, career development, compensation, performance management, and exit management at the unit level. In addition, the Office of Diversity Programs provides guidance on institutional- and unit-level diversity and inclusion strategies across HR processes, and the Health Services Department serves the staff and management of the Bank Group by promoting good health and by contributing to a healthy work environment.

Independent Evaluation Group

The Independent Evaluation Group is an independent unit that reports directly to the Board of Executive Directors. Led by its director-general, the unit assesses the results of all of the Bank Group's work and offers recommendations. The group undertakes its work during the evaluation phase of all World Bank Group projects, as outlined in chapter 2. The goals of evaluation are to provide an objective assessment of the results of the Bank Group's work and to identify and disseminate lessons learned from experience. By promoting evidence-based policy making and accountability, evaluation can help identify ways to achieve better development results.

The unit also supports the development of evaluation capacity in partner countries.

Other units with related missions include the Office of the Compliance Advisor/Ombudsman for IFC and MIGA; the Office of Ethics and Business Conduct, which deals with joint Bank and IFC units; and the Quality Assurance Group at the World Bank.

In addition, the World Bank has set up the independent Inspection Panel, a three-member body to whom citizens of developing countries can bring their concerns if they believe that they or their interests have been or could be directly harmed by a project financed by the World Bank.

Information Management and Technology

Information Management and Technology (IMT) is responsible for the management, support, and construction of the Bank's information management and technology systems. Under the new operating model, IFC and the Finance Complex maintain separate units to provide support in this area. IMT is also responsible for the Bank Group's Library and Archives. IMT falls under the direction of the chief information officer of the World Bank Group.

Internal Justice System

Because of the World Bank's immunities, the Bank cannot be sued in national courts by staff members with employment claims. Therefore, the Bank Group has established the Internal Justice System (IJS) to handle such concerns. The IJS is a group of independent offices that addresses workplace problems such as disputes regarding staff rules, pay, career advancement, performance evaluation, and benefits. The IJS includes the Respectful Workplace Advisors Program, the Ombuds Services Office, the Office of Mediation Services, and Peer Review Services. Another component of the IJS is the Administrative Tribunal, which handles formal claims and is an independent judicial forum of last resort staffed by seven external judges. The Office of Ethics and Business Conduct and the World Bank Integrity Vice Presidency also form part of the IJS; they are discussed separately.

Legal

The World Bank, IFC, and MIGA have separate legal VPUs, each headed by the unit's own general counsel. Each of these units provides legal services for its respective institution and helps to ensure that all activities comport with the institution's charter, policies, and rules. The focus includes legal and judicial reform in developing countries.

Office of the President

This office provides support to the World Bank Group president and maintains information on the president's speeches, interviews, and travels. Visit http://www.worldbank.org/president/ for more information.

Staff Association

The World Bank Group Staff Association (SA) is a member-supported organization; more than half of all eligible Bank Group staff members are dues-paying SA members. The SA is dedicated to fostering a sense of common purpose among staff members by promoting the aims and objectives of the World Bank Group and by promoting and safeguarding the rights, interests, and welfare of all staff members. The SA works with the HR department, senior management, line management, and the World Bank Group's Boards of Executive Directors, as well as with the staff itself, to fulfill these objectives.

Among other activities, the SA maintains a direct line of communication with all levels of management, including the president of the World Bank Group; informs staff members of developments affecting them; urges management to keep the staff informed; provides support for staff members experiencing problems and difficulties on the job; and appoints staff representatives to any joint executive, advisory, or consultative group formed by management to work on issues of common concern.

World Bank Institute

The World Bank Institute (WBI) is the capacity development arm of the World Bank. WBI attempts to transform the way development practitioners operate by equipping them not only with technical skills but also with very practical knowledge on how to make change happen on the ground. By connecting development practitioners with peers in other countries who have successfully addressed similar challenges and by complementing the transfer of technical knowledge with expertise on leadership, coalition building, and innovation, WBI strives to empower its partners in and outside government and to become effective change agents. WBI works in close collaboration with Bank operations staff to provide global and regional programs that address key sectoral issues and that often go beyond country boundaries.

World Bank Integrity Vice Presidency

The World Bank Integrity Vice Presidency (INT) investigates allegations of fraud, corruption, coercion, collusion, and obstructive behavior related to Bank-financed projects and Bank Group operations. INT also investigates allegations of serious staff misconduct. In addition to investigations, INT also helps improve corporate compliance with World Bank procurement policies and works to prevent corruption by a variety of means, including training staff members to detect and deter fraud and corruption in Bank-financed projects and to improve financial accountability, control, and compliance systems. As a result of INT investigations, the World Bank's Independent Sanctions Board debarred (as of April 2011) 423 firms and individuals for fraud and corruption in Bank-financed projects since its establishment in 1999. In April 2010, the World Bank signed a cross-debarment agreement with four other multilateral development banks, bringing into effect the first global enforcement mechanism that is based on a harmonized definition of sanctionable practices.

As part of its disclosure policy, INT publishes an annual integrity report with aggregate data, outcomes, and generic descriptions of significant cases. INT also discloses redacted reports by summarizing the findings of its investigations for which entities have been debarred. INT's vice president reports directly to the president of the World Bank Group.

World Bank Group's Relationship to the IMF and the United Nations

The World Bank Group, which is an independent specialized agency of the United Nations, works in close cooperation with another independent specialized UN agency, the International Monetary Fund. This section explains those relationships (see also the history timeline in appendix B).

The Bretton Woods Institutions

The World Bank and the IMF were both created in 1944 at a conference of world leaders in Bretton Woods, New Hampshire, with the aim of placing the international economy on a sound footing after World War II. As a result of their shared origin, the two entities—the IMF and the expanded World Bank Group—are sometimes referred to collectively as the *Bretton Woods institutions*. The Bank Group and the IMF—which came into formal existence in 1945—work closely together, have similar governance structures, have a similar relationship with the United Nations, and have headquarters in close proximity in Washington, D.C. Although membership in the Bank Group's institutions is open only to countries that are already members of the IMF, the Bank Group and the IMF remain separate institutions. Their work is complementary, but their individual roles are quite different.

Key differences between the work of the World Bank Group and that of the IMF include the following:

- The Bank Group lends only to developing or transition economies, whereas all member countries, rich or poor, can draw on the IMF's services and resources.
- The IMF's loans address short-term economic problems: they provide general support for a country's balance of payments and international reserves while the country takes policy action to address its difficulties. The Bank Group is concerned mainly with longer-term issues: it seeks to integrate countries into the wider world economy and to promote economic growth that reduces poverty.
- The IMF focuses on the macroeconomic performance of economies, as well as on macroeconomic and financial sector policy. The Bank Group's focus extends further into the particular sectors of a country's economy, and its work includes specific development projects as well as broader policy issues.

A few Bank Group and IMF units have joint functions, including the Library Network, Health Services, and the Bank/Fund Conferences Office, which plans and coordinates the joint Annual Meetings and Spring Meetings. The staff members of the two institutions have formed the joint Bank-Fund Staff Federal Credit Union, but this entity is independent of the institutions themselves.

The Development Committee and the International Monetary and Financial Committee

The Development Committee is a forum of the Bank Group and the IMF that facilitates intergovernmental consensus building on development issues. Known formally as the Joint Ministerial Committee of the Boards of the

Bank and Fund on the Transfer of Real Resources to Developing Countries, the committee was established in 1974.

The Development Committee's mandate is to advise the Boards of Governors of the two institutions on critical development issues and on the financial resources required to promote economic development in developing countries. Over time, the committee has interpreted this mandate to include trade and global environmental issues in addition to traditional development matters.

The committee has 25 members, usually ministers of finance and development, who represent the full membership of the Bank Group and the IMF. They are appointed by each of the countries—or groups of countries—represented on the Boards of Executive Directors of the two institutions. The chair is selected from among the committee's members and is assisted by an executive secretary elected by the committee. The Development Committee meets twice a year. For more information, see http://www.worldbank.org/devcom/.

The International Monetary and Financial Committee has a similar structure, selection process for members, and schedule for meetings. It serves in an advisory role to the IMF Board of Governors; however, unlike the Development Committee, the International Monetary and Financial Committee is solely an IMF entity.

Annual Meetings and Spring Meetings

Each September or October, the Boards of Governors of the World Bank Group and the IMF hold joint Annual Meetings to discuss a range of issues related to poverty reduction, international economic development, and finance. These meetings provide a forum for international cooperation and enable the two institutions to serve their member countries more effectively. In addition, the Development Committee and the International Monetary and Financial Committee are officially convened.

These meetings have traditionally been held in Washington, D.C., two years out of three and in a different member country every third year. Recent meetings outside Washington, D.C., have taken place in Dubai, the United Arab Emirates (2003); Singapore (2006); and Istanbul, Turkey (2009). The Bank Group and the IMF organize a number of forums around these meetings to facilitate interaction by government officials and Bank Group and IMF staff members with civil society organizations (CSOs), private sector representatives, and journalists.

The Development Committee and the International Monetary and Financial Committee also meet in March or April of each year to discuss progress on the work of the Bank Group and the IMF. As with the Annual Meetings, a number of activities are organized at these Spring Meetings to involve the press, CSOs, and the private sector. Plenary sessions of the two institutions' Boards of Governors, however, are scheduled only during the Annual Meetings in September or October.

Specialized Agency of the United Nations

Cooperation between the Bank Group and the United Nations has been in place since the founding of the two organizations (in 1944 and 1945, respectively) and focuses on economic and social areas of mutual concern, such as reducing poverty, promoting sustainable development, and investing in people. In addition to a shared agenda, the Bank Group and the United Nations have almost the same membership: only a handful of UN member countries are not members of IBRD.

The World Bank's formal relationship with the United Nations is defined by a 1947 agreement that recognizes the Bank (now the Bank Group) as an independent specialized agency of the United Nations and as an observer in many UN bodies, including the General Assembly. As an independent specialized agency, the Bank Group officially falls under the purview of the United Nations Economic and Social Council. In recent years, the Economic and Social Council has conducted a special high-level meeting with the Bretton Woods institutions immediately after the Spring Meetings of the Bank Group and the IMF. The Bank Group president is also a member of the UN System Chief Executives Board for Coordination, which meets twice annually. In addition, the Bank Group plays a key role in supporting United Nations–led processes, such as the International Conference on Financing for Development and the World Summit on Sustainable Development. It also provides knowledge about country-level challenges and helps formulate international policy recommendations.

In terms of operations, the Bank Group works with other UN funds and programs to coordinate policies, aid, and project implementation. It also helps prepare for and participates in most of the United Nations global conferences and plays an important role in follow-up, especially in relation to the implementation of goals at the country level.

Further information on the Bank Group's collaboration with UN agencies can be found under "Partnerships" in chapter 2.

The empowerment of women is smart economics. Studies show that investments in women yield large social and economic returns. Investing in adolescent girls breaks intergenerational cycles of poverty.

2 How the World Bank Group Operates

This chapter covers the basics of World Bank Group operations, many aspects of which are interconnected. The chapter is organized as follows:

- *Strategies.* This section explains the Bank Group's overall framework for its fight against poverty as well as strategies pertinent to individual countries and specific sectors of development.
- *Policies and Procedures.* This section provides an overview of the policies and procedures that the Bank Group has established for its operations to help ensure quality and fairness in its projects.
- *The Bank Group's Finances.* This section offers a quick primer on how the Bank Group institutions are funded and what they do with their money.
- *Financial Products and Services.* This section describes the financial products and services offered by World Bank Group institutions.
- *Knowledge Sharing.* This section describes the knowledge-sharing services that the Bank Group provides in support of development and poverty reduction activities.
- *World Bank Project Cycle.* This section covers the typical phases of a World Bank project, the documentation that each phase creates, and the resources for locating detailed information about Bank projects.
- *IFC Project Cycle.* This section covers the typical phases of an International Finance Corporation (IFC) project.
- *Partnerships.* This section provides an overview of the types of partners the Bank Group works with, including affiliates whose secretariats are located at Bank Group headquarters.
- *Staff, Consultants, and Vendors.* This section provides details about the Bank Group's staff and related opportunities: job openings, internships, and scholarships. It also provides links to basic information on doing business with the Bank Group.

Strategies

This section covers the main strategies guiding the work of the Bank Group, beginning with the Millennium Development Goals (MDGs). Information on the MDGs and the Bank Group's strategies for meeting them can be found online at http://www.worldbank.org/mdgs/.

Millennium Development Goals

The MDGs (table 2.1) identify—and quantify—specific gains for improving the lives of the world's poor people. The aim of the MDGs is to reduce poverty while improving health, education, and the environment. These goals were endorsed by 189 countries at the September 2000 United Nations (UN) Millennium Assembly in New York. They help focus the efforts of the World Bank Group, other multilateral organizations, governments, and other partners in the development community on significant, measurable improvements in the lives of poor people in developing countries.

Table 2.1 Millennium Development Goals (MDGs)

Goals and Targets from the Millennium Declaration	
Goal 1	Eradicate Extreme Poverty and Hunger
TARGET 1	Halve, between 1990 and 2015, the proportion of people whose income is less than $1 a day
TARGET 2	Halve, between 1990 and 2015, the proportion of people who suffer from hunger
Goal 2	Achieve Universal Primary Education
TARGET 3	Ensure that by 2015, children everywhere, boys and girls alike, will be able to complete a full course of primary schooling
Goal 3	Promote Gender Equality and Empower Women
TARGET 4	Eliminate gender disparity in primary and secondary education, preferably by 2005, and at all levels of education no later than 2015
Goal 4	Reduce Child Mortality
TARGET 5	Reduce by two-thirds, between 1990 and 2015, the under-five mortality rate
Goal 5	Improve Maternal Health
TARGET 6	Reduce by three-quarters, between 1990 and 2015, the maternal mortality ratio

Goal 6	Combat HIV/AIDS, Malaria, and Other Diseases
TARGET 7	Have halted by 2015 and begun to reverse the spread of HIV/AIDS
TARGET 8	Have halted by 2015 and begun to reverse the incidence of malaria and other major diseases
Goal 7	**Ensure Environmental Sustainability**
TARGET 9	Integrate the principles of sustainable development into country policies and programs and reverse the loss of environmental resources
TARGET 10	Halve by 2015 the proportion of people without sustainable access to safe drinking water and basic sanitation
TARGET 11	Have achieved a significant improvement by 2020 in the lives of at least 100 million slum dwellers
Goal 8	**Develop a Global Partnership for Development**
TARGET 12	Develop further an open, rule-based, predictable, nondiscriminatory trading and financial system (including a commitment to good governance, development, and poverty reduction, nationally and internationally)
TARGET 13	Address the special needs of the least developed countries (including tariff- and quota-free access for exports of the least developed countries; enhanced debt relief for heavily indebted poor countries and cancellation of official bilateral debt; and more generous official development assistance for countries committed to reducing poverty)
TARGET 14	Address the special needs of landlocked countries and small island developing states (through the Programme of Action for the Sustainable Development of Small Island Developing States and the outcome of the 22nd special session of the General Assembly)
TARGET 15	Deal comprehensively with the debt problems of developing countries through national and international measures to make debt sustainable in the long term
TARGET 16	In cooperation with developing countries, develop and implement strategies for decent and productive work for youth
TARGET 17	In cooperation with pharmaceutical companies, provide access to affordable, essential drugs in developing countries
TARGET 18	In cooperation with the private sector, make available the benefits of new technologies, especially information and communication

Source: United Nations. 2008. *Report of the Secretary-General on the Indicators for Monitoring the Millennium Development Goals.* Report e/CN.2/2008/29. New York: United Nations.
Note: The Millennium Development Goals and targets come from the *Millennium Declaration* signed by 189 countries, including 147 heads of state, in September 2000. The goals and targets are related and should be seen as a whole. They represent a partnership of countries determined, as the Declaration states, "to create an environment—at the national and global levels alike—which is conducive to development and the elimination of poverty."

The MDGs grew out of the agreements and resolutions that have resulted from world conferences organized by the United Nations in the past 15 to 20 years. Each goal is to be achieved by 2015, with progress to be measured by comparison with 1990 levels. Although the goals are sometimes numbered, the numbers are not intended to indicate any differences in priority or urgency.

The goals establish yardsticks for measuring results, not just for the developing countries but also for the high-income countries that help fund development programs and for the multilateral institutions that work with countries to implement those programs. The first seven goals are mutually reinforcing and are directed at reducing poverty in all its forms. The last goal—to develop a global partnership for development—is directed at the means for reaching the first seven.

Many of the poorest countries will need assistance if the MDGs are to be achieved, and countries that are both poor and heavily indebted will need further help to reduce their debt burdens. But providing assistance is not limited to providing financial aid. Developing countries may also benefit if trade barriers are lowered and therefore allow a freer exchange of goods and services.

Achieving the goals is an enormous challenge. Partnerships between the Bank Group, the UN Development Group (UNDG), and other organizations, as well as between donors and developing countries, are the only way to ensure coordinated and complementary efforts. The UNDG consists of the many UN programs, funds, and agencies engaged in development assistance and related activities. The Bank Group participates in the UNDG and supports its framework for greater coherence and cooperation in UN development operations.

Since 2004, the World Bank—in partnership with the International Monetary Fund (IMF)—has published the annual *Global Monitoring Report*, which monitors the performance of donor countries, developing countries, and international financial institutions in delivering on their commitments to support achievement of the MDGs. The report reviews key developments in the previous year, discusses priority emerging issues, and assesses performance. For more information about this report, go to http://www.worldbank.org/globalmonitoring/.

In 2010, the World Bank launched the eAtlas of the Millennium Development Goals. This online data visualization tool allows users to map the indicators that measure progress on the MDGs. Features include worldwide mapping, timeline graphing, ranking tables, and exporting and sharing of graphics. For more information, visit http://data.worldbank.org/mdg-atlas/.

For the Bank Group, as for other agencies, the challenge of implementing the MDGs provides a starting point for all operations.

Strategic Themes

The World Bank has made the world's challenge—to reduce global poverty—its challenge. The Bank focuses on achievement of the MDGs, which call for the elimination of poverty and the achievement of sustained development. The goals provide the targets and yardsticks for measuring results.

Working with its many partners in development, the Bank addresses global challenges in ways that advance an inclusive and sustainable globalization—with projects that overcome poverty, enhance growth with care for the environment, and create individual opportunity and hope.

Six strategic themes drive the Bank's efforts: the poorest countries, fragile and conflict-affected states, the Arab world, middle-income countries, global public goods issues, and delivery of knowledge and learning services. By focusing on these themes, the Bank delivers technical, financial, and other assistance to those most in need and to places where it can have the greatest influence and promote growth.

Developing countries have determined themselves that for their economies to grow and attract business and jobs, they must build capacity, create infrastructure, develop their financial systems, and fight corruption. These priorities inform all the work of the World Bank Group.

Thematic and Sector Strategies

Thematic and sector strategies address cross-cutting facets of poverty reduction, such as HIV/AIDS, the environment, and participation in and decentralization of the government. In addition, these strategies serve as a guide for future work in a given sector, and they help in assessing the appropriateness and the impact of related Bank Group policies. The strategies are revised on a rolling basis through extensive consultation with a wide variety of stakeholders. The process helps to build consensus within the Bank Group and strengthen relationships with external partners. Figures 2.1 and 2.2 present overall shares of lending by theme and sector for the World Bank, figure 2.3 presents IFC investment projects by industry, and figure 2.4 presents overall shares of Multilateral Investment Guarantee Agency (MIGA) guarantees by sector. Many sector strategies are posted on the World Bank's websites.

Figure 2.1 Total IBRD-IDA Lending by Theme, Fiscal Year 2010
Share of total lending of $58.75 billion

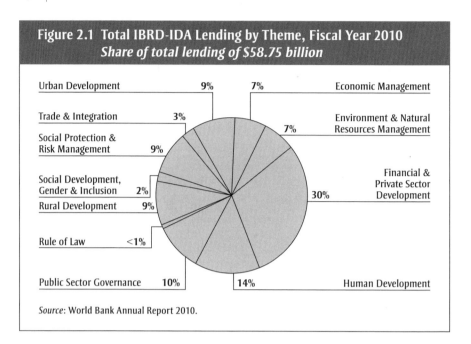

Urban Development — 9%

Trade & Integration — 3%

Social Protection & Risk Management — 9%

Social Development, Gender & Inclusion — 2%

Rural Development — 9%

Rule of Law — <1%

Public Sector Governance — 10%

7% — Economic Management

7% — Environment & Natural Resources Management

30% — Financial & Private Sector Development

14% — Human Development

Source: World Bank Annual Report 2010.

Figure 2.2 Total IBRD-IDA Lending by Sector, Fiscal Year 2010
Share of total lending of $58.75 billion

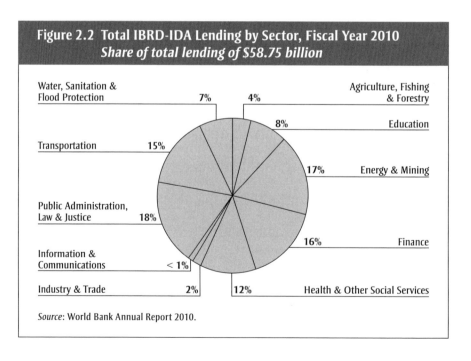

Water, Sanitation & Flood Protection — 7%

Transportation — 15%

Public Administration, Law & Justice — 18%

Information & Communications — < 1%

Industry & Trade — 2%

4% — Agriculture, Fishing & Forestry

8% — Education

17% — Energy & Mining

16% — Finance

12% — Health & Other Social Services

Source: World Bank Annual Report 2010.

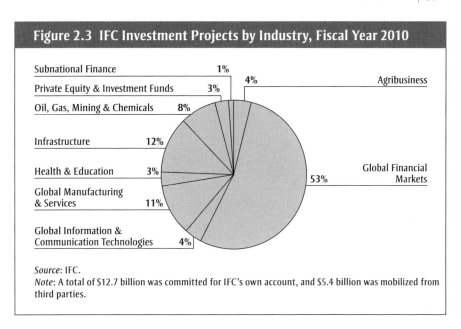

Figure 2.3 IFC Investment Projects by Industry, Fiscal Year 2010

Subnational Finance — 1%

Private Equity & Investment Funds — 3%

Oil, Gas, Mining & Chemicals — 8%

Infrastructure — 12%

Health & Education — 3%

Global Manufacturing & Services — 11%

Global Information & Communication Technologies — 4%

Agribusiness — 4%

Global Financial Markets — 53%

Source: IFC.
Note: A total of $12.7 billion was committed for IFC's own account, and $5.4 billion was mobilized from third parties.

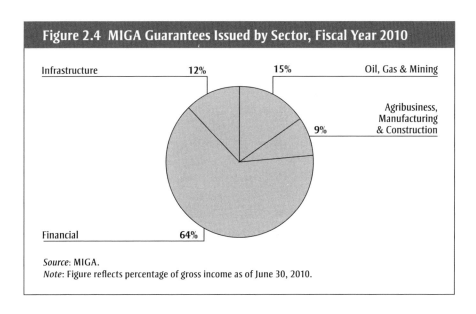

Figure 2.4 MIGA Guarantees Issued by Sector, Fiscal Year 2010

Infrastructure — 12%

Oil, Gas & Mining — 15%

Agribusiness, Manufacturing & Construction — 9%

Financial — 64%

Source: MIGA.
Note: Figure reflects percentage of gross income as of June 30, 2010.

Comprehensive Development Framework

The Comprehensive Development Framework, adopted in January 1999, is an approach to development whereby countries become the leaders and owners of their own development and poverty reduction policies. It emphasizes the interdependence of all aspects of development: social, structural, human, governance, environmental, economic, and financial. It also aims to correct the historical shortcomings of many aid programs, which were often implemented with a limited focus and with little support in the affected countries.

The Comprehensive Development Framework advocates three specific approaches:

- A holistic, long-term strategy with the country taking the lead, both owning and directing the development agenda, while the Bank Group and other partners each define their support in their respective business plans.
- The development of stronger partnerships among governments, donors, civil society, the private sector, and other development stakeholders in implementing the country strategy.
- A transparent focus on accountability for development results to ensure better practical success in reducing poverty.

The Comprehensive Development Framework is not a blueprint to be applied to all countries uniformly, but a way of doing business to make development efforts more effective in a world challenged by poverty and distress. The related website is http://www.worldbank.org/cdf/.

Poverty Reduction Strategies

Poverty reduction strategies represent the tangible outcomes of the approach defined by the Comprehensive Development Framework. In contrast to past approaches, which were applied to countries by donor organizations, developing countries now write their own strategies for reducing poverty (box 2.1). The resulting Poverty Reduction Strategy Papers (PRSPs) then become the basis for International Development Association (IDA) lending from the World Bank, for comparable lending from the IMF's Poverty Reduction and Growth Facility, and for debt relief under the Heavily Indebted Poor Countries (HIPC) Initiative.

PRSPs describe a country's macroeconomic, structural, and social policies and programs to promote growth and reduce poverty, as well as associated external financing needs. Governments prepare PRSPs through a

Box 2.1 Poverty Reduction Strategies: Key Steps

No blueprint is available for building all countries' poverty reduction strategies. Rather, the process reflects countries' individual circumstances and characteristics. Recommended features of Poverty Reduction Strategy Papers (PRSPs) include the following:

- *Description of the participatory process.* The PRSP will describe the format, frequency, and location of consultations; summarize the main issues raised and the views of participants; provide an account of the effect of the consultations on the design of the strategy; and discuss the role of civil society in future monitoring and implementation.
- *Comprehensive poverty diagnostics.* A good understanding of the poor and where they live allows the PRSP to analyze the macroeconomic, social, structural, and institutional constraints to faster growth and poverty reduction.
- *Clearly presented priorities for macroeconomic, structural, and social policies, including assessment of costs.* In light of a deeper understanding of poverty and its causes, the PRSP will set out the macroeconomic, structural, and social policies that together constitute a comprehensive strategy for achieving poverty-reducing outcomes. Costs of implementing policies will be estimated and policies prioritized as far as possible so that they do not become just a "wish list."
- *Appropriate targets, indicators, and systems for monitoring and evaluating progress.* The PRSP will define medium- and long-term goals for poverty-reducing outcomes (monetary and nonmonetary), establish indicators of progress, and set annual and medium-term targets. The indicators and targets will be consistent with the assessment of poverty, the institutional capacity to monitor, and the strategy's policy choices.

participatory process that involves civil society and development partners, including the Bank and the IMF.

The World Bank has produced *A Sourcebook for Poverty Reduction Strategies*, with chapters that address the various sectors of development, as a resource to help countries prepare their PRSPs. A PDF version of this volume is available for free online at http://www.worldbank.org/prsp/.

On receiving the interim or final document, the World Bank and the IMF conduct a joint staff assessment, which helps the boards of the institutions judge whether the document provides a sound basis on which to proceed with assistance and debt relief.

Country Assistance Strategies

Country Assistance Strategies (CASs) identify the key areas in which the Bank Group can best assist a country in achieving sustainable development and poverty reduction. CASs are the central vehicle used by the Bank Group's executive directors to review and guide the Bank Group's support for borrowers from the International Bank for Reconstruction and Development (IBRD) and IDA. Each CAS includes a comprehensive diagnosis—drawing on analytic work by the Bank Group, the government, and other partners—of the development challenges facing the country, including the incidence, trends, and causes of poverty. From this assessment, the level and composition of Bank Group financial, advisory, and technical support to the country are determined. So that implementation of the CAS program can be tracked, CASs are increasingly results focused. Thus, each CAS includes a framework of clear targets and indicators that are used to monitor Bank Group and country performance in achieving stated outcomes.

The key elements of the CAS are discussed with the country's government and often with civil society representatives before the Board of Executive Directors considers the CAS; however, it is not a negotiated document. Any differences between the country's own agenda and the strategy advocated by the Bank Group are highlighted in the CAS. Even though the country owns its development strategy as outlined in the PRSP, the Bank Group provides the CAS to its shareholders specifically to account for its diagnosis of a country's development situation and for the programs it supports.

Some CASs are publicly available. More information on the purpose, process, and content of CASs—as well as a project database—can be found at http://www.worldbank.org/cas/.

IFC and Private Sector Development Strategies

IFC produces an annual document called the *IFC Road Map* that reviews its external environment, assesses the progress it has made in implementing its strategic priorities, and sets goals to be achieved to increase development effects. The paper is available at http://www.ifc.org/ifcext/about.nsf/content/StrategicDirections.

The World Bank Group also has a private sector development strategy that includes activities undertaken by IFC, MIGA, and some World Bank units. The lead unit in this area is the joint World Bank and IFC Financial and Private Sector Development Vice Presidency.

Policies and Procedures

The World Bank Group has established policies and procedures to help ensure that its operations are economically, financially, socially, and environmentally sound. Each operation must follow these policies and procedures to ensure quality, integrity, and adherence to the Bank Group's mission, corporate priorities, and strategic goals. These policies and procedures—including rigorous safeguard policies on projects affecting, for example, women, the environment, and indigenous peoples—are codified in the *World Bank Operational Manual*. They are subject to extensive review while being formulated and to compliance monitoring after being approved.

Operational Manual

The *World Bank Operational Manual* is available online at http://www.worldbank.org/opmanual/. It deals with the Bank's core development objectives and goals and the instruments for pursuing them, in addition to the requirements applicable to Bank-financed lending operations. The manual includes several different kinds of operational statements: operational policies, Bank procedures, and good practices.

Policy definitions and documentation

Operational policies are short, focused statements that follow from the Bank's Articles of Agreement and the general conditions and policies approved by the Board of Executive Directors. They establish the parameters for conducting operations, describe the circumstances in which exceptions to policy are admissible, and spell out who authorizes exceptions. *Bank procedures* explain how staff members carry out the operational policies by describing the procedures and documentation required to ensure consistency and quality across the Bank. *Good practices* are statements that contain advice and guidance on policy implementation, such as the history of an issue, the sectoral context, and the analytical framework, along with examples of good practice. Although they may be included in the manual, good practices are generally maintained and made available by the Bank units responsible for specific policies.

Environmental and social safeguard policies

Environmental and social safeguard policies help to avoid, minimize, mitigate, and compensate for adverse environmental and social impacts in Bank-supported operations that result from the development process. Safeguard policies have helped to ensure that environmental and social issues are thoroughly evaluated by Bank and borrower staff in the identification, preparation, and implementation of Bank-financed programs and projects. The effectiveness and positive development impact of these projects and programs have increased substantially as a result of attention to these policies. The safeguard policies also provide a platform for stakeholder participation in project design and are an important instrument for building ownership among local populations.

The Bank has 10 safeguard policies that cover the following issues: environmental assessment, natural habitats, pest management, involuntary resettlement, indigenous peoples, forests, cultural resources, dam safety, international waterways, and projects in disputed areas. The Bank also has a policy to govern the use of borrower systems for environmental and social safeguards. Bank safeguards require screening of each proposed project to determine the potential environmental and social risks and opportunities and how to address those issues. The Bank classifies the proposed project into risk categories depending on the type, location, sensitivity, and scale of the project and the nature and magnitude of its potential environmental and social impact. This categorization influences the required risk management and mitigation measures for the proposed project. The borrower is responsible for any studies required by the safeguard policies, with general assistance provided by Bank staff members. The Bank's Quality Assurance and Compliance Unit within the Bank's Operations Policy and Country Services (OPCS) Vice Presidency, jointly with the Environmental and International Law Practice Group of the Legal Vice Presidency, provides support to Bank teams that are dealing with environmental and social risks in Bank-supported operations.

Policy formulation and review

The OPCS reviews, updates, and formulates policies and procedures that govern the Bank's operations. Proposals for policy revisions or new policies respond to the strategic priorities set by the Bank's management and the Board of Executive Directors. Formulation or review of a policy entails bringing together experienced regional and network staff members, legal experts, and policy writers. If the policy or proposed revision is complex, the task may entail an iterative process of consultation inside and outside the Bank, including consultation with internal experts, clients, external experts, partners such as civil society organizations, and the public. Following the consultation process, a final draft, usually accompanied by an explanatory paper, is submitted for comment and approval to the appropriate management group, the Bank's managing directors, and the Board of Executive Directors.

The Independent Evaluation Group (IEG) assesses the performance of Bank Group policies, programs, projects, and processes. This work identifies lessons about what works in what contexts and contributes to improving the Bank Group's operations and impact. The group's work also can feed into new policies and Bank strategies as they are being developed. As the scope of the Bank Group operations and its portfolio of products have grown, IEG has continued to adapt its approach to evaluation to ensure that its involvement is relevant and timely. These efforts help improve the Bank Group's contributions to development results by ensuring both accountability and learning.

Recent policy and procedural reforms have included revisions of the Bank's policy on public access to information, its procurement guidelines, and the internal processing of Bank investment lending.

Compliance monitoring

The Bank's credibility rests on effective implementation of its policies. The mission of OPCS is to enhance the Bank's operational effectiveness. It supports and advises the World Bank's staff and management on a wide range of operational areas, from preparing and implementing lending and nonlending programs to applying policies and procedures in Bank priority areas. It works in collaboration with the Bank's other vice presidencies and with other World Bank Group organizations. The Bank has also set up the Inspection Panel, an independent forum for private citizens who believe that their rights or interests have been or could be directly harmed by a Bank-financed project. If people living in a project area believe that harm has resulted from, or will result from, a failure by the Bank to follow its policies and procedures, they or a representative may request a review of the project by the Inspection Panel. The panel's website is at http://www.worldbank. org/inspectionpanel/.

Access to information

In 2010, the Bank launched its Policy on Access to Information. The new policy represents a fundamental shift in the Bank's approach to disclosure of information—moving from an approach that spells out what information it can disclose to one under which the Bank will disclose any information in its possession that is not on a list of exceptions. For some years, the Bank has viewed the disclosure of information as a means of being more open about its activities, explaining its work to the widest possible audience, and promoting overall accountability and transparency in the development process. Now the public can get more information than ever before—information about projects under preparation, projects that are being implemented, analytic and advisory activities, and Board proceedings.

This enhanced transparency and accountability will allow for greater monitoring of Bank-supported projects, thereby enabling better development results as well as providing an opportunity to better track the use of public funds.

The policy also includes a clear process for making information publicly available and gives information seekers a right to appeal if they believe that they were improperly or unreasonably denied access to information or that a public interest case may override an exception that restricts certain information.

Among the newly available documents are minutes of Board committee meetings, chairman's summaries of Board meetings and Committee of the Whole meetings, summaries of discussion, annual reports of Board committees, country portfolio performance reviews, concept notes and consultation plans for policy reviews that are subject to external consultations, consultation plans for CASs, and key decisions at the end of supervision missions and project midterm review.

The Bank continues to regularly review the provisions and implementation of its access to information policy. More about the World Bank Policy on Access to Information is available at http://www.worldbank.org/disclosure/. The free World Bank Infofinder mobile phone application, released in fall 2010, provides the complete Access to Information Policy in seven languages. It is available for iPad and iPhone. Visit http://www.worldbank.org/wbaccess/ or search for "World Bank" in the iTunes app store.

Fiduciary policies

The Bank's fiduciary policies, set forth in the *Operational Manual*, govern the use and flow of Bank funds, including financial management, procurement, and disbursement. The OPCS Vice Presidency provides guidelines for the procurement of goods and services in Bank projects. The guidelines help ensure that funds are used for their intended purposes and with economy, efficiency, and transparency. They also ensure competitive bidding and help protect Bank-funded projects from fraud and corruption (box 2.2). The procurement policy website is at http://www.worldbank.org/procure/.

Box 2.2 Reporting Fraud or Corruption

The World Bank Integrity Vice Presidency investigates allegations of fraud or corruption in operations financed by the World Bank Group, as well as allegations of staff misconduct within the Bank Group.

Examples of issues that should be reported to the World Bank Integrity Vice Presidency for further review include suspected contract irregularities and violations of the Bank's procurement guidelines; bid manipulation; bid collusion; coercive practices; fraudulent bids; fraud in contract performance; fraud in an audit inquiry; product substitution; price manipulation; use of substandard or inferior parts or materials; cost or labor mischarges; kickbacks, bribery, or acceptance of gratuities; abuse of authority; misuse of Bank Group funds or of funds entrusted to the Bank Group; travel-related fraud; theft and embezzlement; benefits and allowances fraud; conflict of interest; misrepresentation; and forgery. The involvement of Bank Group staff members in any of the aforementioned activities should also be reported.

The World Bank Integrity Vice Presidency can be contacted through the following means:

■ Directly at World Bank headquarters:
  Telephone: 1-202-458-7677
  Fax: 1-202-522-7140
  E-mail: investigations_hotline@worldbank.org
  Website: http://www.worldbank.org/integrity/

■ Through a fraud and corruption hotline, hired by the department for this purpose, that is accessible 24 hours a day with translation services available:
  Toll-free: 1-800-831-0463
  Collect calls: 1-704-556-7046
  Mail: PMB 3767
  13950 Ballantyne Corporate Place
  Charlotte, NC 28277

Calls may be anonymous.

Independent firms periodically audit Bank projects to ensure that the procurement rules are being followed. Any allegations of fraud or corruption that surface are referred to the Oversight Committee for follow-up, including investigations where appropriate. If the allegations prove to be true, the Bank may terminate the employment of a staff member, debar the firms implicated, and cancel the funds allocated to the contract in question.

IFC, MIGA, and ICSID Policies

The policies and procedures of the World Bank Group also apply to IFC and to MIGA, with some specific variations in guidelines, as appropriate to their clients:

- For links to IFC's disclosure policy and its environmental and social policy and standards, see http://www.ifc.org/disclosure.
- For links to MIGA's disclosure policy and its environmental and social policy and standards, see http://www.miga.org/policies/.
- The policies of the International Centre for Settlement of Investment Disputes (ICSID) are set forth in its basic documents, additional facility documents, and other documents available at http://www.worldbank.org/icsid/.

World Bank Reforms

The World Bank Group is advancing multiple reforms to promote inclusiveness, innovation, efficiency, effectiveness, and openness. It is increasing the voice and representation of developing and transition economies; promoting accountability and good governance; increasing transparency and access to information; expanding cooperation with the United Nations, the IMF, other multilateral development banks, donors, civil society, and foundations; and modernizing its financial services.

A major effort is under way to reform the Bank's lending model so that it responds better to borrowers' needs and a changing global environment. The new approach calls for more focus on results and risks as well as streamlined processing of low-risk operations and a sharper focus on supervision and higher-risk investments. For example, a new lending instrument—Program for Results (P4R)—is proposed that supports government programs, links disbursements to results, and helps build client institutional capacity.

These efforts will continue until the World Bank Group has reshaped itself to reflect the international economic realities of the 21st century, recognizes the role and responsibility of its growing body of stakeholders, and provides a larger voice for developing countries.

For more information on these reforms, see the introduction of this volume or go to http://www.worldbank.org/worldbankreforms/ or http://www.worldbank.org/open/.

The Bank Group's Finances

This section provides an overview of how the Bank Group institutions are financed, how they provide assistance in developing countries, and how they report on their finances. More details about Bank Group loans and other assistance follow in this chapter, in the sections "Financial Products and Services" and "Knowledge Sharing."

IBRD and IDA Funding and Lending

The World Bank finances its development programs by tapping the world's capital markets (in the case of IBRD) and by receiving contributions from wealthier member governments (in the case of IDA). In addition, specific activities can be funded by donors through trust funds managed by the World Bank.

IBRD, which facilitates more than half of the Bank's annual lending, raises money primarily by selling bonds in international financial markets. It sells AAA-rated bonds and other debt securities to pension funds, insurance companies, corporations, other banks, and individuals around the world. IBRD charges interest to its borrowers at rates that reflect its low cost of funding and offers clients a wide variety of choices to customize the terms of their loans including choice of interest spread; currency; length of maturity up to 30 years including grace period, plus embedded options to manage currency and interest rate risks, among others.

Six percent of the subscription is required to be paid in when countries join the Bank. Member governments purchase shares, the number of which is based on their relative economic strength, but pay in only a small portion of the value of those shares. The unpaid balance is "on call" in case the Bank suffers losses so grave that it can no longer pay its creditors—something that, to date, has never happened. This guaranteed capital can be used only to pay bondholders, not to cover administrative costs or to make loans. IBRD's rules require that the sum of all loans outstanding and disbursed not exceed the combined total of capital and reserves.

The income that IBRD earns each year from the return on its equity and from the small margin it makes on lending pays for its operating expenses, goes into reserves to strengthen the balance sheet, and is used to fund annual transfers to IDA. Because it is a cooperative institution, IBRD seeks not to maximize profit but to earn enough income to ensure its financial strength and to sustain its development activities.

IDA, the world's largest source of low- or no-interest loans (credits) and grant assistance to the poorest countries, is replenished every three years by donor countries. Additional funds are regenerated through repayments of loan principal on its 20- to 40-year credits and net income transfers from IBRD and IFC. IDA accounts for nearly 40 percent of World Bank lending. Fifty-two countries contribute to IDA's funding. Donor nations include not only traditional donors such as France, Germany, Japan, the United Kingdom, and the United States, but also emerging donors such as Brazil, the Republic of Korea, the Russian Federation, and Turkey, some of which were once IDA borrowers.

IDA funds are allocated to the recipient countries in relation to their income levels and record of success in managing their economies and their ongoing IDA projects. IDA's lending terms are highly concessional, meaning that they carry no or low-interest charges. The lending terms are determined with reference to recipient countries' risk of debt distress, level of gross national income per capita, and creditworthiness for IBRD borrowing. Recipients with a high risk of debt distress receive 100 percent of their financial assistance in the form of grants, and those with a medium risk of debt distress receive 50 percent in the form of grants. Other recipients receive IDA credits on regular or blend and hard terms with 40-year and 25-year maturities, respectively.

Cumulative lending by IBRD and IDA as of June 30, 2010, amounted to nearly $745 billion (table 2.2). More information on IBRD and IDA product lines and lending instruments follows in the section "Financial Products and Services." Grants and loans obtained from cofinanciers and partnerships often complement government funds and World Bank lending to make up the total package of assistance to a country.

Funding of IFC, MIGA, and ICSID

IFC and MIGA each have share capital that is paid in by member countries. Member countries vote in proportion to the number of shares they hold.

IFC makes loans and equity investments and provides advisory services. The corporation's equity and quasi-equity investments are funded out of paid-in capital and retained earnings from those investments. Strong

Table 2.2 IBRD and IDA Cumulative Lending by Country, Fiscal Years 1945–2010

Economy	IBRD Number	IBRD Amount ($ millions)	IDA Number	IDA Amount ($ millions)	IBRD and IDA Number	IBRD and IDA Amount ($ millions)
Afghanistan			68	2310.4	68	2,310.4
Africa (regional)	12	265.9	43	3776.1	55	4,042.0
Albania	6	131.6	62	949.9	68	1,081.5
Algeria	71	5,765.8			71	5,765.8
Angola			21	828.6	21	828.6
Argentina	152	27,055.9			152	27,055.9
Armenia	7	149.6	53	1,176.0	60	1,325.6
Australia	7	417.7			7	417.7
Austria	9	106.4			9	106.4
Azerbaijan	12	1,936.6	35	1,042.2	47	2,978.8
Bahamas, The	5	42.8			5	42.8
Bangladesh	1	46.1	218	15,084.5	219	15,130.6
Barbados	13	153.4			13	153.4
Belarus	10	685.3			10	685.3
Belgium	4	76.0			4	76.0
Belize	9	86.2			9	86.2
Benin			69	1,350.3	69	1,350.3
Bhutan			19	188.4	19	188.4
Bolivia	15	314.3	82	2,107.0	97	2,421.3
Bosnia and Herzegovina	4	175.0	57	1,199.6	61	1,374.6
Botswana	22	895.8	6	15.8	28	911.6
Brazil	359	47,445.7			359	47,445.7
Bulgaria	40	2,932.8			40	2,932.8
Burkina Faso		1.9	82	2,450.4	82	2,452.3
Burundi	1	4.8	69	1,480.2	70	1,485.0
Cambodia			36	831.5	36	831.5
Cameroon	45	1,347.8	41	1636.7	86	2,984.5
Cape Verde			26	290.4	26	290.4
Caribbean (regional)	4	83.0	3	52.0	7	135.0
Central African Republic			33	577.4	33	577.4
Central America (regional)			1	8.0	1	8.0
Central Asia (regional)			1	25.0	1	25.0
Chad	1	39.5	50	1,086.6	51	1,126.1
Chile	74	4,115.8		19.0	74	4,134.8
China	252	37,905.2	71	9,946.7	323	47,851.9
Colombia	209	17,874.1		19.5	209	17,893.6
Comoros			22	145.7	22	145.7
Congo, Dem. Rep.	7	330.0	83	4,688.5	90	5,018.5
Congo, Rep.	10	216.7	23	503.8	33	720.5

(continued)

Table 2.2 *continued*

Economy	IBRD Number	IBRD Amount ($ millions)	IDA Number	IDA Amount ($ millions)	IBRD and IDA Number	IBRD and IDA Amount ($ millions)
Costa Rica	45	1,636.0	0	5.5	45	1,641.5
Côte d'Ivoire	62	2,887.9	35	2,962.5	97	5,840.4
Croatia	41	2,963.9			41	2,963.9
Cyprus	29	404.8			29	404.8
Czech Repulic	3	776.0			3	776.0
Denmark	3	85.0			3	85.0
Djibouti			23	193.0	23	193.0
Dominica	3	6.6	5	22.6	8	29.1
Dominican Republic	47	1,792.9	3	22.0	50	1,814.9
Ecuador	82	3,240.0	5	36.9	87	3,276.9
Egypt, Arab Rep.	87	9,812.1	41	1,984.0	128	11,796.1
El Salvador	45	2,032.6	2	25.6	47	2,058.2
Equatorial Guinea			9	45.0	9	45.0
Eritrea			15	548.9	15	548.9
Estonia	8	150.7	0	0.0	8	150.7
Ethiopia	12	108.6	108	8,834.2	120	8,942.8
Fiji	12	152.9			12	152.9
Finland	18	316.8			18	316.8
France	1	250.0			1	250.7
Gabon	16	267.0			16	267.0
Gambia, The			34	304.0	34	304.0
Georgia	4	275.0	48	1,147.5	52	1,422.5
Ghana	9	187.0	136	6,440.7	145	6,627.7
Greece	17	490.8			17	490.8
Grenada	7	26.5	5	42.3	12	68.8
Guatemala	52	2,695.6			52	2,695.6
Guinea	3	75.2	65	1,430.0	68	1,505.2
Guinea-Bissau			30	343.9	30	343.9
Guyana	12	80.0	22	355.3	34	435.3
Haiti	1	2.6	61	1,015.7	62	1,018.3
Honduras	33	717.3	52	1,862.3	85	2,579.6
Hungary	41	5,660.8			41	5,660.8
Iceland	10	47.1			10	47.1
India	232	44,371.6	286	38,720.2	518	83,091.8
Indonesia	291	38,214.4	53	2,875.3	344	41,089.7
Iran, Islamic Rep.	48	3,413.1			48	3,413.1
Iraq	7	406.2	5	508.5	12	914.7
Ireland	8	152.5			8	152.5
Israel	10	254.5			10	254.5
Italy	8	399.6			8	399.6
Jamaica	78	2,096.1			78	2,096.1
Japan	31	862.9			31	862.9
Jordan	66	2,910.2	15	85.3	81	2,995.5

Economy	IBRD Number	IBRD Amount ($ millions)	IDA Number	IDA Amount ($ millions)	IBRD and IDA Number	IBRD and IDA Amount ($ millions)
Kazakhstan	35	5,476.9			35	5,476.9
Kenya	45	1,180.7	102	5,357.7	147	6,538.4
Korea, Rep.	112	15,472.0	6	110.8	118	15,582.8
Kosovo			15	86.3	15	86.3
Kyrgyz Republic			48	894.1	48	894.1
Lao PDR			59	1,038.2	59	1,038.2
Latvia	21	842.5			21	842.5
Lebanon	22	1255.1			22	1,255.1
Lesotho	2	155.0	39	480.9	41	635.9
Liberia	19	156.0	26	750.7	45	906.7
Lithuania	17	490.9			17	490.9
Luxembourg	1	12.0			1	12.0
Macedonia, FYR	30	735.2	15	378.7	45	1,113.9
Madagascar	5	32.9	105	3,380.9	110	3,413.8
Malawi	9	124.1	93	2,726.7	102	2,850.8
Malaysia	87	4,145.6			87	4,145.6
Maldives			13	139.9	13	139.9
Mali		1.9	86	2,506.7	86	2,508.6
Malta	1	7.5			1	7.5
Mauritania	3	146.0	60	929.0	63	1,075.0
Mauritius	40	757.7	4	20.2	44	777.9
Mexico	225	48,597.8			225	48,597.8
Moldova	9	302.8	30	510.6	39	813.4
Mongolia			34	498.1	34	498.1
Montenegro	4	48.5	9	75.0	13	123.5
Morocco	150	10,790.3	3	50.8	153	10,841.1
Mozambique			67	3,790.5	67	3,790.5
Myanmar	3	33.4	30	804.0	33	837.4
Namibia	2	15.0			2	15.0
Nepal			98	3,026.9	98	3,026.9
Netherlands	8	244.0			8	244.0
New Zealand	6	126.8			6	126.8
Nicaragua	27	233.6	51	1,546.0	78	1,779.6
Niger			67	1,580.2	67	1,580.2
Nigeria	84	6,248.2	56	6,678.0	140	12,926.2
Norway	6	145.0			6	145.0
OECS[c] countries	3	11.8	3	32.2	6	43.9
Oman	11	157.1			11	157.1
Pakistan	92	7,600.2	153	12,519.4	245	20,119.6
Panama	57	1,809.6			57	1,809.6
Papua New Guinea	35	786.6	13	220.0	48	1,006.6
Paraguay	48	1,205.6	6	45.5	54	1,251.1
Peru	119	8,784.5			119	8,784.5

(continued)

Table 2.2 *continued*

Economy	IBRD Number	IBRD Amount ($ millions)	IDA Number	IDA Amount ($ millions)	IBRD and IDA Number	IBRD and IDA Amount ($ millions)
Philippines	180	13,558.2	5	294.2	185	13,852.4
Poland	47	10,275.8			47	10,275.8
Portugal	32	1,338.8			32	1,338.8
Romania	89	8,154.0			89	8,154.0
Russian Federation	64	13,856.1			64	13,856.1
Rwanda			75	1,905.3	75	1,905.3
Samoa			15	122.1	15	122.1
São Tomé and Principe			14	90.5	14	90.5
Senegal	19	164.9	106	3,091.2	125	3,256.1
Serbia	11	865.3	19	689.0	30	1,554.3
Seychelles	3	19.7			3	19.7
Sierra Leone	4	18.7	43	949.1	47	967.8
Singapore	14	181.3			14	181.3
Slovak Republic	9	424.6			9	424.6
Slovenia	5	177.7			5	177.7
Solomon Islands			13	65.1	13	65.1
Somalia			39	492.1	39	492.1
South Africa	14	4,052.8			14	4052.8
Spain	12	478.7			12	478.7
Sri Lanka	12	210.7	103	3,900.1	115	4,110.8
St. Kitts and Nevis	5	23.5		1.5	5	25.0
St Lucia	12	36.9	2	54.6	14	91.6
St. Vincent and the Grenadines	5	12.0	1	18.2	6	30.1
Sudan	8	166.0	47	1,352.9	55	1,518.9
Swaziland	12	104.8	2	7.8	14	112.6
Syrian Arab Republic	16	579.6	3	47.3	19	626.9
Taiwan, China	14	329.4	4	15.3	18	344.7
Tajikistan			37	541.3	37	541.3
Tanzania	17	318.9	142	8,197.0	159	8,515.9
Thailand	119	8,106.7	6	125.1	125	8,231.8
Timor-Leste			9	33.1	9	33.1
Togo	1	20.0	48	1,007.7	49	1,027.7
Tonga			6	28.2	6	28.2
Trinidad and Tobago	22	333.6			22	333.6
Tunisia	131	6,028.3	5	69.8	136	6,098.1
Turkey	169	32,506.0	10	178.5	179	32,684.5
Turkmenistan	3	89.5			3	89.5
Uganda	1	9.1	108	6,195.7	109	6,204.8
Ukraine	41	6,702.6			41	6,702.6
Uruguay	63	3,195.8			63	3,195.8
Uzbekistan	13	554.1	7	341.5	20	895.6

Economy	IBRD		IDA		IBRD and IDA	
	Number	Amount (S millions)	Number	Amount (S millions)	Number	Amount (S millions)
Vanuatu			5	18.9	5	18.9
Venezuela, RB	40	3,328.4			40	3,328.4
Vietnam	2	700.0	94	10,810.2	96	11,510.2
Yemen, Rep.			153	3,073.0	153	3,073.0
Yugoslavia, former	89	6,090.7			89	6,090.7
Zambia	27	679.1	66	3,043.2	93	3,722.3
Zimbabwe	24	983.2	12	662.0	36	1,645.2
Total	5,530	523,632.6	4,822	221,190.2	10,352	744,822.8

Note: A blank space equals zero.

a. Effective fiscal 2005, lending includes guarantees and guarantee facilities. Supplemental and additional financing operations (except for projects scaled up through additional financing) are not counted as separate lending operations, although they are included in the amount.

b. Joint IBRD-IDA operations are counted only once, as IBRD operations. When more than one loan is made for a single project, the operation is counted only once. Commitments in regional projects are classified under this table as regional projects and are not counted as commitments of the individual countries involved under the regional project. Figure excludes the HIPC grants of $45.5 million to Côte d' Ivoire in fiscal year 2009.

c. OECS = Organization of Eastern Caribbean States.

shareholder support, AAA ratings, and the substantial paid-in capital base have allowed IFC to raise funds for its lending activities on favorable terms in the international capital markets.

In addition to its share capital, MIGA charges premiums for the investment guarantees it provides.

The operating expenses of the ICSID Secretariat are funded through the World Bank's budget, although the parties involved bear the costs of individual proceedings.

Financial Reporting: Bank Group Annual Reports

Each Bank Group institution provides detailed financial statements in its annual report. The fiscal year for these institutions runs from July 1 of a given year to June 30 of the following calendar year. The reports catalog financial performance and new activities. They also include comparative information on the regions and development sectors in which the institutions have provided assistance. The reports are available for free to the public, both in print and on the Internet. The reports are published in multiple languages, and the websites include past editions. For Web links to the Bank Group's annual reports, see appendix A.

Financial Products and Services

The World Bank Group is best known for its financial services. The following sections describe the financial products and services provided by World Bank Group institutions.

World Bank

Lending instruments

The World Bank offers two basic types of lending instruments to its client governments: investment loans and development policy loans. Depending on its eligibility, a member country will draw on loans from either IBRD or IDA to support a lending project. Whether the money is lent through IBRD or IDA determines the terms of the loan (box 2.3 presents key terms and rates).

The World Bank's business model and products continue to evolve. Clients are seeking—and Bank staff members are developing—innovative lending approaches that are more flexible and provide quicker and more customized solutions. A major effort is under way to reform the Bank's investment lending model so that it responds better to borrowers' needs and the changing global environment.

Reform is organized around five pillars:

- Focusing more on results and risk
- Moving from an emphasis on supervision to one on implementation support
- Revising the options for investment lending and designing a new way to link disbursements more directly to results
- Creating tools, training programs, and templates to support the implementation of reforms
- Simplifying the policy framework for investment lending

Loans are made as part of the comprehensive lending program set out in the CASs, which tailor Bank assistance (both lending and services) to each borrower's development needs. Lending operations are developed in several phases, as outlined in the "World Bank Project Cycle" section later in this

Box 2.3 Financial Terms and Rates

IBRD

Front-end fee: 0.25 percent of the loan amount, payable within 60 days of loan effectiveness

Lending rate: Consists of a variable base rate (6-month LIBOR[a]) plus a spread

Maturity: Up to 30 years final maturity including grace period (weighted average maturity must not exceed 18 years)

IDA

Service charge: 0.75 percent

Commitment fee: 0.0 to 0.5 percent on the undisbursed balance (set annually; 0 percent for fiscal 2011)

Maturity: 40 years, with a 10-year grace period or 25 years, with a 5-year grace period

Interest rate: 1.25 percent for blend credits and the fixed rate equivalent of IBRD interest rate less 2 percent set annually for hard-term credits (3.2 percent for fiscal 2011)

Note: IBRD conducts annual and periodic reviews of lending rates and loan charges to ensure that pricing is aligned with the prevailing needs of the institution and its shareholders and reflect underlying market conditions. For current lending rates and more detailed information on pricing, visit http://treasury.worldbank.org/bdm/htm/ibrd .html.

a. The London Interbank Offered Rate is a floating interest rate at which banks can borrow funds, in marketable size, from other banks in the London interbank market. The LIBOR is fixed on a daily basis by the British Bankers' Association.

chapter. Complete descriptions of the Bank's various lending instruments are available at http://www.worldbank.org/ibrd/, under "Products and Services."

The Bank has a searchable online database of all projects at http://www. worldbank.org/, under "Projects and Operations." In addition, the Bank posts information on the loans and credits most recently approved by the Board of Executive Directors under "News" on the Bank's website. For more information, see the subsection "Project Information" later in this chapter.

Investment lending. Investment operations focus on the long term (5–10 years) and finance goods, works, and services that support economic and social development projects. These investment projects encompass a broad range of sectors—from agriculture to urban development, rural infrastructure, education, and health.

Investment loans, credits, and grants provide financing for a wide range of activities aimed at creating the physical and social infrastructure necessary to reduce poverty and create sustainable development. Over the past two decades, investment operations have, on average, accounted for 75 to 80 percent of the Bank's portfolio.

The nature of investment lending has evolved over time. Originally focused on hardware, engineering services, and bricks and mortar, investment lending has come to focus more on institution building, social development, and the public policy infrastructure needed to facilitate private sector activity.

Examples of areas in which recent projects have been funded include urban poverty reduction, rural development, water and sanitation, natural resource management, postconflict reconstruction, public finance management, education, and health.

Development policy lending. Development policy lending provides quick-dispersing financing to support government policy and institutional reforms. The earlier focus on macroeconomic policy reforms has evolved over the years into a greater emphasis on structural, financial sector, and social policy reforms—for example, improving the management of public resources, strengthening the functioning of the judiciary, or promoting good governance. During the past two decades, development policy lending has accounted, on average, for 20 to 25 percent of total Bank lending.

Grants

The Bank sees grant making as an integral part of its development work and an important complement to its lending and advisory services. The Bank sets out its overall strategy of using grants to encourage innovation, catalyze partnerships, and broaden the scope of Bank services. In addition, all grants must meet sector and institutional priorities, be of high quality, and conform to eligibility criteria. A limited number of grants are available through the Bank, funded either directly or through partnerships. Most are designed as seed money for pilot projects with innovative approaches and technologies. Grants also foster collaboration with other organizations and encourage broader participation in development projects. The Development Grant Facility provides overall strategy, allocations, and management for

Bank grant-making activities. It has supported programs in sectors such as economic policy, health, environmental sustainability, urban infrastructure, investment climate, and rural development. For more information, go to http://worldbank.org/dgf/.

Cofinancing

The World Bank often cofinances its projects with governments, commercial banks, export credit agencies, multilateral institutions, and private sector investors. Cofinancing is any arrangement under which funds from the Bank are associated with funds provided by sources from outside the recipient country for a specific lending project or program. Official cofinancing—through either donor government agencies or multilateral financial institutions—constitutes the largest source of cofinancing for Bank-assisted operations.

Trust funds

Trust funds are financial arrangements between the World Bank and a donor or a group of donors under which the donor entrusts the Bank with funds for a specific development-related activity. Trust funds enable the Bank, along with bilateral and multilateral donors, to expand their response to specific needs, as in the case of fragile states or natural disasters or in support of global public goods. Bank-administered trust funds support poverty reduction activities across a wide range of sectors and regions, thereby supporting clients in achieving development results at the global, regional, and country levels.

Much of the recent growth in these funds reflects the international community's desire for the Bank to help manage broad global initiatives through multilateral partnerships, such as the Global Fund to Fight AIDS, Tuberculosis, and Malaria; the Global Environment Facility; the HIPC Initiative; and carbon funds. Trust funds also support the World Bank's own development operations and work programs. Cash contributions from donors in fiscal 2010 totaled $11.5 billion, an increase of 33 percent over fiscal 2009. The main Web page for Bank trust funds is at the Concessional Finance and Global Partnerships site, http://www.worldbank.org/cfp/.

IFC also manages trust funds; see http://www.ifc.org/tatf for more information.

Guarantees and risk management

Guarantees promote private financing by covering risks that the private sector is not normally ready to absorb or manage. All World Bank guarantees are partial guarantees of private debt; hence, risks are shared by the Bank and private lenders. The Bank's objective is to cover risks that it is in a unique position to bear, given its experience in developing countries and its relationships with governments.

IBRD also offers hedging products for risk management. These are available in one of three ways: as part of the original terms of the IBRD flexible loan, on a stand-alone basis to manage risk on the entire portfolio of World Bank loans, or on a stand-alone basis to manage debt owed to other creditors. These products give borrowers improved risk management capability in the context of projects, lending programs, or sovereign asset and liability management. IBRD hedging products include interest rate swaps, interest rate caps and collars, currency swaps, and—on a case-by-case basis—commodity swaps.

Additional information on guarantees and risk management services follows in the sections on IFC and MIGA financial products and services.

International Finance Corporation

IFC invests primarily in enterprises that are majority owned by the private sector in almost all developing countries. For details of the corporation's products and services, go to "About IFC" or "Products and Services" at http://www.ifc.org/.

Asset management

The IFC Asset Management Company (AMC) is a private equity fund manager. It was created to tap the substantial financial resources held by sovereign funds, pension funds, and other institutional investors—channeling them to profitable investment opportunities in countries that most need the capital. AMC allows IFC to make more investments than it could alone. A wholly owned subsidiary of IFC, AMC invests third-party capital alongside IFC across the developing world. In the process, it helps "crowd in" commercial investors, expanding IFC's development influence. By demonstrating the financial benefits, growth opportunities, and development effect of investing in these markets, AMC aims to encourage investors to shift the long-term composition of their portfolios.

Lending and investments

IFC's investments in emerging market companies and financial institutions create jobs, build economies, and generate tax revenues. IFC brings its extensive knowledge of social and environmental issues and corporate governance to each investment to strengthen the financial health of the enterprise and ensure its long-term sustainability.

IFC offers clients a variety of investment services, including short-term liquidity, loans and intermediary services, trade finance, and subnational finance, as well as a choice of interest rates (namely, fixed and variable rate loans and, on occasion, loans indexed to the price of a commodity). Loans are issued at market rates. Most are denominated in major currencies, but an increasing number are in local currencies. IFC lending includes credit lines for on-lending to intermediary banks, leasing companies, and other financial institutions, particularly those that serve small businesses or microenterprises.

IFC also makes equity investments, risking its own capital by buying and holding shares in companies, other project entities, financial institutions, and portfolio or private equity funds. IFC is always a minority shareholder, generally limiting its shareholding to 5 to 15 percent or less of a company's equity, and it will never be the largest shareholder in a project. In addition, IFC invests through quasi-equity instruments (that is, products that have both debt and equity characteristics).

IFC offers clients risk management products that provide them with access to long-term derivatives markets. Instruments such as swaps and options help clients manage their currency, interest rate, and commodity price risks.

Working closely with the World Bank, IFC has also begun making new financial products and services and access to capital markets available to subnational entities—states, municipalities, and municipally controlled institutions—in developing countries. The goal is to help such local public entities deliver key infrastructure services and improve their efficiency and accountability. As with the IFC's other investments, subnational transactions do not require sovereign guarantees.

Resource mobilization

Through its syndicated loan program, IFC offers commercial banks and other financial institutions the chance to lend to IFC-financed projects that they might not otherwise consider. These loans are a key part of IFC's efforts to mobilize additional private sector financing in developing countries, thereby broadening the IFC's development impact. Through this mechanism, financial institutions share fully in the commercial credit risk of projects, while IFC remains the lender of record.

Participants in IFC's B-loans share the advantages that IFC derives as a multilateral development institution, including preferred creditor access to foreign exchange in the event of a foreign currency crisis in a particular country. Where applicable, these participant banks are also exempted from the mandatory country-risk provisioning requirements that regulatory authorities may impose if these banks lend directly to projects in developing countries.

Structured finance

IFC has developed products that provide clients with forms of cost-effective financing not otherwise available to them. These products include credit enhancement structures for bonds and loans through partial credit guarantees, participation in securitizations, and risk-sharing facilities.

Trust funds

IFC's advisory services are funded by donor countries and from IFC's own resources. Donor trust funds and IFC's own funding mechanisms are managed by IFC Trust Funds. Coordination among IFC's regional facilities, all of which support development of small and medium-size enterprises, is provided by the Partnerships and Advisory Services Operations Department. Agencies that donate to IFC facilities and trust funds are closely involved in decisions about which technical assistance projects should be taken on. Prospective clients may also contact the individual facilities directly to request assistance.

For details of IFC's advisory activities, see chapters 3 and 4, or select "Investment and Advisory Services" at http://www.ifc.org/about.

Multilateral Investment Guarantee Agency

MIGA provides political risk insurance (investment guarantees) against certain noncommercial risks (that is, political risk insurance) to eligible foreign investors for qualified investments in developing member countries. MIGA's investment guarantees cover the following risks: currency transfer restrictions, expropriation, breach of contract, war and civil disturbance, and failure to honor sovereign financial obligations. A preliminary application for a guarantee is available on MIGA's website, http://www.miga.org/guarantees/.

Knowledge Sharing

Knowledge sharing at the World Bank Group has evolved over time. From an early emphasis on capturing and organizing knowledge, the focus now is on adopting, adapting, and applying knowledge in a way that helps World Bank staff members, clients, and partners work more effectively to reduce global poverty.

Analytic and Advisory Services

World Bank

The World Bank's vast research, analytical, and technical capabilities are a vital part of the Bank's contribution to development. Use of these services can help member governments adopt better policies, programs, and reforms that lead to greater economic growth and poverty reduction. Products range from reports on key economic and social issues, to policy notes, to knowledge-sharing workshops and conferences.

Most of the Bank's analytic and advisory services—that is, its nonlending activities—consist of economic and sector work and technical assistance. Economic and sector analysis examines a country's economic prospects—including, for example, its banking or financial sectors—and its trade, poverty, and social safety net issues. The results often form the basis for assistance strategies, government investment programs, and projects supported by IBRD and IDA lending. Much of this economic research output is available through the World Bank's research website at http://econ.worldbank.org/.

The Bank's advisory services correspond with the thematic networks and sectors. They provide information on such topics as environmentally and socially sustainable development; the financial sector; health, nutrition, and population; and law and justice. Advisory services serve the Bank's clients and staff members, other development organizations, and the general public. For more information, go to http://www.worldbank.org/about/, select "Operations," and see the discussion on "Analytic and Advisory Services."

Some of the Bank's networks and sectors have also prepared topical toolkits for development practitioners. These toolkits cover, for example, food and nutrition, gender, labor standards, public health, infrastructure, and early childhood.

International Finance Corporation

IFC's advisory services are organized into five business lines: access to finance, corporate, environmental and social sustainability, investment climate, and infrastructure. Much of IFC's advisory services work is conducted through facilities—both regional and thematic—that are managed by IFC but funded through partnerships with donor governments and other multilateral institutions. Examples of thematic, cross-regional facilities include those focused on carbon finance, cleaner technologies, social responsibility, sustainable investing, investment climate, gender, and global environment. For more information, visit http://www.ifc.org/ifcext/about. nsf/Content/TAAS.

Capacity Development

The World Bank Institute (WBI) is the Bank Group's capacity development arm. It has delivered training courses and seminars since the 1950s, mostly for government officials in developing countries on such topics as macroeconomic policy, poverty reduction, health, education, and policy reform in other economic sectors. During the past decade, WBI has increased its activities on a broader range of subjects aligned with the World Bank's regional and country development priorities. It has also expanded its audiences to include nonstate actors such as civil society organizations, the private sector, journalists, and parliamentarians. More recently, WBI has expanded its understanding of capacity development to focus beyond investment in human capital: the challenge is to transform the way in which development practitioners operate by equipping them not only with technical skills but also with very practical knowledge on how to make change happen on the ground.

Many of WBI's initiatives are described in chapter 4 and on its website at http://wbi.worldbank.org/wbi/.

Also coordinated by the World Bank, the Global Development Learning Network (GDLN) is a fully interactive, multichannel network that harnesses video, Internet, and satellite communications to build local capacity, learning, and knowledge in the developing world and to create a global community dedicated to fighting poverty. The network comprises about 120 partners who collaborate in the design of customized learning solutions for those working in development. Telemedicine, microfinance, postconflict, leadership, climate change, the food crisis, HIV/AIDS, and water are among the pressing issues GDLN has addressed. The GDLN website is http://www.gdln.org/.

Research

The Bank Group's economic analysis identifies specific development indicators that provide a big picture of economic trends, the cumulative effectiveness of development programs, and other factors that affect economic progress. The website for World Bank research is http://econ.worldbank.org/; the e-mail for general queries is research@worldbank.org.

The World Bank's Development Economics Vice Presidency supports studies on the implications of a range of development issues, such as the global financial crisis, the environment and climate change, poverty, trade, and globalization. The findings from these studies bring about a deeper understanding of development challenges and can be used to influence policy, thereby leading to better outcomes for poor people. The Development Prospects Group provides information, analysis, and advice on global trends in the world economy—especially on trade, financial flows, commodity prices, and remittances flows—and the effect of these trends on developing countries. The group's global projections and other vital information can be found at http://www.worldbank.org/prospects/.

The World Bank and IFC also conduct economic research through the joint Financial and Private Sector Development Vice Presidency. The website for this vice presidency is http://www.worldbank.org/fpd/.

Other Resources

Various other resources are available on the Internet:

- *Poverty Reduction and Economic Management (PREM) Network.* The PREM Network focuses on economic policy, gender, governance and public sector reform, and poverty, among other issues. *PREM Notes*, published by the network, summarizes good practice and key policy findings on those topics. The network's website is at http://www.worldbank.org/prem/. The e-mail address is premadvisory@worldbank.org.
- *Journals.* The *World Bank Research Observer* and *World Bank Economic Review* are published by the World Bank and Oxford University Press.

  - *The World Bank Research Observer* seeks to inform nonspecialist readers about research being undertaken within and outside the Bank in areas of economics relevant for development policy. Requiring only a minimal background in economic analysis, its surveys and overviews of key issues in development economics research are intended for policy makers, project officers, journalists, and teachers and students of development economics and related disciplines.
  - *The World Bank Economic Review* is one of the most widely read scholarly economic journals in the world. It is the only journal of its kind that specializes in quantitative development policy analysis. Subject to

strict refereeing, articles examine policy choices and therefore emphasize policy relevance rather than theory or methodology. Readers
include economists and other social scientists in government, business, international agencies, universities, and research institutions.

Current issues are available by subscription. The archive database is searchable on the journals' home pages, but back issues older than 18 months
are available in the World Bank's document library at www.worldbank.
org/documents. The journals' home pages can be reached through links
on the Bank's website at http://www.worldbank.org/research/journals.

Legal Counsel

MIGA's Legal Affairs and Claims group advises on all legal activities related to
the encouragement of foreign private investment in developing member countries, including operational support for the provision of guarantees against
political risks, advice to member countries on varied aspects of foreign investment legal matters, and assistance in resolving investment disputes between
investors and a host country. The group also cooperates with other entities of
the World Bank Group and with other international and national agencies or
institutions on legal aspects of investment protection and guarantees.

Conciliation and Arbitration

ICSID provides facilities for and coordination of the conciliation and arbitration of investment disputes between contracting states and nationals of
other contracting states. ICSID's objective in making such facilities available is to promote an atmosphere of mutual confidence between states and
foreign investors—an atmosphere that is conducive to increasing the flow of
private international investment.

Open Data, Open Knowledge, Open Solutions

The World Bank Group is actively working to make its data and research
open and user friendly. In 2010, the Bank Group began enacting a range of
reforms that enable free and open access to the Bank Group's data, knowledge products, and tools that previously either had not been available or
had been available only for sale. This new Open Data, Open Knowledge,
Open Solutions initiative represents a fundamentally new way of searching
for development solutions where none dominates and all can play a part.

Through this initiative, the Bank is supplementing its "elite retail" model of economic research, which had economists focusing on specific issues and then writing papers, with a "wholesale" and networked model that gives outsiders the data, research, and software to reach their own findings.

Key examples of the Bank's work in promoting openness and transparency in development, from tools and knowledge resources to Bank-wide initiatives, can be found at http://www.worldbank.org/open/. Highlights include the following:

- *Open Data Initiative.* The World Bank launched its Open Data Initiative in 2010. This initiative made available an array of data sets—including World Development Indicators, Africa Development Indicators, and Millennium Development Goal Indicators—free of charge, in accessible nonproprietary machine-readable formats, through an open license for use and reuse. More than 7,000 financial, business, health, economic, and human development indicators for more than 200 countries (some going back 50 years) are now accessible through the Bank's applications programming interface. In addition, World Development Indicators' 1,200 indicators are available in Arabic, Chinese, English, French, and Spanish. To access the datasets, visit http://data.worldbank.org/.
- *World Bank DataFinder.* The World Bank DataFinder 2.0 lets you access 50 years of World Bank data on more than 1,100 global economic indicators for around 200 countries, chart and visualize those data, and share those data and charts for use in presentations and projects. Visit http://data.worldbank.org/news/datafinder-for-iphone or download the app at http://bit.ly/DataFinder.
- *Data visualization tools.* In recent years, the Bank has been developing a series of data visualization tools to display development indicators in a more engaging and user-friendly way:

  - *eAtlas of Global Development.* The eAtlas of Global Development allows users to easily and quickly transform data into customized visual comparisons across time, countries, and regions. Users can map more than 175 indicators for up to 200 countries over time, including creating two maps to compare progress. Other features include scalable maps, timeline graphing, ranking tables, and import and export functions. Critical issues such as poverty, food production, population growth, climate change, international trade, and foreign direct investment are covered. Visit http://data.worldbank.org/atlas-global/ to access the eAtlas.

☐ *Mapping for Results.* The Mapping for Results platform provides detailed information about the World Bank's work to reduce poverty and promote sustainable development around the world. This interactive platform visualizes the location of Bank projects and provides access to information about indicators, sectors, funding, and results. It overlays poverty and MDG data such as infant mortality rates with the geographic location of more than 1,000 World Bank–financed products. For more information, visit http://maps.worldbank.org/.

☐ *AidFlows.* AidFlows is a tool to visualize how much development aid is provided and received around the world. Users can select individual donor countries (providing the aid) and beneficiary countries (receiving the aid) to track the sources and uses of aid funding. For all countries, two different sources of aid data are available: (a) Organisation for Economic Co-operation and Development (OECD) data showing global development aid and (b) World Bank data on development funding provided by members of the World Bank Group. In addition, AidFlows provides data on development indicators by country. AidFlows is the result of a partnership between the World Bank and the OECD Development Assistance Committee. For more information, visit http://data.worldbank.org/data-catalog/aidflows.

■ *Apps for Development competition.* The Bank launched an Apps for Development competition in 2010, challenging developers around the world to transform World Bank data sets and create innovative software applications that address one of the eight MDGs. Winners were announced in April 2011. To learn more about the competition and to see the winners and the apps, visit http://appsfordevelopment.challenge-post.com/.

■ *Results at a Glance mobile application.* World Bank Results at a Glance is a free app that highlights more than 450 results profiles across more than 85 countries and a diverse range of projects over the past decade. It includes stories and data collected from projects in which the World Bank partnered with developing countries toward progress on one or more of the MDGs and on projects that advanced sectoral or thematic work in core international development areas. For more information, visit http://www.worldbank.org/open/.

■ *Open knowledge tools.* The Bank now provides a variety of tools and software applications to empower more collaborative and effective solutions to global challenges and to help development practitioners interpret and analyze the data themselves. These tools include the following:

☐ *ADePT.* This innovative software program is designed to simplify and speed up the production of tables and graphs in economic data.

☐ *PovCalNet.* This tool allows users to replicate the Bank's global poverty counts and make their own estimates on the basis of different assumptions.

☐ *iSimulate.* This web-based forecasting model of more than 100 countries not only gives users access to Bank forecasts but also allows them to design their own forecasts and simulations and to share them with others.

☐ *WITS.* This tool allows the user to access trade data. For example, it lets a producer anywhere in the world who has a laptop, an Internet connection, and an agricultural or manufactured product identify trade barriers that he or she will face in export markets around the world.

For more information about these tools, visit http://www.worldbank.org/ open/.

■ Collaborations with commercial information providers Google and Microsoft are also broadening access to the Bank's development data.

The World Bank Group continues to publish a wide range of publications in print and electronic formats, including its annual flagship reports. Major titles include *World Development Report, World Development Indicators, Africa Development Indicators, Global Development Finance, Global Monitoring Report, Global Development Horizons, Doing Business, Atlas of Global Development,* and *World Bank Annual Report.* To find out more about World Bank publications, visit http://www.worldbank.org/ publications/. Information about obtaining publications can be found in box 2.4.

Events: Conferences, Forums, and Summits

The Bank Group sponsors, hosts, or participates in numerous conferences, both on its own and in conjunction with other organizations. Among the best known is the Annual World Bank Conference on Development Economics. For major World Bank events, see http://www.worldbank.org/ events/. Many of the websites of specific Bank Group units also list upcoming events.

Box 2.4 Obtaining World Bank Group Publications

World Bank Group publications can be obtained through the World Bank InfoShop as follows:

World Bank InfoShop
MSN: J1-100
701 18th Street, NW
Washington, DC 20433
Fax: 1-202-458-4500
E-mail: infoshop@worldbank.org.
Website: http://www.worldbank.org/publications/ or
http://www.worldbank.org/infoshop/
E-library: http://www.worldbank.org/elibrary/

World Bank Project Cycle

In recent years, the World Bank has lent an average of $43.4 billion annually ($24.7 billion in fiscal 2008, $46.9 billion in fiscal 2009, and $58.7 billion in fiscal 2010) for projects in the more than 100 countries it works with. Projects range across the economic and social spectrum, including infrastructure, education, health, and government financial management.

The projects the Bank finances are conceived and supervised according to a well-documented project cycle (figure 2.5). Documents produced as part of the project cycle can be valuable sources of information for interested stakeholders wanting to keep abreast of the work the Bank is financing and for businesses wishing to participate in Bank-financed projects. The following text provides a step-by-step guide to the project cycle and the documents that are produced as part of the process. Most of this information is specific to World Bank projects; information about IFC's project cycle follows in the next section. Information about how to access information about World Bank projects appears at the end of this section.

How the Process Begins: Poverty Reduction and Country Assistance Strategies

The Bank recognizes that many past assistance efforts, including some of its own, failed because donors, rather than the governments they were trying to assist, drove the agenda. Under its current development policy, the Bank

Figure 2.5 World Bank Project Cycle

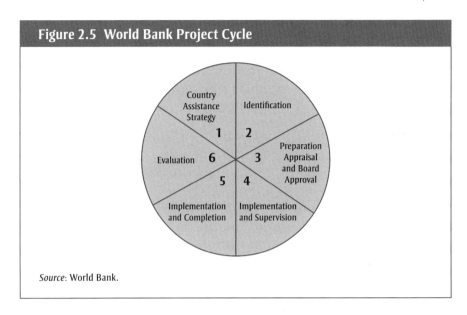

Source: World Bank.

helps governments take the lead in preparing and implementing development strategies, in the belief that if the country owns the program and it has
widespread stakeholder support, the program has a greater chance of success.

In low-income countries, the Bank approaches poverty reduction through
widespread consultation and consensus building on how to boost development. Under that process, the country devises a national poverty reduction
strategy and creates a framework that enables donors to better coordinate
their programs and align them with national priorities. The government
consults a wide cross-section of local groups and combines such consultations with an extensive analysis of poverty in the country and of the country's economic situation. The government determines its own priorities from
this process and produces targets for reducing poverty over a period of three
to five years. These priorities and targets are outlined in a Poverty Reduction
Strategy Paper. The Bank and other aid agencies then align their assistance
efforts with the country's own strategy—a proven way of improving development effectiveness.

The Bank's blueprint for its work with a country is based on a Country
Assistance Strategy that, in the case of low-income countries, is derived from
the priorities contained in the countries' PRSPs. The CAS is produced in
cooperation with the government and interested stakeholders. The CAS may
draw on analytical work conducted by the Bank or other parties on a wide
range of sectors, such as agriculture, education, fiscal management, health,
public expenditure and budgeting, and procurement.

Country Strategy and Identification

The World Bank works with a borrowing country's government and other stakeholders to determine how financial and other assistance can be designed to have the greatest influence. After analytical work is conducted, the borrower and the Bank produce strategies and priorities for reducing poverty and improving living standards.

The World Bank and the government agree on an initial project concept and its beneficiaries, and the Bank's project team outlines the basic elements in a Project Concept Note. This document identifies proposed objectives, imminent risks, alternative scenarios, and a likely timetable for the project approval process. Two other Bank documents are generated during this phase. The Project Information Document contains useful public resources for tailoring bidding documents to the proposed project, and the publicly available Integrated Safeguards Data Sheet identifies key issues related to the Bank's policies for environmental and social safeguards.

The following project documentation is required at this stage:

- Project Information Document
- Integrated Safeguards Data Sheet

Project Preparation

The borrower government and its implementing agency or agencies are responsible for the project preparation phase, which can take several years. The government contracts with consultants and other public sector companies for goods, works, and services, if necessary, not only during this phase but also later in the project's implementation phase. Beneficiaries and stakeholders are also consulted at this stage to obtain their feedback and enlist their support for the project. Because of the time, effort, and resources involved, the full commitment of the government to the project is vital.

The World Bank generally takes an advisory role and offers analysis and advice, when requested, during this phase. However, the Bank itself assesses the relevant capacity of the implementing agencies at this point, to reach agreement with the borrower about arrangements for overall project management, such as the systems required for financial management, procurement, reporting, and monitoring and evaluation.

Earlier screening by Bank staff members may have determined that a proposed project could have environmental or social impacts that are included under the World Bank's environmental and social safeguard policies. If necessary, the borrower prepares an Environmental Assessment

Report that analyzes the planned project's likely environmental impact and describes steps to mitigate possible harm. In the event of major environmental issues in a country, the borrower's Environmental Action Plan will describe the problems, identify the main causes, and formulate policies and concrete actions to deal with them. For planning of social safeguards, various studies aimed at analyzing a project's potentially adverse effects on the health, productive resources, economies, and cultures of indigenous peoples may be undertaken. An Indigenous Peoples Development Plan identifies the borrower's planned interventions that may be needed in affected areas with indigenous populations, with the objective of avoiding or lessening potential negative impacts on the people. These plans are integrated into the design of the project.

Project documentation at this stage includes the following:

- Environmental Assessment Report
- Indigenous Peoples Development Plan
- Environmental Action Plan

Project Appraisal

Appraisal gives stakeholders an opportunity to review the project design in detail and resolve any outstanding questions. The government and the World Bank review the work done during the identification and preparation phases and confirm the expected project outcomes, intended beneficiaries, and evaluation tools for monitoring progress. Agreement is reached on the viability of all aspects of the project at this time. The Bank team confirms that all aspects of the project are consistent with all World Bank operations requirements and that the government has institutional arrangements in place to implement the project efficiently. All parties agree on a project timetable and on public disclosure of key documents and identify any unfinished business required for final Bank approval. The final steps are assessment of the project's readiness for implementation and agreement on conditions for effectiveness (agreed-on actions prior to implementation). The Project Information Document is updated and made publicly available when the project is approved for funding.

Project Approval

Once all project details are negotiated and accepted by the government and the World Bank, the project team prepares the Project Appraisal

Document (for investment lending) or the Program Document (for development policy lending), along with other financial and legal documents, for submission to the Bank's Board of Executive Directors for consideration and approval. When funding approval is obtained, the conditions for effectiveness are met, and the legal documents are accepted and signed, the implementation phase begins. Project documentation at this stage includes the following:

- Project Appraisal Document
- Program Document
- Loan and credit documents

Project Implementation

The borrower government implements the development project with funds from the World Bank. With technical assistance and support from the Bank's team, the implementing government agency prepares the specifications for the project and carries out all procurement of goods, works, and services needed, as well as any environmental and social impact mitigation set out in the agreed-on plans. Financial management and procurement specialists on the Bank's project team ensure that adequate fiduciary controls on the use of project funds are in place. All components at this phase are ready, but project delays and unexpected events can sometimes prompt the restructuring of project objectives.

Once the project is under way, the implementing government agency reports regularly on the project's activities. The government and the Bank also join forces and prepare a midterm review of the project's progress. In addition, the World Bank's Report on the Status of Projects in Execution, which is a brief summary of all Bank-funded projects active at the end of each fiscal year, is available to the public. As projects close during the fiscal year, they are removed from this report, because their individual Implementation Completion and Results Reports are publicly disclosed at that time.

The government and the Bank monitor the project's progress, outcomes, and effects on beneficiaries throughout the implementation phase to obtain data for evaluating and measuring the ultimate effectiveness of the operation and the project in terms of results.

Project documentation at this stage includes the following:

- Report on the Status of Projects in Execution

Project Completion

When a project is completed and closed at the end of the loan disbursement period—a process that can take anywhere from 1 to 10 years—the Bank and the borrowing government document the results, the problems, and the lessons learned from the project in a report. The knowledge gained from this results-measurement process is intended to benefit similar projects in the future. Project documentation at this stage includes the following:

- Implementation Completion Reports

Evaluation

The Bank's Independent Evaluation Group assesses the performance of roughly 1 project out of 4 (about 70 projects a year), to measure outcomes against the original objectives, sustainability of results, and institutional development effects. From time to time, IEG also produces impact evaluation reports to assess the economic worth of projects and the long-term effects on people and the environment against an explicit counterfactual.

Project documentation at this stage includes the following:

- Project Performance Assessment Reports
- Impact evaluation documents

These documents, which are produced by IEG, are described further in the following subsections.

Other Monitoring

An independent body, the Quality Assurance Group, monitors the quality of the Bank's activities during implementation to improve management. It examines project quality both for loans (shortly after project approval by the Board) and for advisory services (after delivery to country clients). It also monitors the quality of project supervision and reports to the Board of Executive Directors on the overall health of the portfolio of ongoing projects through the *Annual Report on Portfolio Performance.* The Quality Assurance Group's website is at http://go.worldbank.org/ J4OO0PFYM0/.

Another independent body within the World Bank, the Inspection Panel, provides a forum for citizens who believe they have been or could be harmed by a Bank-financed project. For details, go to http://www.worldbank.org/inspectionpanel/.

PPARs

Completed projects are evaluated through Project Performance Assessment Reports (PPARs), which rate projects in terms of their outcome (taking into account relevance, efficacy, and efficiency); sustainability of results; and institutional development effect. PPARs, completed after Bank funds have been fully disbursed to a project, are similar to the completion evaluations carried out by many agencies. PPARs are the main project-level evaluations conducted by IEG.

Impact evaluation documents

In international development, impact evaluation is principally concerned with the final results of interventions—such as programs, projects, policies, or reforms—on the welfare of communities, households, and individuals. This type of evaluation seeks to identify the extent to which changes can be attributed specifically to the interventions being evaluated. IEG impact evaluations have increased as the unit has collaborated more with other international development evaluation units and networks, such as the Evaluation Cooperation Group, the Network of Networks for Impact Evaluation, the United Nations Evaluation Group, the International Initiative for Impact Evaluation, and the OECD Development Assistance Committee Evaluation Network.

Project Information

Several major sources provide project documents, which are also referred to as *operational documents*, and other project information (see box 2.5 for additional Web links):

- *Projects database.* Available online at http://www.worldbank.org/projects/, this database enables users to search the entire World Bank project portfolio from the founding of IBRD to the present. Users can search in the projects database or in project documents, contract awards, or documents on analytical and advisory work. The search can be defined by any combination of the following: keyword, region, country or area, theme, sector, project status, product line, lending instrument, year approved,

Box 2.5 Web Links for Project Information, Disclosure, and Evaluation

WORLD BANK

Loans and credits: http://www.worldbank.org/loansandcredits/

Projects, policies, and strategies: http://www.worldbank.org/projects/

Project cycle: http://www.worldbank.org/projectcycle/

Operational procedures: http://www1.worldbank.org/operations/

Country assistance strategies: http://www.worldbank.org/cas/

Operational documents: http://www.worldbank.org/infoshop/

Poverty Reduction Strategy Papers: http://www.worldbank.org/prsp/

Public information services: http://www.worldbank.org/pics/

Policy on disclosure of information: http://www.worldbank.org/disclosure/

Independent Evaluation Group: http://www.independentevaluation.worldbankgroup.org/

Inspection Panel: http://www.worldbank.org/inspectionpanel/

Development Impact Evaluation program: http://www.worldbank.org/dime

IFC

Projects: http://www.ifc.org/projects

Project cycle: http://www.ifc.org/ifcext/proserv.nsf/content/IFCprojectcycle

Policy on disclosure of information: http://www.ifc.org/disclosure

Environmental and social standards: http://www.ifc.org/projects and http://www.ifc.org/ifcext/sustainability.nsf/Content/EnvSocStandards

Independent Evaluation Group: http://www.ifc.org/ieg

IFC AND MIGA

Office of the Compliance Advisor/Ombudsman:
http://www.cao-ombudsman.org/

MIGA

Projects insured by MIGA: http://www.miga.org/

Disclosure policies: http://www.miga.org/policies/

ICSID

Cases: http://www.worldbank.org/icsid/

and environmental category. Results show the basic project information with links to available project documents.

- *Recent loans, credits, and grants.* The World Bank also posts information on the loans, credits, and grants most recently approved by the Board of Executive Directors under "News" on the Bank's website (http://www.worldbank.org/loansandcredits/). Here, users can view information by date, by topic (sector), by region, or by country. The listings generally include the names of contacts who can provide additional information.

- *Documents and reports.* This feature of the World Bank's website, available at http://www-wds.worldbank.org/, provides more than 130,000 World Bank documents—the full range of material that is made available to the public under its access to information policy. This approach to accessing project documents is an alternative to searching the projects database. This site also includes documents created through the Bank's country economic and sector work; reports concerning the Bank's Board; and various working papers, publications, and informal series from departments around the Bank. Users of the site can access documents as both text and PDF files.

- *InfoShop* is the World Bank Group's bookstore and Public Information Center. It is located at Bank headquarters, at the corner of 18th Street and Pennsylvania Avenue NW, across from the main complex. InfoShop provides computer access to project documents and sells all of the Bank Group's formal publications, books on development topics by other publishers, souvenirs, and gifts. InfoShop also hosts events, nearly all of which are open to the public and feature internationally known and up-and-coming speakers. For more information, go to http://www.worldbank. org/infoshop/ or contact the InfoShop at (202) 458-4500 or infoshop@ worldbank.org.

- *Public Information Centers (PICs).* These centers, which are maintained at World Bank country offices, make Bank information available to the public and disseminate the Bank's work to the widest possible audience. PIC Europe, in Paris, and PIC Tokyo offer the complete range of project documents for all member countries, and they maintain libraries of recent World Bank publications. Other country office PICs and libraries worldwide have project documents specific to the country in which the office is located and often offer a library of recent Bank publications. Each PIC serves as the central contact in the country for people seeking Bank documents and information on the Bank's operations. InfoShop coordinates with all PICs to ensure broad dissemination of information in compliance with the Bank's disclosure policy. For more information, see appendix F.

IFC Project Cycle

IFC offers a wide variety of financial products to projects of private sector companies in developing countries. The project cycle, outlined here, illustrates the stages a business idea goes through as it becomes an IFC-financed project:

- *Business development.* Guided by IFC's strategic goals, IFC's investment officers and business development officers identify suitable projects. The initial conversation with clients is critical to understanding their needs and determining whether there is a role for IFC.
- *Early review.* The investment officer prepares a description of the project, IFC's role, the anticipated contribution to development and benefits to stakeholders, and any reasons the project would potentially not work. Lessons from previous projects are considered, and in some cases, a preappraisal visit is conducted to identify any potential problems in advance. IFC senior management then decides whether to authorize project appraisal.
- *Appraisal and due diligence.* The investment team assesses the full business potential, risks, and opportunities associated with the investment through discussions with the client and visits to the project site. The following questions are asked: Is the investment financially and economically sound? Can it comply with IFC's social and environmental performance standards? Have lessons from prior investments been taken into account? Have the necessary disclosure and consultation requirements been met? How can IFC work with the client to further improve the sustainability of the project or enterprise?
- *Investment review.* The project team makes its recommendations to IFC's departmental management, which decides whether to approve the project. Investment review is a key stage in the investment cycle. The project team and departmental management must be confident that the client is able and willing to meet IFC standards and will work to improve the sustainability of the enterprise.
- *Negotiations.* The project team starts to negotiate the terms and conditions of IFC's participation in the project, including conditions of disbursement, performance and monitoring requirements, agreement of action plans, and resolution of any outstanding issues.

- *Public disclosure.* Once environmental and social due diligence are completed, review summaries and action plans are issued. These documents describe key findings and list actions to be taken by the client to close any significant compliance gap. The documents, as well as a summary of proposed investment, are posted on IFC's website before being submitted to IFC's Board of Directors for review. The length of the disclosure period is determined by the category of the project.

- *Board review and approval.* The project is submitted to IFC's Board of Directors for consideration and approval through regular or streamlined procedures. *Streamlined* means that the members of the board review the documents but do not meet to discuss the project. This option is available to low-risk projects. IFC management can approve certain small projects under delegated authority. The due diligence process and public disclosure remain the same in all cases. The board demands that each investment have economic, financial, and development value and reflect IFC's commitment to sustainability.

- *Commitment.* IFC and the private sector company sign the legal agreement for the investment. Under the agreement, the private sector client agrees to comply with IFC's sustainability requirements, to immediately report any serious accident or fatality, and to provide regular monitoring reports. The legal agreement also formalizes the client's environmental and social action plan.

- *Disbursement of funds.* Funds are often paid out in stages or on completion of certain steps documented in the legal agreement.

- *Project supervision and development outcome tracking.* IFC monitors its investments to ensure compliance with the conditions in the loan agreement. The company submits regular reports on financial and social and environmental performance, as well as information on factors that might materially affect the enterprise. Project site visits are scheduled to verify that environmental and social requirements are met. Ongoing dialogue allows IFC to partner with clients to solve issues and identify new opportunities. IFC also tracks the project's contribution to development against key indicators identified at the start of the investment cycle.

- *Evaluation.* To help improve its operational performance, IFC conducts annual evaluations based on a random sample of projects that have reached early operating maturity.

- *Closing.* IFC closes its books on the project when the investment is repaid in full or when it exits by selling its equity stake. In some cases, IFC may decide to write off the debt. Its goal is to work with the client to develop practices and management systems that support a project's sustainability and that will continue long after IFC's involvement has ended.

All project information is posted on the Web at http://www.ifc.org/projects. Users can narrow their searches by document type, project country, sector, IFC region, environmental category, or keywords.

Partnerships

The World Bank Group has a large array of partners in the global fight against poverty. As discussed in the "Strategies" section earlier in this chapter, the most important partnership is with the developing countries themselves, not only with the many government agencies but also with the whole range of civil society, especially the poor, who are most affected by Bank Group activities.

The Bank Group also partners with other international institutions and donors, the private sector, civil society, and professional and academic associations to improve the coordination of aid policies at the country, regional, and global levels. Partnerships for financing, such as trust funds and cofinancing arrangements, are described in the earlier sections on Bank Group financial products and services. See also http://www.world bank.org/, select "About," and then choose "Partners."

Partnerships with International Institutions

In addition to the IMF, the United Nations, and the many UN agencies and programs (see chapter 1), the Bank Group works with many other organizations whose membership is made up of country governments, for example, the European Union, the World Trade Organization, and multilateral development banks and other multilateral financial institutions.

The banking institutions provide financial support and professional advice for economic and social development activities in developing countries. The term *multilateral development bank* typically refers to the World Bank Group and four regional development banks: the African Development Bank, the Asian Development Bank, the European Bank for Reconstruction and Development, and the Inter-American Development Bank. The Bank Group also works with several other banks and funds—multilateral financial institutions—that lend to developing countries but have a narrower membership and focus. These institutions include, among others, the European Commission and the Islamic Development Bank. Subregional banks owned by groups of countries and established for development purposes also work with the Bank Group. Among these are the Caribbean Development Bank, the Central American Bank for Economic Integration, the East African Development Bank, the Eurasian Development Bank, and the West African Development Bank.

Global and Regional Partnership Programs

Global and regional partnership programs (GRPPs) represent organized collective action in a globalizing world. GRPPs are programmatic partnerships in which the partners dedicate financial, technical, staff, and reputational resources toward achieving agreed-on objectives over time. The activities of GRPPs are global, regional, or multicountry (not single country) in scope, and the partners establish a new organization with shared governance and a management unit to deliver those activities. Global partnership programs (such as the Prototype Carbon Fund, the Stop TB Partnership, and the Cities Alliance) and regional partnership programs (such as the African Programme for Onchocerciasis Control and the Child Protection Initiative) are now an important and growing line of business for the World Bank for addressing global challenges and sharing knowledge. As of April 2011, the Bank is involved in nearly 120 GRPPs with shared governance arrangements and spends about $7 billion annually.

Partnerships with Bilateral Development Agencies

The World Bank Group works with the development agencies of individual countries to coordinate aid and achieve development goals, sometimes formally through trust funds and often with such countries' representatives in the field. Work is coordinated by various committees and through consultations that take place throughout the year.

Programmatic Partnerships

The World Bank hosts the secretariats of several closely affiliated organizations at its headquarters, including the following:

- *Consultative Group on International Agricultural Research (CGIAR).* This association supports agricultural research and related activities carried out by 15 autonomous research centers. CGIAR's priorities include increasing productivity, protecting the environment, saving biodiversity, improving policies, and strengthening research at the national level. Members of

CGIAR include industrial and developing countries, foundations, and international and regional organizations. The group's website is at http://www.cgiar.org/.

- *Consultative Group to Assist the Poor (CGAP).* This independent policy and research center is dedicated to advancing financial access for the world's poor. CGAP is supported by more than 30 development agencies and private foundations that share a common mission to alleviate poverty. Housed at the World Bank, CGAP provides market intelligence; promotes standards; develops innovative solutions; and offers advisory services to governments, microfinance providers, donors, and investors. CGAP's website is at http://www.cgap.org/.

- *Development Gateway.* The Development Gateway is an Internet portal for information and knowledge sharing on sustainable development and poverty reduction. Features include AidData, a comprehensive database of development projects; dgMarket, an international procurement marketplace; Country Gateways, a network of nearly 50 locally owned and managed public-private partnerships, each of which promotes innovative and effective use of the Internet and other information and communication technologies in a country to reduce poverty and promote sustainable development; and Zunia, an online network for knowledge exchange among development professionals worldwide. Users from all over the world visit the portal to access news, events, best practices, and publications on a wide range of development topics. The Development Gateway website is at http://www.developmentgateway.org/.

- *Education for All Fast-Track Initiative.* This secretariat was created as the first-ever global compact on education, to help low-income countries achieve a free, universal basic education. It was launched in 2002 as a global partnership between donor and developing countries to ensure accelerated progress toward the MDG of universal primary education by 2015. All low-income countries that demonstrate a serious commitment to achieving universal primary completion can join the Fast-Track Initiative. For more information, visit http://www.educationfasttrack.org/.

- *GAVI Alliance.* The GAVI Alliance (formerly known as the Global Alliance for Vaccines and Immunisation) is a public-private partnership focused on increasing children's access to vaccines in poor countries. Partners include the GAVI Fund, national governments, the United Nations Children's Fund, the World Health Organization, the World Bank, the Bill & Melinda Gates Foundation, the vaccine industry, public health institutions, and nongovernmental organizations (NGOs). The GAVI Fund provides resources for the GAVI Alliance's programs. The GAVI Alliance provides a forum where partners can agree on mutual goals, share strategies, and coordinate efforts. Its website is at http://www.gavialliance.org/.

■ *Global Environment Facility.* This independent entity provides grants and concessional loans to developing countries so that they can meet the costs of measures designed to achieve global environmental benefits. The focus is on climate change, biological diversity, international waters, ozone layer depletion, land degradation, and persistent organic pollutants. The World Bank, the United Nations Development Programme, and the United Nations Environment Programme are the three implementing agencies of the Global Environment Facility, which is supported administratively by the World Bank but remains functionally independent. Each agency finances the facility's activities within its respective areas of competence. The Global Environment Facility's website is at http://www.worldbank.org/gef/.

NGOs and Civil Society

Most development projects approved by the Bank Group involve the active participation of NGOs in project implementation, and most of the Bank Group's country strategies benefit from consultations with civil society organizations. The Bank Group uses the term *civil society organizations* to refer to the wide array of nongovernmental and not-for-profit organizations that have a presence in public life and that express the interests and values of their members, as well as other organizations that are based on ethical, cultural, political, scientific, religious, or philanthropic considerations.

The Bank Group's outreach in this area encompasses trade unions, community-based organizations, social movements, faith-based institutions, charitable organizations, research centers, foundations, student organizations, professional associations, and many other entities. Staff members working in country offices around the world reach out to and collaborate with NGOs in a variety of areas, ranging from education and HIV/AIDS to the environment. The home pages of the Bank Group's civil society efforts are at http://www.worldbank.org/civilsociety/ (for the World Bank) and http://www.ifc.org/ngo (for IFC).

Staff, Consultants, and Vendors

World Bank Group Staff

The World Bank Group recognizes its staff as its most strategic asset. The institutions of the Bank Group together have a full-time staff of close to

15,000 professionals and administrative personnel (as of April 2011) from some 170 countries. Of these individuals, about 40 percent are located in offices in more than 110 developing countries. The proportion of staff members based in country offices has grown in recent years, reflecting the Bank Group's commitment to operating in close partnership with its clients. Staff members typically have strong academic backgrounds, a broad understanding of development issues, and international work experience.

The staff's diversity reflects the Bank Group's global membership, bringing a wide range of perspectives to bear on its poverty reduction work. Bank Group management includes a record number of women and nationals of developing countries. In addition to gender, nationality, and race, the Bank Group supports diversity of sexual orientation, disabilities, education, and experience.

Job Openings, Internships, and Scholarships

The World Bank Group is continually looking for experienced professionals with a demonstrated record of professional and academic achievement. A broad understanding of development issues and international work experience, preferably at the policy level, are desirable. In addition to proficiency in English, language skills are needed in Arabic, Chinese, French, Portuguese, Russian, or Spanish.

The World Bank provides information on its job openings, job opportunities for professionals, consultancies, internships, and secondment opportunities through a careers website maintained by Human Resources, http://www.worldbank.org/careers/. For information about opportunities at IFC, go to http://www.ifc.org/careers/. For information specific to MIGA, see the "About" section at http://www.miga.org/.

Programs at the World Bank that are geared specifically to younger professionals are as follows:

■ *Young Professionals Program.* This program is for highly qualified and motivated people younger than 32 years of age who are skilled in areas relevant to the World Bank's operations. Candidates must hold the equivalent of a master's degree and have significant work experience or continued academic study at the doctoral level.
■ *Junior Professional Associates Program.* This program is for recent graduates younger than 29 who have superior academic records and an interest in international work. Candidates must hold the equivalent of a bachelor's or master's degree or be a doctoral candidate. This is a

two-year entry-level program. Associates are not eligible for employment with the World Bank for two years following the end of their appointments.

■ *Junior Professionals Program for Afro-Descendants (JPPAD).* This program is for individuals of Sub-Saharan African ancestry and U.S. minorities. JPPAD is a two-year pipeline-building program managed by the Office of Diversity Programs. JPPAD provides young talent with an opportunity to gain experience in global development and enables the Bank Group to benefit from the knowledge and diversity of these professionals.

■ *Bank Internship Program.* This program is for nationals of a World Bank member country who are enrolled in a master's or doctoral program. Interns work either in the winter (November–January) or the summer (May–September). Interns in this program receive a salary.

The World Bank's Partnership Programs reflect a broader commitment to building and sustaining strategic alliances throughout the global community. The following programs provide opportunities for qualified junior and midcareer professionals to contribute to the Bank's work program and to gain skills, exposure, and experience from the Bank's internal perspective:

■ *Global Secondment Program.* This program is for professionals from member countries, regional agencies, development banks, international organizations, and private organizations (including NGOs and academia).

■ *Donor-Funded Staffing Program.* This program is for professionals from partner countries.

■ *Kingdom of Saudi Arabia Recruitment Program.* Professionals from Saudi Arabia are eligible for this program.

■ *Kuwait Recruitment Program.* Professionals from Kuwait are eligible for this program.

■ *Voice Secondment Program.* This capacity-building program is for civil servants from member developing and transition countries.

In addition, the World Bank Group offers scholarship and fellowship programs. Details are available at http://www.worldbank.org/wbi/scholarships/. Specific programs include the following:

■ *Joint Japan–World Bank Graduate Scholarship Program.* This program covers up to two years of study toward a master's degree. Candidates must be nationals of a World Bank member country, have been accepted at a university outside their country, study in a field related to development, be younger than 45 years of age, and have at least two years of professional experience. The program is funded by the Japanese government, but it does not require study in Japan.

- *Robert S. McNamara Fellowships Program.* This program is part of the Woodrow Wilson School of Public Affairs at Princeton University. It provides a full-tuition scholarship, a travel allowance, and a stipend for living expenses. The student must be a national of a World Bank member country and have at least seven years of professional experience. Candidates apply directly to the Master's in Public Policy program at Princeton University and indicate that they are applying for admission as a McNamara Fellow.

Procurement Opportunities in Projects Financed by IBRD and IDA

Every year, investment projects financed by the World Bank generate billions of dollars in opportunities for suppliers of goods and services. Government agencies from the Bank's borrowing countries are responsible for the purchase of goods and services to support these projects. Bank procedures have been established to ensure that procurement is conducted efficiently and in an open, competitive, and transparent manner.

The procurement policies and procedures in Bank-financed projects are explained in "Guidelines: Procurement under IBRD Loans and IDA Credits" and "Guidelines: Selection and Employment of Consultants by World Bank Borrowers," which are available at http://www.worldbank.org/procure/ under the "Bidding/Consulting Opportunities" tab. Also under that tab is the "Resource Guide to Consulting, Supply, and Contracting Opportunities in Projects Financed by the World Bank," which provides detailed guidance on how to identify and track business opportunities.

Opportunities for Supplying Directly to the World Bank Group

The Bank Group regularly seeks qualified vendors for assistance in running its operations in Washington, D.C., and in offices around the world. Opportunities range from supplying printer toner cartridges to managing complex communications systems. For information on how to sell goods and services to the Bank Group, including vendor registration, the key website is the vendor kiosk at http://www.worldbank.org/corporateprocurement/.

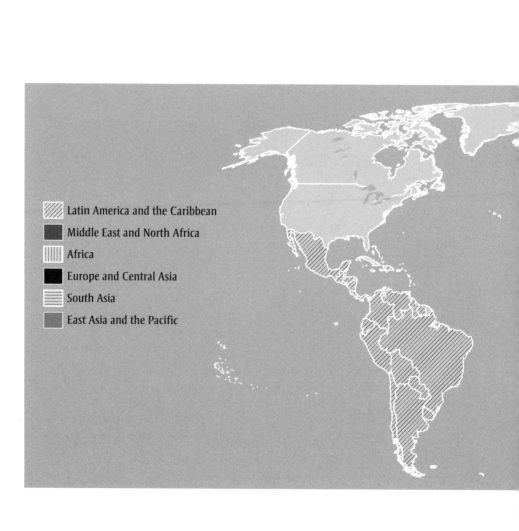

Latin America and the Caribbean

Middle East and North Africa

Africa

Europe and Central Asia

South Asia

East Asia and the Pacific

3 World Bank Group Countries and Regions

This chapter provides information on the countries of the World Bank Group: the mechanics of membership, the ways that countries are classified, and the initiatives focusing on groups of countries with shared characteristics or concerns. The chapter then reviews each of the regions into which the Bank Group organizes its member countries as it provides development assistance.

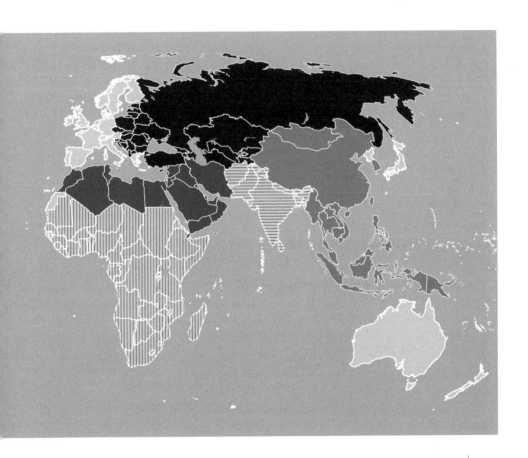

Member Countries

The five institutions of the Bank Group are owned by their member countries (see box 3.1 for Web links).

Membership

To become a member of the International Bank for Reconstruction and Development (IBRD), a country must first join the International Monetary Fund (IMF). Similarly, membership in the International Development Association (IDA), the International Finance Corporation (IFC), and the Multilateral Investment Guarantee Agency (MIGA) is contingent on membership in IBRD. In each of these cases, member countries buy shares in the institution, thereby helping to build the institution's capital and borrowing power. This arrangement is known as *capital subscriptions*. Member countries also sign the founding document of each institution: the Articles of Agreement for IBRD, IDA, and IFC and the MIGA Convention. Membership in the International Centre for Settlement of Investment Disputes (ICSID) entails signing and ratifying the ICSID Convention but does not involve capital subscriptions. Links to the founding documents for each institution can be found at http://www.worldbank.org/articles/. As of April 2011, IBRD had 187 members, IDA had 170, IFC had 182, MIGA had 175, and ICSID had 146.

The Bank Group's Corporate Secretariat keeps up-to-date lists of membership, handles official country names used by the Bank Group, and deals with communications regarding membership status and capital subscriptions. In its maps and publications, the Bank Group sometimes indicates contested boundaries or territorial claims between member countries, but

---

Box 3.1 Web Links for Country Membership Information

- *IBRD and IDA member countries:*
  see "Members" at http://www.worldbank.org/about/
- *IFC member countries:*
  see "Member Countries" at http://www.ifc.org/about
- *MIGA member countries:*
  see "About" and click on "MIGA Member Countries" at
  http://www.miga.org/
- *ICSID contracting states:*
  see "Member States" at http://www.worldbank.org/icsid/

it does not endorse any member country's position where such disputes exist.

As covered in chapter 1, member countries govern the Bank Group through the Boards of Governors and the Boards of Directors. The voting power of each executive director is determined by the value of the capital subscriptions held by the countries that he or she represents. For each of the four shareholding institutions—IBRD, IDA, IFC, and MIGA—the executive director for the United States has the greatest voting power, followed by the executive director for Japan.

Member countries can withdraw from Bank Group institutions at any time by giving notice. A member may also be suspended and, after a year, expelled if it fails to fulfill any of its obligations to a Bank Group institution. A country that ceases to be an IMF member automatically ceases to be a member of the Bank Group unless, within three months, the Bank Group decides by a special majority to allow the country to remain a member. When a country ceases to be a member, it continues to be liable for its contractual obligations, such as servicing its loans. It also continues to be liable for calls on its unpaid subscription resulting from losses sustained by a Bank Group institution on guarantees or loans outstanding on the date of withdrawal.

Member countries are listed by geographic region later in this chapter. A master list—with dates of membership and each country's voting power—is provided in appendix D.

Ways of Classifying Countries

Several designations for member countries commonly used at the Bank Group reflect important distinctions among the member countries. Although the meanings of the terms overlap—and they are all based on wealth—they are not interchangeable.

Low-income, middle-income, and high-income economies

In its analytical and operational work, the Bank Group characterizes country economies as low income, middle income (subdivided into lower-middle income and upper-middle income), and high income. It makes these classifications for most nonsovereign territories as well as for independent countries. Low-income and middle-income economies are sometimes referred to as *developing economies*. On the basis of gross national income in 2009, low-income economies are those with average annual per capita incomes of $995 or less. For lower-middle-income economies, the figures are $996 to

$3,945; for upper-middle-income economies, $3,946 to $12,195; and for high-income economies, $12,196 or more. Classification by income does not necessarily reflect development status.

Developing and industrial countries

In general, the term *developing* refers to countries whose economies are classified as low income or middle income. The terms *industrial* or *developed* refer to countries whose economies are high income. The use of these terms is not intended to imply that all economies in the group are experiencing similar development or that other economies have reached a preferred or final stage of development.

Part I and Part II countries

In IDA, countries choose whether they are Part I or Part II primarily on the basis of their economic standing. Part I countries are almost all industrial countries and donors to IDA, and they pay their contributions in freely convertible currency. Part II countries are almost all developing countries, some of which are donors to IDA. Part II countries are entitled to pay most of their contributions to IDA in local currency.

MIGA makes a similar distinction between Category I and Category II member countries. The breakdown of countries into these categories differs slightly from the breakdown within IDA.

Donors and borrowers

In general, the term *donor* refers to a country that makes contributions specifically to IDA. In contrast, the term *borrower* refers to a country that borrows from IDA or IBRD or both. Note, however, that all member countries pay capital subscriptions, and this payment is distinct from a given country's lending and borrowing.

IBRD, IDA, and blend countries and graduates

The distinctions between IBRD and IDA borrowers—and the circumstances in which a country may be eligible to receive a blend of IBRD loans and IDA credits and grants—are based on per capita income and the country's creditworthiness. These distinctions are discussed in detail in chapter 1. Note that as a country's per capita income increases, it can graduate out of eligibility for IDA credits and grants and, in turn, become eligible for

Box 3.2 IBRD Graduates

The following countries are IBRD graduates:

1947: France	1971: Taiwan,	1989: The Bahamas
1948: Luxembourg	China	and Portugal
1957: Netherlands	1972: New Zealand	1992: Cyprus
1958: Belgium	1974: Iceland	1994: Barbados
1962: Australia and	1975: Finland,	2004: Slovenia
Austria	Israel, and	2005: Czech Republic
1964: Denmark,	Singapore	2006: Estonia and
Malta, and	1976: Ireland	Lithuania
Norway	1977: Spain	2007: Hungary and
1965: Italy	1979: Greece	Latvia
1967: Japan	1987: Oman	2008: Slovak Republic

The following graduates have returned to borrower status:

Country	Last year borrowed (before relapse)	Year of reinitiated borrowing
Costa Rica	1994	2000
Malaysia	1994	1998
Republic of Korea	1995	1998
Chile	1996	1999

IBRD loans (box 3.2). Wealthier countries remain members of Bank Group organizations, however, even if they or the enterprises operating within their borders do not draw on Bank Group services.

Country Activities and Operations

As indicated in chapter 2, the Bank Group's project databases enable users to search for information on individual institutions' activities in a given country. The Bank Group's key resource for comparative data on countries is *World Development Indicators*, which is published each year in April and is available in both print and online formats. In addition, the World Bank has numerous country-specific websites, some maintained by the regional vice presidencies and some by the country offices. The website showing World Bank information on countries and regions is http://www.worldbank.org/countries/. Country information for IFC is accessible through the websites of the investment regions; see http://www.ifc.org/sitemap for links to these sites.

The appendixes to this book provide a number of resources covering both borrower and donor countries:

- A comprehensive table of member countries, including their memberships in the various Bank Group institutions, the years they joined, and their individual voting power can be found in appendix D.
- A list of country groupings that form the constituencies of the 24 executive directors, with the total voting power that each director represents, can be found in appendix E.
- A description of additional country resources and where information about them can be found in appendix F. These resources include country offices and websites, public information centers, depository libraries, and distributors of World Bank publications.

Initiatives for Groups of Countries

Some Bank Group initiatives target groups of countries with key features in common, such as their income level, their degree of indebtedness, or the strength of their institutions.

Fragile and conflict-affected countries

Many of the world's poorest countries have faced a vicious cycle of conflict and poverty. Some 80 percent of the 20 poorest countries have suffered a major war in the past 15 years, bringing extraordinary suffering to their people and often affecting the larger region. Peace can also be fragile: countries emerging from war face a 44 percent chance of relapsing within five years. Even with rapid progress on economic recovery, a generation or more can be needed just to return to prewar living standards. Helping to prevent conflict and support reconstruction remains a critical part of the World Bank's global mission of poverty reduction. It is working with many partners, including donor trust funds and the United Nations, to offer more responsive, flexible, and comprehensive solutions in difficult environments.

Middle-income countries

Middle-income countries are still home to most of the world's poor people, often with a heavy concentration in specific regions or ethnic groups. These countries are generally creditworthy and have some access to financial markets, but they face constraints in mobilizing the funds they need to invest in infrastructure and essential services. They also need assistance in reforming policies and institutions in ways that improve the investment climate. The Bank Group is working to meet middle-income countries' specific needs with tailored assistance that draws on an array of competitive financial products and knowledge and learning services. These countries are also increasingly important partners in the Bank's work to address critical cross-border and global issues, such as clean energy, trade integration, environmental protection, international financial stability, and the fight against infectious diseases.

Multilateral Debt Relief Initiative

Established by the World Bank, IMF, and member countries in 1996 and significantly expanded in 1999, the Heavily Indebted Poor Countries (HIPC) Initiative is a comprehensive approach to reducing the external debt of the world's poorest, most heavily indebted countries. Its goals are to work with countries so they can move from endless restructuring of debt to lasting debt relief, to reduce multilateral debt, and to free up resources for countries that pursue economic and social reforms targeted at measurable poverty reduction.

The Multilateral Debt Relief Initiative (MDRI), introduced in 2006, has built on the HIPC Initiative to cut the debt burdens of many of the world's poorest countries to acceptable levels. Debt relief provided under both initiatives has substantially alleviated the debt burdens of these very poor countries. As of March 2011, 36 of the 40 eligible countries were benefiting from HIPC assistance, and 28 had also received 100 percent debt relief from major multilateral creditors under MDRI. To qualify for these benefits, countries must maintain sufficient macroeconomic stability, carry out key structural and social reforms, and satisfactorily implement a poverty reduction strategy. For more information about the Bank's efforts to work with poor countries in managing their debt, including a list of eligible countries, visit www.worldbank.org/debt/.

Small states

Small states is a term applied to a diverse group of sovereign developing countries—some quite wealthy, some very poor, some islands or groups of islands, some landlocked, and many with populations of 1.5 million or less. More than 40 developing countries meet that definition, almost all of them members of the World Bank.

Many of these countries are especially vulnerable to external events, including natural disasters that cause high volatility in national incomes; many suffer from limited capacity in the public and private sectors; and many currently face an uncertain and difficult economic transition under a changing world trade regime. World Bank engagement with small states has addressed these challenges through specific country and regional programs and through advocacy and corporate initiatives, including lending, economic sector work and technical assistance, and sponsorship of the Annual Small States Forum, which raises the profile of issues affecting small states and provides an opportunity for officials of those states to bring their views and ideas to the attention of the international community. For more information, see http://www.worldbank.org/smallstates/.

Regional groupings

Most Bank Group institutions approach their work by grouping developing countries into geographic regions. As discussed in chapter 1, these regions are one dimension of an organizational matrix, the other dimension being the thematic network or sector aspects of development that cut across regions. The following sections provide a brief overview of Bank Group regions: which countries they include, a few essential facts, and some information on the Bank Group's activities and priorities. They also offer information on major regional initiatives, which in most cases are partnership initiatives between the Bank Group and other organizations or governments.

Additional issue briefs for world regions can be found at http://www. worldbank.org/issuebriefs/. More comprehensive information on regions can be found in the annual reports of the Bank Group institutions.

The regional sections hereafter follow the organization of the World Bank's regional vice presidencies (see figure 3.1 for the share of total lending provided to each region). These vice presidencies largely correspond to IFC's regional departments, except that IFC assigns a few countries to different regions (see figure 3.2 for the share of total investments provided to each region). A small number of IFC investment projects are classified as global because they involve private enterprises that are active in more than one developing region.

In its annual report, MIGA includes East Asia and the Pacific and South Asia as a single region (see figure 3.3 for MIGA's outstanding portfolio distribution by region). ICSID does not organize its work by regions.

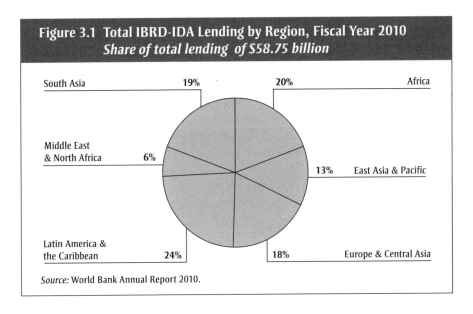

Figure 3.1 Total IBRD-IDA Lending by Region, Fiscal Year 2010
Share of total lending of $58.75 billion

South Asia 19% 20% Africa

Middle East & North Africa 6%

13% East Asia & Pacific

Latin America & the Caribbean 24% 18% Europe & Central Asia

Source: World Bank Annual Report 2010.

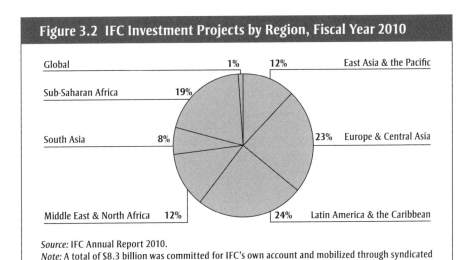

Figure 3.2 IFC Investment Projects by Region, Fiscal Year 2010

Global 1% 12% East Asia & the Pacific

Sub-Saharan Africa 19%

South Asia 8% 23% Europe & Central Asia

Middle East & North Africa 12% 24% Latin America & the Caribbean

Source: IFC Annual Report 2010.
Note: A total of $8.3 billion was committed for IFC's own account and mobilized through syndicated loans. Some amounts include regional shares of investments that are officially classified as global projects.

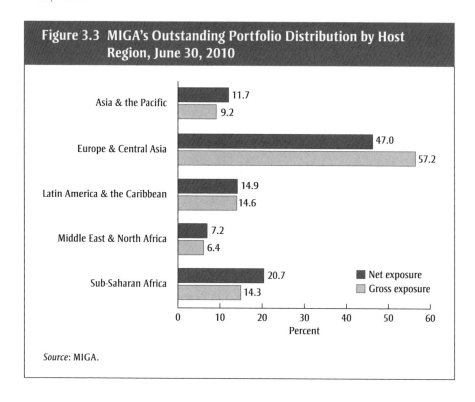

Figure 3.3 MIGA's Outstanding Portfolio Distribution by Host Region, June 30, 2010

Source: MIGA.

Note that, strictly speaking, Bank Group regions refer only to the countries that are eligible for borrowing or other services. Wealthier member countries that lie within these geographic areas—for example, Barbados, Oman, and Singapore—are not normally included in lists of countries within these regions. The Bank Group gathers economic information on all countries, however, and operates offices in a number of donor countries.

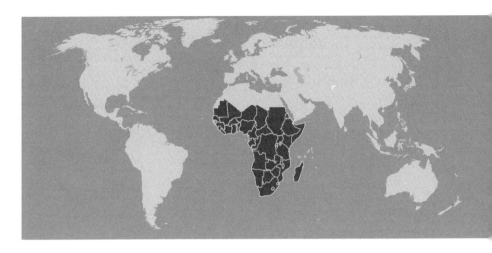

Africa

This World Bank region includes the following countries that are eligible for borrowing:

Angola	Ethiopia	Niger
Benin	Gabon	Nigeria
Botswana	The Gambia	Rwanda
Burkina Faso	Ghana	São Tomé and Principe
Burundi	Guinea	Senegal
Cameroon	Guinea-Bissau	Seychelles
Cape Verde	Kenya	Sierra Leone
Central African Republic	Lesotho	Somalia
Chad	Liberia	South Africa
Comoros	Madagascar	Sudan
Democratic Republic of Congo	Malawi	Swaziland
Republic of Congo	Mali	Tanzania
Côte d'Ivoire	Mauritania	Togo
Equatorial Guinea	Mauritius	Uganda
Eritrea	Mozambique	Zambia
	Namibia	Zimbabwe

All these countries are members of IBRD. As for the other institutions,

- Namibia and the Seychelles are not members of IDA.
- Djibouti is included in IFC's Sub-Saharan Africa region.
- the Comoros, Niger, São Tomé and Principe, and Somalia are not members of MIGA.

■ Angola, Eritrea, Ethiopia, Guinea-Bissau, Namibia, São Tomé and Príncipe, and South Africa are not members of ICSID.

The World Bank in Africa

Africa is a priority for the development community and the World Bank Group. It is the Bank Group's largest region with the greatest number of client countries and the highest volume of IDA lending, and it presents some of the greatest challenges to the development community. Box 3.3 presents key regional facts.

The region was heavily affected by the global food, fuel, and financial crises. Despite the severity of these crises, Africa is recovering rapidly, thanks to more than a decade of prudent macroeconomic policies by many countries and to the sound responses of policy makers. Rather than slowing or reversing reforms, policy makers have, by and large, continued to pursue prudent economic policies.

With Africa facing an unprecedented opportunity to transform itself and improve the lives of its people, the World Bank is responding with a new, ambitious strategy that could help African economies to take off, as the economies of Asia did 30 years ago. The new approach marks a significant shift in the way the organization views Africa and its own role as a supporter of the continent's progress.

Laid out in three main business lines, the program was crafted over more than a year through extensive research and international consultations, especially with the people of Africa.

Box 3.3 Africa Fast Facts

0.8 billion	Total population
2.5 percent	Population growth
52 years	Life expectancy at birth
86	Infant mortality per 1,000 births
67 percent	Female youth literacy
$1,096	Gross national income per capita
22 million	Number of people living with HIV/AIDS

Source: World Bank Annual Report 2010.

The plan, titled "Africa's Future and the World Bank's Support to It," shifts from a more general focus on seeking economic stability and sound fundamentals to emphasizing the need for attention in three key areas:

1. *Competitiveness and employment.* The plan will assist countries in diversifying their economies and generating jobs, especially for the 7 million to 10 million young people entering the labor force each year. It will help close the gap between infrastructure needs and investments—currently about $48 billion annually—and support efforts to make it easier for business to operate. In addition, the plan will focus on building the skills of workers.
2. *Vulnerability and resilience.* Africa's poor are directly affected by shocks—economic shocks, health-related problems, natural disasters, and conflict—which keep them in poverty. By focusing on better health care, dealing preemptively with the effects of climate change through improved irrigation and water management, and strengthening public agencies to share resources more fairly and build consensus, the plan seeks to reduce the number of shocks and limit the damage from those that do occur.
3. *Governance and public sector capacity.* Critical services in education, health, and basic infrastructure are too often either not delivered or delivered badly because of weak management of public funds. The Bank's program of support aims to give citizens better information on what they should expect from their governments, as well as the capacity to report on instances when services are not delivered properly. The Bank will also work directly with governments in their efforts to improve their systems and capacity to deliver basic services and manage accounts.

Significantly, the new strategy reverses the order of importance of the Bank's instruments to support Africa. The most important ingredient will be partnerships, then knowledge, and finally finance. The goal is to make sure that the Bank's interventions complement what others—including the African governments, the private sector, and other agencies—are doing.

To improve the delivery of its services, the Bank has increased its presence on the ground: the number of internationally recruited staff members based in field offices, including offices in postconflict and fragile states, rose to 267 in 2010, up from 153 in 2007. Field-based offices have also been granted greater decision-making authority, with the share of Bank tasks directly managed from the field rising from 25 percent in 2007 to 32 percent in 2010.

Funding to the region has risen substantially in recent years: in fiscal 2010 combined IDA and IBRD funding reached $11.4 billion (figures 3.4 and 3.5).

Most African countries remain off track for meeting the Millennium Development Goals, their advances further slowed by global crises. Since the mid-1990s, however, Africa has made enormous progress in improving social development indicators. Poverty has declined at a rate of about 1 percentage point a year, and some evidence indicates that child mortality is beginning to fall sharply in some countries. However, though progress has been made in a number of areas, including poverty, achieving other targets remains a major challenge in Africa.

For more information, visit the region's website at http://www.worldbank.org/africa/.

IFC in Africa

IFC is the largest multilateral source of loan and equity financing for private sector projects in Africa. The corporation's investments in the region continue to grow and cover a wide range of sectors, including microfinance and other financial sector projects, renewable energy, agriculture, infrastructure,

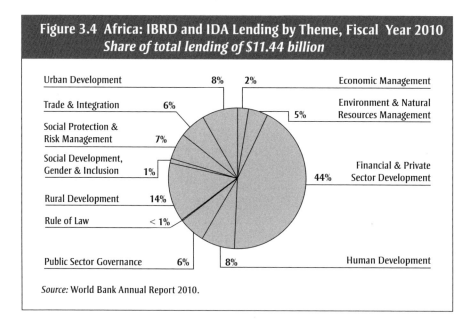

Figure 3.4 Africa: IBRD and IDA Lending by Theme, Fiscal Year 2010
Share of total lending of $11.44 billion

Urban Development	8%
	2% Economic Management
Trade & Integration	6%
	5% Environment & Natural Resources Management
Social Protection & Risk Management	7%
Social Development, Gender & Inclusion	1%
	44% Financial & Private Sector Development
Rural Development	14%
Rule of Law	< 1%
Public Sector Governance	6%
	8% Human Development

Source: World Bank Annual Report 2010.

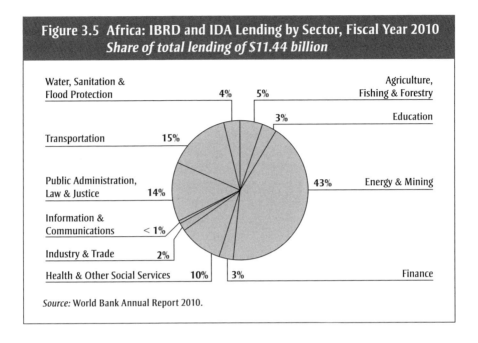

Figure 3.5 Africa: IBRD and IDA Lending by Sector, Fiscal Year 2010
Share of total lending of $11.44 billion

Water, Sanitation & Flood Protection — 4%

Agriculture, Fishing & Forestry — 5%

Education — 3%

Transportation — 15%

Public Administration, Law & Justice — 14%

Energy & Mining — 43%

Information & Communications — < 1%

Industry & Trade — 2%

Health & Other Social Services — 10%

Finance — 3%

Source: World Bank Annual Report 2010.

and health. The region is also a focus of many trade finance transactions through IFC's Global Trade Finance Program.

Through its investments, its advisory services, and its asset management company, IFC is focusing on improving the investment climate, creating economic opportunities for women, supporting economic recovery in conflict-affected countries, catalyzing investment from the private sector, and promoting sustainable agriculture.

The Sub-Saharan Africa Department is managed from IFC's regional hub in Johannesburg. Its website is http://www.ifc.org/africa.

MIGA in Africa

Sub-Saharan Africa is a priority area for MIGA, which works to attract new investment in the region. MIGA's support for projects on the continent underscores its commitment to the poorest countries as well as its capacity to assist fragile states and countries emerging from conflict. Its efforts are focused on investments in infrastructure, agribusiness, green energy, financial services, and small-scale enterprises.

Regional Initiatives

Regional initiatives in Sub-Saharan Africa include the following:

- *Booster Program for Malaria Control in Africa.* Launched in 2005 by the World Bank, the Booster Program was established to assist African governments in scaling up effective interventions to bring malaria under control on the continent. The program translates the Bank's global strategy for malaria control into a concrete plan within the framework of the Roll Back Malaria Partnership. It creates a 10-year horizon and supports country-level efforts to deliver concrete and measurable results, break health care bottlenecks, and enhance progress toward achieving their national malaria control targets. The World Bank and its partners have worked together to develop a Malaria Scorecard that tracks monetary investments and coverage progress for key interventions.
- *Chad-Cameroon Pipeline Project.* The objective of this project is to develop the oil fields in southern Chad and construct a pipeline to offshore oil-loading facilities on Cameroon's Atlantic coast. The unprecedented framework for this project will transform oil wealth into direct benefits for the poor and vulnerable, as well as for the environment. The World Bank and the government of Chad signed a memorandum of understanding in July 2006 under which Chad committed 70 percent of its 2007 budget spending to priority poverty reduction programs.
- *East Africa Agricultural Productivity Program.* Approved at the end of fiscal 2009, this program is supporting cooperation by Ethiopia, Kenya, and Tanzania in generating and disseminating new technology, particularly for growing wheat, rice, fodder, and cassava and for raising dairy cattle.
- *HIV/AIDS Agenda for Action.* This initiative is allowing a growing number of African countries to provide increased access to HIV/AIDS prevention, care, and treatment programs, with an emphasis on vulnerable groups.
- *Knowledge Partnerships for Africa.* A major area of focus and activity for this partnership is sharing knowledge and learning from clients and partners to improve the quality and outcomes of World Bank assistance.
- *Regional integration.* Most African countries have already recognized the benefits of regional integration and participate in at least one regional arrangement. Although past performance has been mixed, renewed momentum exists for a more pragmatic approach to regional integration.
- *Regional Program on Enterprise Development.* This ongoing research project aims at generating business knowledge and policy advice useful to the development of private sector manufacturing in Sub-Saharan Africa.

- *Rehabilitation of the Northern Corridor Transport System.* This IDA project, which links Burundi, Kenya, Rwanda, Tanzania, and Uganda, has already cut transit times by 40 percent at some border crossings. Related projects are improving road, rail, and port infrastructure and resulting in more fluid trade and reductions in transit times in Cameroon, the Central African Republic, and Chad.

- *Roll Back Malaria Partnership.* This global initiative, made up of more than 500 partners, is a coordinated international approach to fighting malaria. The disease kills more than 1 million people each year, most of them children. The partnership's overall strategy aims to reduce malaria morbidity and mortality by reaching universal coverage and strengthening health systems. The website is http://www.rbm.who.int/.

- *Sub-Saharan Africa Transport Policy Program.* This international partnership facilitates policy development and related capacity building in the transport sector. The objective is to ensure that safe, reliable, and cost-effective transport plays its full part in achieving the development objectives of Sub-Saharan Africa (poverty reduction, pro-poor growth, and regional integration) and to allow countries to compete internationally.

- *TerrAfrica.* This partnership between Sub-Saharan African countries, donor countries and agencies, civil society, and the research community has the collective goal of scaling up harmonized support of effective and efficient land management approaches that are sustainable and country driven. The website is http://www.terrafrica.org/.

- *Transitional Demobilization and Reintegration Program.* This multidonor initiative supports the return of ex-combatants to civilian life in the African Great Lakes region. Its ultimate goal is to enhance peace and security in the region, a precursor for recovery and development.

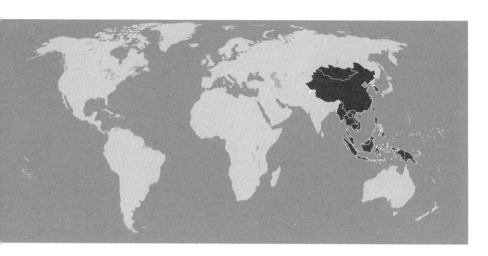

East Asia and the Pacific

This World Bank region includes the following countries that are eligible for borrowing:

Cambodia	Marshall Islands	Samoa
China	Federated States of	Solomon Islands
Fiji	Micronesia	Thailand
Indonesia	Mongolia	Timor-Leste
Kiribati	Myanmar	Tonga
Lao People's	Palau	Tuvalu
Democratic Republic	Papua New Guinea	Vanuatu
Malaysia	Philippines	Vietnam

All these countries are members of IBRD and IDA. As for the other institutions,

- Tuvalu is not a member of IFC.
- Kiribati, the Marshall Islands, Myanmar, Tonga, and Tuvalu are not members of MIGA.
- Kiribati, Lao PDR, the Marshall Islands, Myanmar, Palau, Thailand, Tuvalu, Vanuatu, and Vietnam are not members of ICSID.

The World Bank in East Asia and the Pacific

In its approach to East Asia and the Pacific, the Bank focuses on supporting broad-based economic growth, finding means of effective poverty reduction, increasing levels of trade and integration within the region and with the global economy, improving the environment for governance at both national and subnational levels, increasing regional engagement on global issues and disaster response capacity, and achieving the 2015 Millennium Development Goals. Box 3.4 presents key regional facts.

East Asian output, exports, and employment have mostly returned to the levels before the global financial crisis. China, today the world's second-largest economy and its leading exporter and manufacturer, will remain a powerful source of external demand for East Asian producers in the foreseeable future. Real gross domestic product (GDP) growth in East Asia has been moderating after a sharp rebound from the global crisis. GDP growth is projected to settle at about 8 percent in 2011 and 2012 from about 9.6 percent in 2010. A return to the private sector–driven growth rates that prevailed before the crisis will require that countries return to the medium-term reform agenda and implement it with vigor. Given the region's diversity, priorities will be different in different countries:

- *China.* Rebalancing the economy, as emphasized in the country's development plan, will be key. In addition, support for China's western region, rapid urbanization, and improvement of social safety nets are priority areas.
- *Middle-income countries.* The priorities for these countries are (a) investing more in physical and human capital, which will allow them to move up the value chain in production and exports; (b) maintaining competiveness;

Box 3.4 East Asia and the Pacific Fast Facts

1.9 billion	Total population
0.7 percent	Population growth
72 years	Life expectancy at birth
23	Infant mortality per 1,000 births
98 percent	Female youth literacy
$3,163	Gross national income per capita
2.3 million	Number of people living with HIV/AIDS

Source: World Bank Annual Report 2010.

(c) developing their infrastructure; (d) promoting a knowledge economy; and (e) protecting against macroeconomic shocks. In addition, improving social protection and increasing the sophistication of public services are key.

- *Low-income countries.* These countries need to seize opportunities of regional growth, break into manufacturing, and become part of global and regional production networks. Other priority areas include improving governance and the investment climate.
- *Commodity exporters.* These countries need to strengthen their fiscal rules and frameworks to translate volatile external revenues into long-term sustainable growth.
- *The Pacific Islands.* These countries need deeper integration with their nearest large market. Other key priorities include increasing private sector development, protecting against climate change, and managing the challenge of size and location.

Five priorities guide Bank strategy for the region:

- Working with middle-income countries so that they can move up the value chain
- Supporting the poorest and most fragile states in the region to achieve effective poverty reduction and inclusive growth by strengthening social protection, health, and education systems
- Promoting country-based governance and anticorruption strategies
- Supporting greater knowledge exchange and regional cooperation on global issues
- Preparing for risks and crises such as natural disasters and rising commodity prices

For many countries in the region, the global economic crisis highlighted the need to protect core spending, strengthen safety nets, improve service delivery, and move toward a greener growth path.

The urban population of East Asia is likely to increase by 50 percent in the next 20 years, and energy demand is projected to more than double. In their efforts to address climate change, some of the larger economies in the region could stabilize their greenhouse gas emissions while increasing energy security and improving local environments by major annual investments in energy efficiency and a concerted switch to renewable sources of power.

The Bank continues to strengthen its relationships with its core development partners across the region. It works closely with the Association of South East Asian Nations, the Asia Pacific Economic Cooperation forum, and the

Pacific Islands Forum, regularly attending their regional meetings and providing analytical and advisory support. In Samoa, Tonga, and Vanuatu, the Bank has established shared offices with the Asian Development Bank to expand the reach of its development activities in the Pacific.

Figures 3.6 and 3.7 present thematic and sectoral breakdowns of lending for fiscal 2010. The region's website is http://www.worldbank.org/eap/.

IFC in East Asia and the Pacific

In East Asia and the Pacific, IFC is focusing on expanding the private sector's role in addressing climate change while promoting inclusive rural growth, sustainable urbanization, and the creation of competitive markets.

IFC's investment volume in the region has grown by 50 percent since 2008—from about $1 billion before 2008 to more than $1.5 billion in 2010–11. Its focus is on the most vulnerable countries and people, with more than 40 percent of IFC investments supporting private sector development in the region's poorest nations.

IFC is supporting access to finance in rural areas across East Asia and the Pacific. Landmark transactions, among others, include a 10 percent

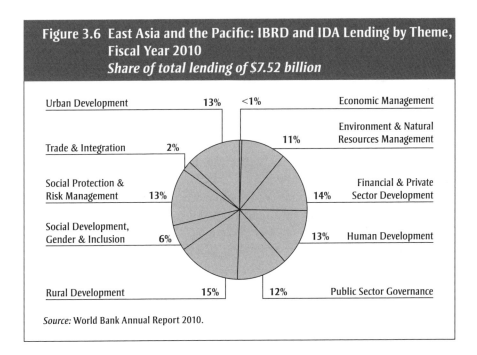

Figure 3.6 East Asia and the Pacific: IBRD and IDA Lending by Theme, Fiscal Year 2010
Share of total lending of $7.52 billion

- Urban Development 13%
- <1% Economic Management
- 11% Environment & Natural Resources Management
- Trade & Integration 2%
- Social Protection & Risk Management 13%
- 14% Financial & Private Sector Development
- Social Development, Gender & Inclusion 6%
- 13% Human Development
- Rural Development 15%
- 12% Public Sector Governance

Source: World Bank Annual Report 2010.

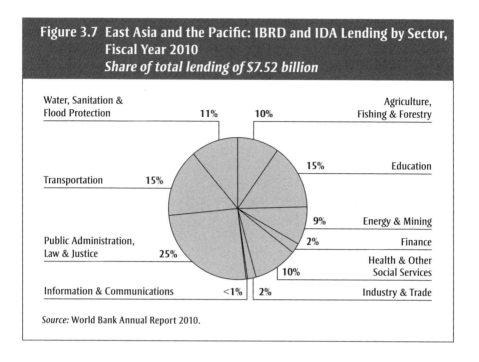

Figure 3.7 East Asia and the Pacific: IBRD and IDA Lending by Sector, Fiscal Year 2010

Share of total lending of $7.52 billion

Water, Sanitation & Flood Protection 11%

Agriculture, Fishing & Forestry 10%

Education 15%

Transportation 15%

Energy & Mining 9%

Finance 2%

Public Administration, Law & Justice 25%

Health & Other Social Services 10%

Information & Communications <1%

Industry & Trade 2%

Source: World Bank Annual Report 2010.

equity investment in Bank South Pacific of Papua New Guinea and support for developing renewable energy in China with an investment in China WindPower. IFC is also working with AusAID, the Australian Government's overseas aid program, on a microfinance program across the region.

The East Asia and Pacific Department is managed from IFC's regional hub in Hong Kong SAR, China. Its website is http://www.ifc.org/eastasia.

MIGA in East Asia and the Pacific

MIGA has provided political risk insurance for a wide range of projects in this region that offer opportunities for foreign investors. Support in the region has included guarantees for the construction of a comprehensive solid waste treatment center in China and projects to support improved water quality. MIGA launched its Asian hub in 2010, operating from Hong Kong SAR, China, and from Singapore—expanding the agency's reach beyond its Washington, D.C., headquarters and signaling a strong emphasis on inbound and outbound Asian investment. MIGA has signed memoranda of understanding with both the Japan Bank for International Cooperation and Korea's Eximbank to cooperate in promoting private sector investment in developing countries. These memoranda are in addition to a reinsurance agreement signed between MIGA and Japan's Nippon Export and Investment Insurance.

Regional Initiatives

The following initiatives are in place in East Asia and the Pacific:

- *Regional Governance Hub.* Established in January 2009, the East Asian and Pacific Regional Governance Hub seeks to improve the effectiveness of the World Bank's work on governance in the region. The hub assists groups seeking greater accountability and transparency in both the public and the private sectors. It aids coalitions for change and serves as a partner in forums, workshops, and roundtables, addressing specific governance issues. The website is at http://www.worldbank.org/eapgovernancehub/.
- *World Bank–Singapore Urban Hub.* Launched in June 2009, the World Bank–Singapore Urban Hub represents the partnership between the World Bank Group and the government of Singapore around urban development and financing solutions. The hub leverages (a) Singapore's recognized expertise in urban development and financing and (b) the Bank Group's global development knowledge and operational experience for the benefit of developing countries. The hub has already established a sizable portfolio of joint World Bank–Singapore projects in several countries, and a strategic partnership has been established with the Australia Treasury. Discussions are ongoing to expand the partnership with other developed economies. In November 2010, the World Bank and the government of Singapore established the Infrastructure Finance Centre of Excellence (IFCOE). IFCOE provides unbiased policy advice and hands-on, step-by-step technical assistance to governments on how to identify, prepare, and negotiate projects with private investors.

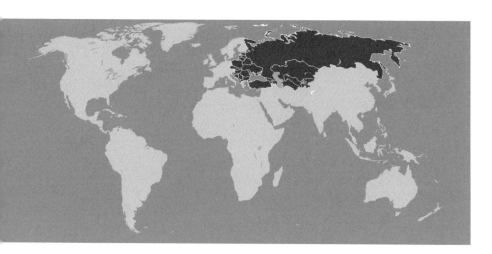

Europe and Central Asia

This World Bank region includes the following countries that are eligible for borrowing:

Albania	Kazakhstan	Romania
Armenia	Kosovo	Russian Federation
Azerbaijan	Kyrgyz Republic	Serbia
Belarus	Former Yugoslav Republic	Tajikistan
Bosnia and Herzegovina	of Macedonia	Turkey
Bulgaria	Moldova	Turkmenistan
Croatia	Montenegro	Ukraine
Georgia	Poland	Uzbekistan

All the countries listed are members of IBRD, IFC, and MIGA. As for the other institutions,

- Belarus, Bulgaria, Lithuania, Romania, and Turkmenistan are not members of IDA.
- the Czech Republic, Estonia, Lithuania, and Slovenia are included in IFC's Central and Eastern Europe region.
- the Kyrgyz Republic, Montenegro, Poland, the Russian Federation, Serbia, and Tajikistan are not members of ICSID.

Box 3.5 presents key regional facts.

Box 3.5 Europe and Central Asia Fast Facts

0.4 billion	Total population
0.3 percent	Population growth
70 years	Life expectancy at birth
19	Infant mortality per 1,000 births
99 percent	Female youth literacy
$6,793	Gross national income per capita
1.5 million	Number of people living with HIV/AIDS

Source: World Bank Annual Report 2010.

The World Bank in Europe and Central Asia

Europe and Central Asia was hit harder than any other region by the global financial and economic crisis and will be the slowest region to recover. In 2009, economic growth fell more than in any other developing region, fiscal balances worsened most, and capital inflows declined most sharply. What started as a financial crisis has taken an economic and social toll, with rising unemployment and worsening economic prospects making life even tougher for those already poor.

To assist the countries in the region in addressing their considerable challenges, the World Bank programs focus on three strategic directions: increasing competitiveness to achieve faster growth, supporting fiscal adjustment and social sector reforms to achieve more inclusive growth, and aiding climate action to achieve more sustainable growth.

In response to requests from countries in the region for assistance in addressing the crisis, the Bank has substantially increased its support, especially its development policy lending. It has also expanded its partnership with the European Union, cofinancing international reform packages, providing advisory services to member states, and expanding work on regional energy issues. Along with the European Bank for Reconstruction and Development and the European Investment Bank, the World Bank has recently launched the Joint International Financial Institutions Action Plan, which supports banking systems and lending to the real economy in Central and Eastern Europe. The Bank also participated in the European Bank Coordination Initiative—or Vienna Initiative—a forum for deepening the dialogue between home- and host-country banking supervisors, private banks, the European Commission, and international financial institutions.

At the same time that the Bank is supporting measures to improve the efficiency of government spending, stabilize the financial sector, mitigate food and fuel emergencies, strengthen social protections, and create jobs, it is not losing sight of other important long-term goals: working with countries to improve governance, better their business climate, and adapt to climate change and invest in energy efficiency.

Figures 3.8 and 3.9 present thematic and sectoral breakdowns of lending for fiscal 2010. The region's website is http://www.worldbank.org/eca/.

IFC in Europe and Central Asia

To promote inclusive growth in Europe and Central Asia, IFC focuses on several cross-cutting objectives: addressing climate change, developing the agribusiness sector, increasing access to and quality of infrastructure services, and enhancing competitiveness. IFC does so through a combination of investment and advisory services.

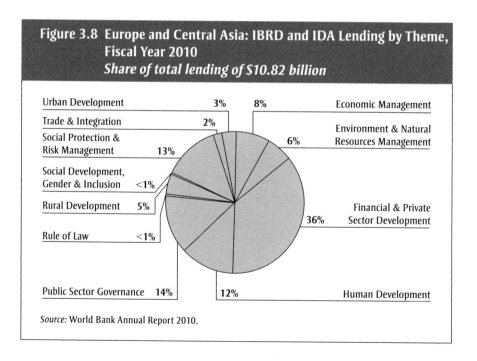

Figure 3.8 Europe and Central Asia: IBRD and IDA Lending by Theme, Fiscal Year 2010
Share of total lending of $10.82 billion

Urban Development — 3%
Trade & Integration — 2%
Social Protection & Risk Management — 13%
Social Development, Gender & Inclusion — <1%
Rural Development — 5%
Rule of Law — <1%
Public Sector Governance — 14%

Economic Management — 8%
Environment & Natural Resources Management — 6%
Financial & Private Sector Development — 36%
Human Development — 12%

Source: World Bank Annual Report 2010.

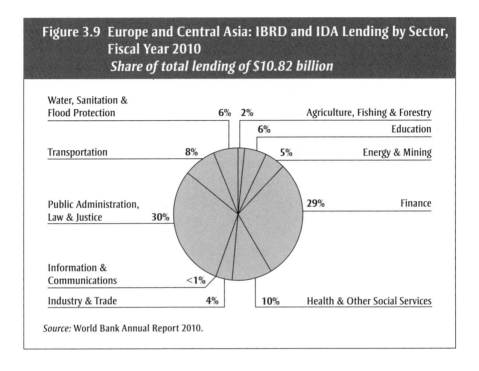

Figure 3.9 Europe and Central Asia: IBRD and IDA Lending by Sector, Fiscal Year 2010
Share of total lending of $10.82 billion

Water, Sanitation & Flood Protection — 6%
Agriculture, Fishing & Forestry — 2%
Education — 6%
Transportation — 8%
Energy & Mining — 5%
Public Administration, Law & Justice — 30%
Finance — 29%
Information & Communications — <1%
Industry & Trade — 4%
Health & Other Social Services — 10%

Source: World Bank Annual Report 2010.

IFC's investment activity is focused on strengthening the financial sector while also supporting key sectors such as agribusiness and manufacturing and the development of infrastructure. In the financial sector, IFC aims to improve access to finance for small and medium-size enterprises while working with companies and banks to strengthen their risk management capacity. Supported by funds from donor partners, IFC also provides advisory services to address climate change, improve the business climate for small and medium-size enterprises, and strengthen local agribusiness and infrastructure.

In the area of climate change, IFC is working to develop a market for renewable energy while collaborating with companies to increase resource efficiency and with local banks to expand financing for energy efficiency, particularly in the residential sector. In Ukraine, where agribusiness potential is significant, IFC is working to strengthen agricultural supply chains and to increase farmers' access to finance through the introduction of new insurance and finance products. Across the region, IFC is working with agricultural producers to improve food safety standards, which should make the producers more competitive in the international marketplace. IFC is also seeking to improve local infrastructure through public-private partnerships.

IFC's investment and advisory work in Europe and Central Asia is coordinated from an operations center in Istanbul. Its regional website is http://www.ifc.org/eca.

MIGA in Europe and Central Asia

Undoubtedly, the perception of commercial and noncommercial risk in Europe and Central Asia increased as a result of the recent global financial crisis. As a result, MIGA continued to guarantee projects under its Financial Sector Initiative to support financial flows from banks to their European and Central Asian subsidiaries hit by the downturn, thus allowing for recapitalization and addressing near-term liquidity needs. These projects formed part of the World Bank Group's ongoing response to the crisis and recovery that was implemented in tandem with other international financial institutions. MIGA has provided support for projects in infrastructure, manufacturing, and other sectors coming into the region, while also supporting regional investors pursuing opportunities in developing countries in other parts of the world.

Regional Initiatives

Regional initiatives include the following:

- *Black Sea and Danube Basin Partnership.* The Black Sea and Danube Basin have become polluted over the past four decades, resulting in reduced revenues from tourism and fisheries, loss of biodiversity, and increased prevalence of waterborne diseases. This initiative aims to promote investment and capacity building to return the environment to its condition in the 1960s. Ten World Bank projects supported by the Investment Fund for Nutrient Reduction financed by the Global Environment Facility since 2002 have been very successful in piloting measures to reduce nutrient loads entering the Black Sea and Danube Basin. See "Regional Initiatives" at http://www.worldbank.org/eca/.
- *European Union integration.* In recent years, the World Bank has actively partnered with the accession candidate countries and the European Commission in relation to the European Union's enlargement process. See "Regional Initiatives" at http://www.worldbank.org/eca/.

- *Forest law enforcement and governance in Europe and North Asia.* In 2005, 48 countries committed to cracking down on illegal logging by improving forest law enforcement and governance. To this end, they signed the St. Petersburg Declaration. See "Regional Initiatives" at http://www.worldbank.org/eca/.
- *Southeast Europe Social Development Initiative.* This regional initiative aims to provide the governments of Southeast Europe and the donor community involved in the region (in particular, the World Bank) the capacity to carry out social analyses, promote institution building, and launch pilot projects to address interethnic tensions and social cohesion issues. See "Regional Initiatives" at http://www.worldbank.org/eca/.

Latin America and the Caribbean

This World Bank region includes the following countries that are eligible for borrowing:

Antigua and Barbuda	El Salvador	Peru
Argentina	Grenada	St. Kitts and Nevis
Belize	Guatemala	St. Lucia
Bolivia	Guyana	St. Vincent and the
Brazil	Haiti	Grenadines
Chile	Honduras	Suriname
Colombia	Jamaica	Trinidad and Tobago
Costa Rica	Mexico	Uruguay
Dominica	Nicaragua	República Bolivariana
Dominican Republic	Panama	de Venezuela
Ecuador	Paraguay	

All these countries are members of IBRD. As for the other institutions,

- Antigua and Barbuda, Jamaica, Suriname, Uruguay, and República Bolivariana de Venezuela are not members of IDA.
- The Bahamas and Barbados are included in IFC's Latin America and Caribbean region; St. Vincent and the Grenadines and Suriname are not members of IFC.
- Antigua and Barbuda, Belize, Bolivia, Brazil, Dominica, the Dominican Republic, Ecuador, Mexico, and Suriname are not members of ICSID.

The World Bank in Latin America and the Caribbean

Latin America and the Caribbean is a region of broad diversity, with people who speak Spanish, Portuguese, English, French, and some 400 indigenous languages. Its topography and ecosystems range from tropical islands to high sierras and altiplanos, rain forests, deserts, and sprawling plains. It is the most urbanized region in the developing world, with three-quarters of its people living in and around cities, but natural resources and agriculture are also important to many of its economies, which include some of the developing world's largest, such as Brazil and Mexico, and some of the smallest. Despite immense resources and dynamic societies, deep inequalities of wealth persist in most countries. Box 3.6 presents key regional facts.

In 2011, Latin America and the Caribbean remained on a steady growth path, reaping the fruits from the longest and most comprehensive commodity price boom in recorded history. Thanks to its solid macroeconomic and fiscal policy framework, the region emerged from the global financial meltdown of 2008–09 more resilient and stable than in past crises.

Fueling the region's momentum was a global commodity and food price surge that largely benefited agrocommodity-producing countries, mostly South American net food exporters, which jointly account for between 30 percent and 50 percent of several key food exports globally. By contrast, non-export-based Central American and Caribbean economies faced the double peril of a food crisis and price hikes in other commodities that could hurt their most vulnerable populations. Overall, the region showed a strong capacity for staying on the right side of development.

Box 3.6 Latin America and the Caribbean Fast Facts

0.6 billion	Total population
1.1 percent	Population growth
73 years	Life expectancy at birth
20	Infant mortality per 1,000 births
97 percent	Female youth literacy
$6,971	Gross national income per capita
1.8 million	Number of people living with HIV/AIDS

Source: World Bank Annual Report 2010.

In response to the financial crisis, the Bank stepped up its commitment to Latin America and the Caribbean, approving $13.9 billion in new loans in fiscal 2010. By March 2011, lending for the new fiscal year was at $7.9 billion, with a renewed focus on social protection, human development, and the environment.

The Bank is working with the countries in the region to reduce their vulnerability to natural disasters, such as the 2010 earthquakes in Chile and Haiti, by providing both financial support and technical assistance. In Haiti, the Bank Group has supported safety inspections of 400,000 homes, provided grant financing for repair and reconstruction, assisted in stabilizing government operations, addressed the cholera epidemic, and worked to get thousands of children back to school. The Bank also works with development partners such as the United Nations, the Inter-American Development Bank, and the European Union to assist countries coping with the aftereffects of such disasters. Bank experts have provided satellite imagery analysis to assess infrastructure damage and other technical expertise as part of the Bank's alliance with volunteers from catastrophe assessment network GEO-CAN and the Crisis Camp—a grassroots movement of developers that provides critical solutions to communications on the ground in disaster-stricken areas.

Improving early childhood development is a priority for the region. National investments in early childhood development are a very small part of total educational expenditures in the region, and programs reach only a small fraction of those who need assistance. In response, the World Bank established the Early Childhood Initiative: An Investment for Life. The program invests in improvements and expansion of early childhood development programs in a region where 9 million children under five years old suffer from chronic malnutrition and 22 million lack access to early basic health care.

Addressing climate change is another priority. Many countries in Latin America and the Caribbean have taken steps to reduce emissions although the region produces only 6 percent of global greenhouse gas emissions—or 13 percent when deforestation and agriculture are included. The Bank provides resources to stimulate green growth and assists countries in the region in meeting their low-carbon growth goals. It also supports the transformation of urban transport by developing equipment, infrastructure, and operational strategies that reduce carbon dioxide emissions and promotes sustainable growth in key sectors such as mining, fishing, and urban transportation. Currently more than 170 green programs are active in the region with Bank support.

Beyond the postcrisis scenario, the region needs to close key gaps in education, innovation, and infrastructure if it is to generate a growth trend above the world's average after trailing behind it for more than a century. Critical reforms in education standards, logistics, and infrastructure are needed to make the region more competitive globally.

Figures 3.10 and 3.11 provide thematic and sectoral breakdowns of lending for fiscal 2010. The region's website is http://www.worldbank.org/lac/.

IFC in Latin America and the Caribbean

IFC focuses on key development challenges facing Latin America and the Caribbean. It follows an integrated approach of investment and advisory services targeting several strategic priorities:

- Improving the business environment
- Supporting projects that reach underserved people at the base of the economic pyramid
- Increasing its focus on smaller countries, especially in the Caribbean and Central America

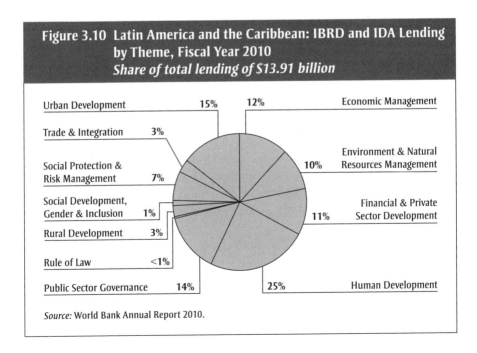

Figure 3.10 Latin America and the Caribbean: IBRD and IDA Lending by Theme, Fiscal Year 2010
Share of total lending of $13.91 billion

Urban Development 15%
Trade & Integration 3%
Social Protection & Risk Management 7%
Social Development, Gender & Inclusion 1%
Rural Development 3%
Rule of Law <1%
Public Sector Governance 14%

Economic Management 12%
Environment & Natural Resources Management 10%
Financial & Private Sector Development 11%
Human Development 25%

Source: World Bank Annual Report 2010.

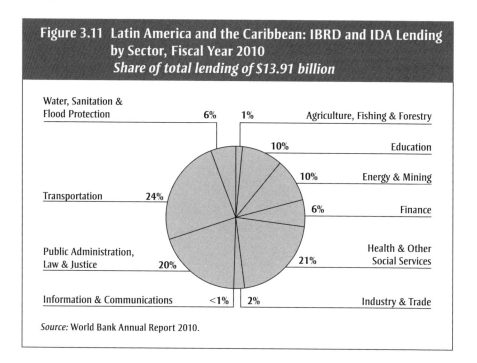

Figure 3.11 Latin America and the Caribbean: IBRD and IDA Lending by Sector, Fiscal Year 2010
Share of total lending of $13.91 billion

Water, Sanitation & Flood Protection — 6%
Agriculture, Fishing & Forestry — 1%
Education — 10%
Energy & Mining — 10%
Finance — 6%
Transportation — 24%
Health & Other Social Services — 21%
Public Administration, Law & Justice — 20%
Information & Communications — <1%
Industry & Trade — 2%

Source: World Bank Annual Report 2010.

- Promoting investments in clean technology to mitigate climate change
- Supporting private sector participation in infrastructure
- Increasing access to finance, with an emphasis on microenterprises and small and medium-size enterprises

IFC is a long-term partner that promotes sustainability by strengthening social, environmental, and corporate governance standards. In the Caribbean and Central America, which have some of the highest levels of income inequality, IFC is working with businesses and communities to strengthen their comparative advantages. In middle-income countries, such as Brazil, Colombia, and Mexico, it promotes access to education, telecommunications, renewable energy, and financial services to underserved segments. IFC emphasizes inclusive business models across Latin America, especially investments that serve the working poor, who make up 70 percent of the population in the region.

The Latin America and the Caribbean Department is managed from IFC's regional head office in Rio de Janeiro. Its website is http://www.ifc.org/lac.

MIGA in Latin America and the Caribbean

Since its inception, MIGA has issued more than $7 billion in guarantees for more than 190 projects in Latin America and the Caribbean, covering all sectors and spanning 20 countries. Among the projects have been toll roads in Costa Rica and the Dominican Republic that had a strong development impact. The agency has also supported microlending organizations to help close the existing gap between the demand and supply of financial services to low-income sectors. MIGA also provided support for a project that converts methane generated by a landfill in San Salvador to less harmful carbon dioxide. Sale of the resulting certified carbon credits helped finance the project.

Regional Initiatives

The following initiatives are among those in place in Latin America and the Caribbean:

- *Central American integration.* Central American countries are making progress with the regional integration agenda along different dimensions: democratic stability, disaster risk management and climate change, social inclusion, economic integration, and strengthening of democratic institutions. The Bank is providing both financial and technical support, including advisory services, training, and a program to support judicial transparency and accountability.
- *Conditional cash transfer programs.* For more than a decade, the Bank has worked with countries in the region to develop homegrown conditional cash transfer programs, which alleviate poverty by providing small cash payments to families to ensure that children and youth receive regular health checkups and attend school. These programs have been implemented in 15 countries in the region, where they are improving the lives of some 100 million people. The Bank provides support to most of these programs through funding, technical support, and the coordination of South-South learning. Conditional cash transfer programs are moving from first-generation operational issues, such as ensuring that money reaches beneficiaries in a timely, transparent manner, to future challenges, such as improving coordination with other social programs and linking beneficiaries to opportunities to move out of poverty. Lessons learned in IBRD countries are providing guidance for the expansion of conditional cash transfer programs to IDA countries.

■ *Disaster response.* The Bank is providing assistance to two countries in the region hit by earthquakes in 2010. To restore the necessary economic and financial functions of the government of Haiti in the aftermath of the earthquake and to carry out emergency rehabilitation of critical public infrastructure, the Bank is providing technical assistance to support key institutions and reconstruction planning. The Bank is assisting the country with disaster risk management, infrastructure, community-driven development, education, and economic governance. In Chile, the Bank mobilized a grant from the Spanish Fund for Latin America and the Caribbean to support initial damage assessment. It also provided technical expertise in remote sensing for analyzing aerial images and data from the stricken area.

■ *Early Childhood Initiative: An Investment for Life.* This partnership with the ALAS Foundation was launched at Bank headquarters in 2010. One year later, this pioneering initiative to improve the well-being of Latin American children has benefited more than half a million young children and has received over $100 million in funding from the World Bank—one-third of the initial three-year pledge of $300 million—to support early childhood development policies and programs. These programs provide nutrition, health care, and stimulating environments to infants from birth through six years of age—a period of development crucial for achieving a child's full potential.

■ *Dialogues for Development, Social Cohesion, and Democracy in Latin America.* This initiative aims to create a space for dialogue on key issues for development and social cohesion in Latin America as the region moves forward in a postcrisis scenario. Through consultation and debate, the dialogues include leading figures in government, the private sector, trade unions, media, academia, and civil society. The debate seeks to generate concrete policy proposals in the areas of democratic governance, opportunities for all (including the generation of good jobs and social security reforms), competitiveness, and economic growth. The dialogues are facilitated through a partnership between the Chile-based think tank CIEPLAN (Corporación de Investigaciones Económicas para Latinoamérica, or Corporation for Latin American Studies) and the World Bank. The initiative has an advisory council composed of eminent persons with credibility and gravitas in the region, including Fernando Henrique Cardozo, the former president of Brazil; Tabaré Vázquez, the former president of Uruguay; and Enrique Iglesias, secretary general of the Ibero-American Secretariat.

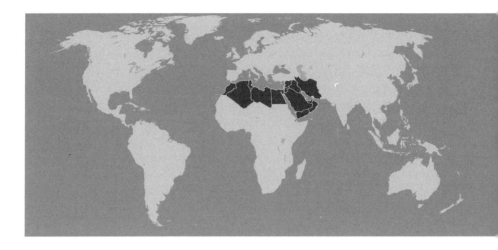

Middle East and North Africa

This World Bank region includes the following countries that are eligible for borrowing:

Algeria	Jordan	Syrian Arab Republic
Djibouti	Lebanon	Tunisia
Arab Republic of Egypt	Libya	Republic of Yemen
Islamic Republic of Iran	Morocco	

All these countries are members of IBRD. The World Bank also has activities in the West Bank and Gaza. As for the other institutions,

- Afghanistan, Kuwait, Oman, Pakistan, Saudi Arabia, and the United Arab Emirates are included in IFC's Middle East and North Africa region, which also covers the West Bank and Gaza; Djibouti is included in IFC's Africa region.
- Djibouti, the Islamic Republic of Iran, Iraq, and Libya are not members of ICSID.

The World Bank in the Middle East and North Africa

Since the beginning of 2011, the 20 Middle Eastern and North African countries where the World Bank Group is engaged have been experiencing extraordinary change in one way or another. Whether this change has had the watershed effect of events in the Arab Republic of Egypt and Tunisia or whether the contest for political voice continues, the "Arab Spring" opens an opportunity for better governance and a potentially profound change of the political and social landscape. Of the 355 million people living in the region, 85 percent live in middle-income countries, 8 percent in high-income countries, and 7 percent in low-income countries. Before the recent popular uprisings, the region made significant progress on key social indicators with an average life expectancy of 70 years, a primary education completion rate of 90 percent, and a mortality rate of 38 of 1,000 children under five years old (box 3.7). Absolute poverty was low, with approximately 4 percent of the population living under $1.25 a day. The disruptions to economic life that are accompanying the political changes of early 2011 in the Middle East and North Africa are expected to lower growth in many countries of the region because of a decline in tourism revenue, a wider spread in debt markets, instability in national stock markets, and higher subsidies and public sector salaries. Furthermore, the potential for instability to spread beyond Libya to other large oil-exporting economies has serious political and economic implications.

The protests and popular uprisings across many Middle Eastern and North African countries are driven by fatigue with long-standing authoritarian rule. Citizens have articulated demands for a voice, for social justice, for accountability, for access to services, and for a fair shot on a level economic playing field. The region came into its Spring with many strengths too: its youth, its resource base, and the economic resilience shown during the global crisis. Economies across the region were rebounding. Egypt and Tunisia had strong reserve cushions and had benefited from tourism and foreign flows. The economic impacts of the popular uprisings will be sharply felt but manageable if they can be confined to the short term.

Box 3.7 Middle East and North Africa Fast Facts

0.3 billion	Total population
1.8 percent	Population growth
71 years	Life expectancy at birth
29	Infant mortality per 1,000 births
86 percent	Female youth literacy
$3,594	Gross national income per capita
0.5 million	Number of people living with HIV/AIDS

Source: World Bank Annual Report 2010.

In the longer term, Middle Eastern and North African countries are profoundly challenged by many of the structural problems that existed before the Arab Spring and indeed drove much of the discontent. Among these challenges are inequitable growth and high unemployment rates (between 20 and 25 percent in some countries and steeper for university graduates and women). Poverty is low at the $1.25 level, but in Egypt, for example, it doubles at the $2.50 mark, with millions of Egyptians experiencing the vulnerability and uncertainty of crossing in and out of this threshold.

The region's main challenge, loudly proclaimed now, is to create sustainable jobs. These jobs must be generated by the private sector, and key to such job creation is improving the enabling environment for private sector players, big and small. Key, too, is fair competition and reduction of privileges that have benefited only the elites. Countries must also deal with long-standing issues such as low and depleting water resources (the region has the lowest renewable resources in the world) and the challenge of food insecurity, coupled with high food and social subsidies.

The World Bank Group stepped up its program in the region following the global financial crisis. IBRD and IDA lending increased from $1.8 billion in fiscal year 2009 to $3.8 billion in fiscal year 2010 and is expected to be $3.2 billion in fiscal year 2011. IDA support to the Republic of Yemen was significantly less in fiscal year 2011 at a projected $100 million and will be $6 million for Djibouti—very close to the previous year's level. High-value knowledge services increased from $6 million in 2007 to nearly $11 million in 2010. The number of nonlending economic analytic and advisory products increased from approximately 90 in 2007 to nearly 140 in 2010. The World Bank has also prepared a regional poverty study; reports on regional private sector development, migration, and integration; and notes on the impact and long-term challenges stemming from the financial crisis as well as the current crisis, especially as it related to the employment challenge.

With the historic political and economic changes reshaping the region, the World Bank's support will intensify. The World Bank's strategy and assistance will include a range of products:

- Quick budgetary support to meet growing financing requirements
- A rapid investment response to support the required poverty interventions
- Help with employment generation and programs in special areas
- Advisory support
- Strengthening of institutional capacities
- Provision of entrepreneurship and other training programs

Key to sustaining a manageable transition in Middle Eastern and North African countries will be strengthening the region's governance framework (transparency, accountability, and social justice); fostering inclusive growth; establishing sustainable social protection; helping to reduce food price volatility; and supporting global and regional economic integration. The World Bank Group's longer-term strategy is focusing its attention in these areas.

Figures 3.12 and 3.13 provide a thematic and sectoral breakdown of lending for fiscal 2010. The region's website is http://www.worldbank.org/mena/.

IFC in the Middle East and North Africa

IFC focuses on providing long-term finance to the private sector in the Middle East and North Africa in ways that benefit underserved communities. Its priorities are in areas with high development effect and in areas where it can make the greatest contribution, including access to finance for the underserved, especially microenterprises, small and medium-size enterprises, and mortgage and student borrowers; investments in infrastructure; and opportunities in IDA, conflict-affected, and resource-poor

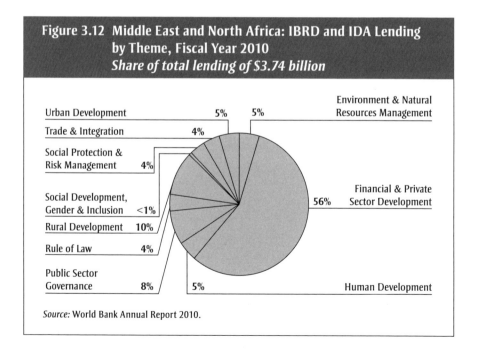

Figure 3.12 Middle East and North Africa: IBRD and IDA Lending by Theme, Fiscal Year 2010
Share of total lending of $3.74 billion

Urban Development 5%
Trade & Integration 4%
Social Protection & Risk Management 4%
Social Development, Gender & Inclusion <1%
Rural Development 10%
Rule of Law 4%
Public Sector Governance 8%
Human Development 5%
Financial & Private Sector Development 56%
Environment & Natural Resources Management 5%

Source: World Bank Annual Report 2010.

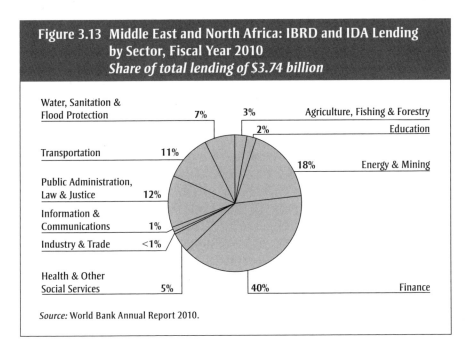

Figure 3.13 Middle East and North Africa: IBRD and IDA Lending by Sector, Fiscal Year 2010
Share of total lending of $3.74 billion

- Water, Sanitation & Flood Protection — 7%
- Agriculture, Fishing & Forestry — 3%
- Education — 2%
- Transportation — 11%
- Energy & Mining — 18%
- Public Administration, Law & Justice — 12%
- Information & Communications — 1%
- Industry & Trade — <1%
- Health & Other Social Services — 5%
- Finance — 40%

Source: World Bank Annual Report 2010.

middle-income countries. IFC pursues these objectives by combining investment and advisory services and facilitating South-South investments.

IFC advisory services in the Middle East and North Africa are a multidonor facility, which supports private sector development across the region. Some of the similar challenges countries in the region face include the following:

- High unemployment rates
- Complex legal and regulatory environments
- Weak financial institutions
- Insufficient infrastructure services
- Increasing pressures on existing resources, such as water and energy supplies

IFC's first operations center outside Washington, D.C., is in Istanbul. This center serves IFC operations in Central and Eastern Europe, Central Asia, Southern Europe, and the Middle East and North Africa. Establishment of this center will be followed by a phased rollout of other operations centers globally, incorporating lessons learned from the Istanbul center.

The Middle East and North Africa Department is managed from IFC's regional hub in Cairo. Its website is http://www.ifc.org/mena.

MIGA in the Middle East and North Africa

MIGA offers guarantee services in the Middle East and North Africa and provides support to regional investors making investments outside the region. To continue to support the World Bank Group's Arab World Initiative, MIGA has expanded its potential for activities in the Middle East and North Africa by partnering with the Dubai International Financial Centre (DIFC) to launch the joint MIGA-DIFC Political Risk Insurance Program for the Arab World. This program encourages foreign direct investment in enterprises and projects located in Arab countries by providing a means for investors to mitigate noncommercial risks. The agency also appointed a local representative in the West Bank and Gaza to be a point of contact for MIGA's West Bank and Gaza Investment Guarantee Trust Fund. The agency also underscored its commitment to supporting investment in Iraq that brings potential private sector development with an announcement in 2011 of its first contract of guarantee for that country.

Regional Initiatives

Regional initiatives in the Middle East and North Africa include the following:

- *Arab World Initiative.* This World Bank Group initiative aims to promote development and opportunity in the Arab world by strengthening partnerships, scaling up successful regional programs, and piloting new regional and country-specific initiatives with strong potential for results. Recent projects include development of an integrated index for education performance; technical assistance for launching the Regional Academy for Learning and Leadership in Education, based in Jordan; assessments of energy integration in the Arab world; investments in ports, airports, and logistics in the Arab Republic of Egypt, Jordan, and Tunisia; and assessments of cross-border facilitation and infrastructure in Iraq, Jordan, Lebanon, the Syrian Arab Republic, and the West Bank and Gaza. The Arab World Initiative piloted a study on barriers to female employment in Jordan, scaled up support to countries severely hit by soaring food prices, and increased support to community projects in fragile and conflict-affected economies, including Iraq, Lebanon, Mauritania, Sudan, and the West Bank and Gaza. See http://arabworld.worldbank.org/.
- *Initiative on Governing Development and Developing Governance in the Middle East and North Africa.* This initiative seeks to improve governance

institutions and processes, the weaknesses of which may lead to disappointing economic performance. It is a partnership of individual researchers from the region, local think tanks, and donor agencies. The website is http://www.worldbank.org/mena/governance/.

■ *Knowledge Networks Agency.* In response to increasing demand from the Middle East and North Africa for expertise and knowledge services, the World Bank Group, with technical and financial support from the city of Marseilles, has opened a technical office, the Knowledge Networks Agency (KNA) for the Middle East and North Africa Region, in Marseilles, France. The objective of KNA is to build capacity for knowledge sharing and learning in the region. KNA's proximity to the region enables it to work with institutions in the Middle East and North Africa to identify the demand for knowledge in key areas and to organize learning activities in response. These national, subregional, and regional institutions (centers of excellence, training centers, thematic networks, and communities of practice) are playing a leading role as knowledge connectors and providers.

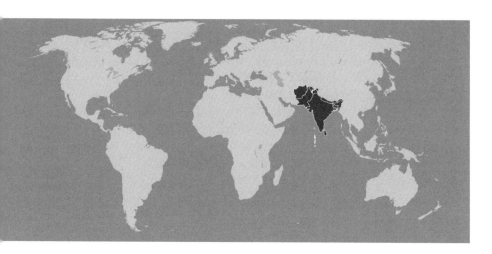

South Asia

This World Bank region includes the following countries that are eligible for borrowing:

Afghanistan	India	Pakistan
Bangladesh	Maldives	Sri Lanka
Bhutan	Nepal	

All these countries are members of IBRD and IDA. As for the other institutions,

- Afghanistan and Pakistan are included in IFC's Middle East and North Africa region.
- Bhutan is not a member of MIGA.
- Bhutan, India, and the Maldives are not members of ICSID.

The World Bank in South Asia

South Asia has experienced a long period of robust economic growth, averaging 6 percent a year over the past 20 years. This strong growth has translated into declining poverty and impressive improvements in human development. Yet poverty remains rampant in many areas, and South Asia has the world's largest concentration of poor people—more than 1 billion people living on less than $2 a day. Box 3.8 presents key regional facts.

> ### Box 3.8 South Asia Fast Facts
>
> | | |
> |---:|:---|
> | 1.6 billion | Total population |
> | 1.5 percent | Population growth |
> | 64 years | Life expectancy at birth |
> | 58 | Infant mortality per 1,000 births |
> | 72 percent | Female youth literacy |
> | $1,079 | Gross national income per capita |
> | 2.6 million | Number of people living with HIV/AIDS |
>
> *Source:* World Bank Annual Report 2010.

During the financial crisis, the region's growth prospects dimmed. Regional growth decelerated from 8.9 percent in 2007 to 6.3 percent in 2009, driven largely by the drop in investment growth and private consumption. South Asia is now rebounding strongly, however, with the World Bank projecting GDP growth of 7 percent in 2010 and 8 percent in 2011. Despite the impressive growth, however, the region faces serious development challenges. Although its high growth has led to declining poverty rates, that growth has not been fast enough to reduce the number of poor people. Weak governance and conflict are serious impediments to inclusive growth in a region with deteriorating security and very little integration. In addition, two of the countries in the region—Bangladesh and Maldives—are among the countries most affected by climate change.

The Bank's strategy for South Asia was updated in fiscal 2011. The strategy builds on the unprecedented access to client governments and strong momentum of demand for Bank services and lending to enable a dynamic private sector to drive growth, a skilled labor force to respond to new demands, world-class rural and urban infrastructure, greater gender equality, better governance and service delivery, regional integration, and protection of the environment and mitigation of the impact of climate change. Greater emphasis will be put on leveraging resources through partnerships, for example, with the Asian Development Bank and bilateral donors.

The Bank remains active in the many areas of South Asia that are affected by conflict. It has provided debt relief for Afghanistan under the enhanced HIPC Initiative and has funded programs to boost employment and incomes in rural areas, where 75 percent of the people live with financial assistance to the government's community-driven National Solidarity Program. The

National Solidarity Program is present in 359 of 364 districts in all 34 provinces in the country.

With the end of armed confrontations in May 2009, Sri Lanka is facing a historic opportunity for development and reconciliation. In fiscal 2010, the Bank approved a $77 million package designed to support the return of 100,000 internally displaced persons to their places of origin in the Northern Province and to restore their livelihoods, which had been destroyed by three decades of civil war. The Bank supported the rehabilitation of provincial roads in Northern Province, Eastern Province, and the southern province of Uva with a $105 million credit. It also provided $75 million for the second phase of Gemi Diriya, a community-driven development program that has touched the lives of nearly 1 million poor Sri Lankans in more than 1,000 villages.

Figures 3.14 and 3.15 provide thematic and sectoral breakdowns of lending for fiscal 2010. The region's website is http://www.worldbank.org/sar/.

IFC in South Asia

Despite the financial crisis, South Asia has been one of the world's fastest-growing regions in recent years, with particularly strong growth in India.

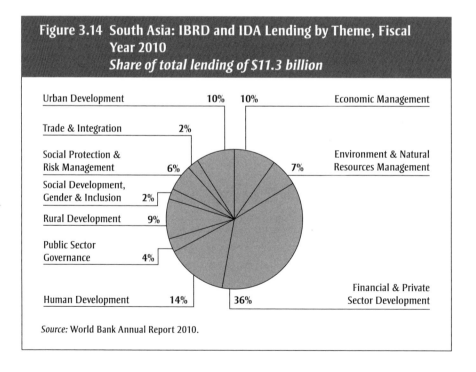

Figure 3.14 South Asia: IBRD and IDA Lending by Theme, Fiscal Year 2010
Share of total lending of $11.3 billion

Urban Development	10%
Economic Management	10%
Trade & Integration	2%
Social Protection & Risk Management	6%
Environment & Natural Resources Management	7%
Social Development, Gender & Inclusion	2%
Rural Development	9%
Public Sector Governance	4%
Human Development	14%
Financial & Private Sector Development	36%

Source: World Bank Annual Report 2010.

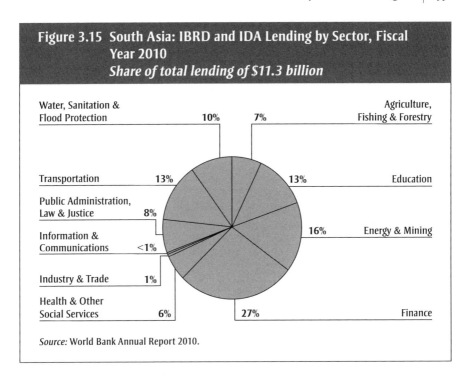

Figure 3.15 South Asia: IBRD and IDA Lending by Sector, Fiscal Year 2010
Share of total lending of $11.3 billion

Water, Sanitation & Flood Protection 10%

Agriculture, Fishing & Forestry 7%

Transportation 13%

Education 13%

Public Administration, Law & Justice 8%

Information & Communications <1%

Energy & Mining 16%

Industry & Trade 1%

Health & Other Social Services 6%

Finance 27%

Source: World Bank Annual Report 2010.

IFC's strategic priorities in the region are centered on sustaining growth by increasing access to infrastructure and finance; focusing on low-income, rural, and fragile areas; and making climate change central to its approach in both investments and advisory services. Through investments that have a high effect on development, IFC is working with companies in the region to improve their international competitiveness and pursue new investment opportunities in South Asia and beyond.

IFC provides advisory services to improve the business environment, strengthen providers of business services, and increase financial services for smaller businesses. The South Asia Department is managed from IFC's regional hub in New Delhi. Its website is http://www.ifc.org/southasia.

MIGA in South Asia

MIGA supports projects in South Asia through guarantees and technical assistance. MIGA's portfolio includes projects in Afghanistan, Bangladesh, Nepal, and Pakistan. For example, since 2007, MIGA has issued over $78 million in guarantee coverage for investments in Afghanistan, including a portable brick-making device known as the GreenMachine, which had an enormous effect on the home-building industry, as well as a large telecommunications project that has delivered mobile phone capability and much-needed connectivity to many people throughout the country. In Pakistan, MIGA has supported a microfinance project that provides lending to owners of microenterprises and small businesses, especially women, in areas across the country.

Regional Initiatives

Regional initiatives include the following:

- *Child labor and South Asia.* Although legislation banning child labor has been enacted in all South Asian countries, the region remains home to a high number of working children. Faced with the need to promote inclusive growth, many South Asian countries are focusing on expanding social protection programs and improving their administration. The World Bank is partnering with South Asian countries in this area to provide technical and financial assistance to strengthen safety net systems (as opposed to a program- or project-specific approach). The long-term solution to child labor problems lies in reducing poverty, improving the quality of education, and expanding access to schooling for disadvantaged social groups. These areas are central objectives of the Bank's assistance programs in the South Asian countries.
- *HIV/AIDS and South Asia.* Between 2 million and 3.5 million people in South Asia are living with HIV and AIDS. The World Bank has focused on mobilizing South Asian countries to improve and accelerate their responses to HIV and AIDS. It has supported national efforts to slow the spread of HIV since the first India project in 1992 and has committed $661 million to support national programs to date. The main components of these projects are surveillance, monitoring and evaluation, targeted interventions for vulnerable populations, blood safety programs, efforts to reduce stigma among the general population, and strengthening of public and private institutions for a multisector response. In addition, the Bank has undertaken analytical work to inform policy and evidence-based decision making.
- *Investing in infrastructure.* Poor access to transport infrastructure and services leaves hundreds of millions of people in South Asian countries without access to basic social and economic services. By assisting in infra-

structure investments, the World Bank seeks to contribute to growth and poverty alleviation. Some examples follow:

☐ To improve connectivity and boost opportunities for people in south-west Bangladesh, the World Bank approved a $1.2 billion IDA credit for the Padma Multipurpose Bridge Project. Spanning the Padma River, the world's third largest, the 6.1-kilometer bridge will connect nearly 30 million people in the southwest region to the rest of the country, thereby enhancing their access to markets and services and accelerating growth in the country as a whole.

☐ In Afghanistan, the Bank provided an additional $40 million grant to the National Emergency Rural Access Project. Launched in 2002, the project has rehabilitated some 10,370 kilometers of rural roads connecting 8,726 villages in 358 districts of Afghanistan's 34 provinces, thus reducing travel times and increasing rural Afghans' access to key services. The project has also rehabilitated 15,000 hectares of land by improving irrigation and drainage and has provided employment opportunities to impoverished rural men, creating about 700,000 temporary jobs over a month-long period and facilitating reintegration of ex-combatants into society. The additional grant will continue supporting the government's ongoing efforts to provide year-round access to basic services and facilities in rural areas.

☐ In India, almost half of all households—44 percent—lack access to electricity. To increase access and meet rising consumer demand, the Bank loaned $1 billion to Powergrid, the national power transmission utility, in fiscal 2010. The loan will help expand the power transmission network, especially in the western, northern, and southern parts of the country. The Bank also approved a $330 million loan to strengthen the electricity transmission and distribution system in the Indian state of Haryana. In addition, the Bank approved $430 million to finance Mumbai Urban Transport Project 2A. This project will further improve the suburban railway system in the Mumbai Metropolitan Region, one of the world's largest urban centers, with a population of 18 million in 2010.

■ *Regional integration.* South Asia is the least integrated region in the world, but the region could see significant gains from increased regional cooperation. Regional trade is less than 2 percent of GDP in South Asia, compared with 40 percent for East Asia, so significant gains could be realized from goods and services. Lagging, landlocked regions are home to an estimated 50 percent of South Asia's poor. Increasing connectivity and integrating markets would be the best strategy for growth and equality; such a strategy represents a large opportunity to reduce poverty and inequality. Less than 1 percent of Afghanistan's and Nepal's hydropower capacity of over 100 gigawatts is actually used because of lack of regional cooperation, so gains from trade in electricity could benefit both countries and others as well. More regional cooperation has the potential to reduce vulnerability from natural disasters. For example, cross-border cooperation on water between Bangladesh, India, and Nepal offers the only long-term solution to flood control and water shortages in Bangladesh and in the Indian states of Bihar and Uttar Pradesh.

■ *Gender equality.* Gender issues in South Asia represent a complex challenge. In most countries, women have experienced improved access to services and credit markets. However, despite the recent economic growth, dramatic gender inequities persist in South Asia and still need to be addressed. Through the self-help groups supported by the Andhra Pradesh Rural Poverty Reduction Project, more than 8 million women and their spouses have life and disability insurance coverage, and more than 800,000 lives are insured against health risks. Significantly, given the importance of livestock to rural families, about 500,000 cattle (primarily cows and buffaloes) have been insured. The Female Secondary School Assistance Program in Bangladesh has provided tuition stipends to girls, aiming to increase their access to secondary education. Since the program's inception in 1993, overall enrollment of girls in secondary schools in Bangladesh has increased to more than 4 million in 2006 from 1.1 million in 1991.

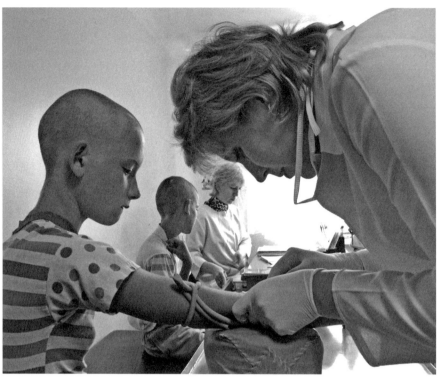

Poor families often tap into savings or sell what they own to cover the costs of medical care. Ensuring adequate levels of basic health and nutrition lies at the heart of poverty reduction and economic development.

4 Topics in Development

This chapter provides an overview of major aspects of development in which the World Bank Group is involved. These topics are listed alphabetically with a focus on key initiatives, websites, and publications. Because of space constraints, the listing of topics is not intended to be comprehensive.

The broad themes in Bank Group work are covered under "Strategies" in chapter 2. A key organizing principle of its work is the Millennium Development Goals (MDGs) as defined by the United Nations (UN).

Another key aspect of Bank Group activities, as explained in chapter 1, is the matrix in which units focused on development sectors (called networks) intersect with units focused on world regions. The networks correspond to many of the topics covered in this chapter. These topics are as follows:

- Agriculture and rural development
- Aid effectiveness
- Children and youth
- Climate change
- Combating corruption
- Debt relief
- Education
- Energy access and renewable energy
- Environment
- Extractive industries
- Financial crisis
- Financial sector
- Food crisis
- Fragile and conflict-affected countries
- Gender
- Governance
- Health, nutrition, and population
- Information and communication technologies
- Infrastructure
- Labor and social protection
- Law and development
- Migration and remittances
- Poverty
- Private sector development
- Social development
- Sustainable development
- Trade
- Transport
- Urban development
- Water
- World Bank reform

Agriculture and Rural Development

Seventy-five percent of the world's poor live in rural areas, and most are involved in farming. In the 21st century, agriculture and rural development remain fundamental for economic growth, poverty reduction, and environmental sustainability. The Bank Group pursues its work in agriculture and rural development through the units and programs discussed in this section.

Agriculture and Rural Development Department of the World Bank

The Agriculture and Rural Development (ARD) Department—one of the departments that make up the Sustainable Development Network (SDN)—provides analytic and advisory services to the Bank's regions on a wide range of agriculture and rural development topics. These services include preparing and implementing the World Bank's corporate strategy on agriculture and rural development, monitoring the Bank's portfolio of agriculture and rural projects, and promoting knowledge sharing among agriculture and rural development practitioners inside and outside the Bank to continually improve the Bank's activities in rural areas. ARD's focus includes agribusiness, agricultural technology, climate-smart agriculture, commodities risk management, fisheries, forestry, gender and rural development, land tenure, livestock, rural finance, and water. For more information on ARD, visit http://www.worldbank.org/ard/. For more information on SDN, visit http://www.worldbank.org/sustainabledevelopment/.

Agribusiness Department of IFC

The technical, financial, and market expertise necessary to evaluate agribusiness projects is centralized in the Agribusiness Department of the International Finance Corporation (IFC). Its staff comprises investment officers, engineers, and economists, all with specialized international experience. IFC supports projects involving primary agricultural production, aquaculture, and fishing, as well as marketing (for example, silos, cold and controlled-atmosphere storage facilities, and wholesale markets); food processing; and distribution. As a rule, preference is given to investment projects that have the largest demonstrated benefits for the efficiency and competitiveness of the supply chain and that have the highest overall contribution to economic development. For more on IFC and agribusiness, see http://www.ifc.org/agribusiness.

Other Resources

The Multilateral Investment Guarantee Agency (MIGA) also has extensive experience supporting projects in agribusiness. For more on MIGA and agribusiness see http://www.miga.org/sectors/.

Other resources include the following:

- *The Consultative Group on International Agricultural Research (CGIAR).* CGIAR is a strategic alliance of members, partners, and international agricultural centers that mobilizes science to benefit the poor. More information on CGIAR can be found at http://www.cgiar.org/.
- *The Global Agriculture and Food Security Program (GAFSP).* GAFSP is a multilateral mechanism that supports country-led agriculture and food security plans and helps to promote investments in smallholder farmers. For more information on GAFSP, visit http://www.gafspfund.org/.
- *The World Bank's response to the global food crisis.* For more information on projects and programs, visit http://www.worldbank.org/foodcrisis/.

For more information on ARD, visit http://www.worldbank.org/ard/. Additional research can be found by selecting "Agricultural Research" under "Topics." *World Development Report 2008: Agriculture for Development* and its related background research papers can be found at http://www.worldbank.org/wdr2008/.

Aid Effectiveness

The effectiveness of aid in reducing poverty, improving lives, and stimulating economic growth has always been a central concern of the Bank Group. The international community's broad acceptance of the MDGs brought aid effectiveness into even sharper relief as the Bank Group (among others) began focusing on measuring progress toward achieving the MDGs. This effort helps influence the global agenda and coordinates the technical work of the Organisation for Economic Co-operation and Development (OECD). That work, done through the OECD's Development Assistance Committee (DAC) Working Party on Aid Effectiveness clusters, covers aid transparency and aid predictability, financial management, procurement, results, and South-South cooperation. It brings country partner perspectives and country-level experiences on what has and has not worked to the Working Party's discussions.

Independent Evaluation

The World Bank's Independent Evaluation Group (IEG) assesses the effectiveness of specific World Bank Group programs and projects for the people and countries participating in them. IEG provides advice to the Boards of Directors based on evaluations at the project, country, and sector levels. Each year, evidence from those evaluations is marshaled to produce a summary report on the Bank's development effectiveness. As covered in chapter 2, evaluation is an integral part of the life cycle of every project, as is monitoring for quality while a project is under way. The website for the IEG is http://www.worldbank.org/ieg/.

Other Resources

The following websites are also useful:

- *Development Impact Evaluation (DIME) Initiative.* This Bank-wide initiative evaluates active projects and programs in collaboration with donor partners. More information on the DIME initiative can be found at http://www.worldbank.org/dime/.
- *Independent Evaluation Group Help Desk.* IEG can be contacted through the website (http://www.worldbank.org/ieg/contact.html/) or by e-mail (ieg@worldbank.org).
- *World Bank research.* Research on aid effectiveness can be found at http://www.worldbank.org/aideffectiveness/.

Children and Youth

More than 3 billion people under the age of 24 years are living in the world today, representing about 47 percent of the world's population. The demand for policy advice on how to develop the enormous potential of the world's children and youth is large and growing. The World Bank has an array of programs that support young people on the path to adulthood, including safe and healthy habitats, health and nutrition, early childhood development, lifelong learning, healthy behaviors, livelihoods and employment, and protection of the most vulnerable. More information is available at http://www.worldbank.org/childrenandyouth/. *World Development Report 2007: Development and the Next Generation* and its related background research papers can be found at http://www.worldbank.org/wdr2007/.

The following resources are also useful:

- *Youth in Numbers.* The Youth in Numbers series comprises six booklets, one for each operational region of the World Bank. They bring together data tables and sources of information to provide a handy reference guide for young people and for practitioners who are concerned with understanding and improving the well-being of young people. The data sources and presentation of the information are as similar as possible between the booklets to allow for intraregional and cross-regional comparisons. The booklets are available under "Data and Statistics," at http://www.worldbank.org/childrenandyouth/.
- *YouThink.* The World Bank's website for youth can be found at http://www.youthink.org/. The site aims to inform youth on development issues and to inspire them to get involved.
- *Y2Y (Youth to Youth) Community.* Y2Y Community is the first attempt to bring together all young staff members and external youth to engage them in the Bank's work. For information, visit http://www.worldbank.org/y2ycommunity/.

Climate Change

Climate change is expected to hit developing countries the hardest, and they are the least prepared to cope with the impact. Climate change effects—higher temperatures, changes in precipitation patterns, rising sea levels, and more frequent weather-related disasters—pose risks for agriculture, food, and water supplies. At stake are recent gains in the fight against poverty, hunger, and disease and the lives and livelihoods of millions of people in developing countries. Tackling this immense challenge must involve both mitigation and adaptation, while maintaining a focus on the social dimensions of the phenomenon.

The International Development Association (IDA), International Bank for Reconstruction and Development (IBRD), MIGA, and IFC have all adopted the World Bank Group's Strategic Framework on Development and Climate Change. The framework supports Bank Group clients in developing countries by facilitating growth objectives and poverty reduction goals while recognizing the added costs and risks of climate change. The framework also helps promote the new economic opportunities that arise from the development of global climate policies. The framework guides the specific strategies and business plans of IFC, MIGA, and World Bank regions and climate-sensitive sectors, such as agriculture and natural resources, water, energy, and health. The website for the Bank Group's climate change work is http://www.worldbank.org/climatechange/.

IFC and Climate Change

Standing between the public and private sectors, IFC brings market-based solutions to the challenge of creating low-carbon economic growth that meets the needs of the poor. IFC helps private companies in emerging markets identify business risks and opportunities associated with climate change.

IFC provides financing, in the form of loans and equity, to climate-friendly projects, such as renewable energy power plants, sustainable forest plantations, and clean technologies. IFC also provides its client companies with expert advice on reducing their greenhouse gas emissions and on adapting to potential impacts of climate change on their businesses. See "Climate Change" at http://www.ifc.org/topics.

Other Resources

The following resources are also useful:

- *Development and Climate Change research series.* This series provides in-depth analyses on key issues at the nexus of development and climate change, covering areas as diverse as climate-resilient development, low-carbon growth, and climate finance. Reports in this series offer timely new analyses, advice, and operational recommendations.
- *Climate finance instruments.* The World Bank's main tools for addressing climate change are its own lending instruments (almost all country assistance and partnership strategies emphasize climate action), carbon finance, the Climate Investment Funds, the Carbon Partnership Facility, the Forest Carbon Partnership Facility, the Global Environment Facility, the Global Facility for Disaster Reduction and Recovery, the Adaptation Fund, the Least Developed Countries Fund, and the Special Climate Change Fund. These mechanisms channel resources toward specific needs in developing countries.
- *World Bank Institute's climate change website.* The World Bank Institute (WBI) climate change practice has a website with information about this topic. Visit http://wbi.worldbank.org/wbi/topic/climate-change.
- *Regional studies.* Climate change is a global issue, but the needs differ across the countries and regions that the World Bank Group serves. The Bank tailors its approaches and brings clients together to address the many concerns that cut across borders.

For more information on these studies and the Bank Group's approach to climate change, visit http://www.worldbank.org/climatechange/. *World Development Report 2010: Development and Climate Change* and its related background research papers can be found at http://www.worldbank.org/wdr2010/.

Combating Corruption

The Bank Group has identified corruption as one of the single greatest obstacles to economic and social development. Through bribery, fraud, and the misappropriation of economic privileges, corruption diverts resources away from those who need them most. Since the mid-1990s, the Bank Group has supported more than 600 anticorruption programs and governance initiatives developed by its member countries. The goals include increasing political accountability, strengthening civil society participation, creating a competitive private sector, establishing institutional restraints on power, and improving public sector management.

Hundreds of governance and anticorruption activities take place throughout the World Bank. These activities focus on monitoring staff conduct at the Bank, minimizing corruption in World Bank–funded projects, and working with countries to improve their public sector and control corruption.

As outlined in the World Bank's Strategy on Governance and Anticorruption, the Bank will continue to expand efforts in these areas on three fronts. At the country level, the Bank is collaborating with countries to build capable, transparent, and accountable institutions and to design and implement anticorruption programs. In Bank-funded projects, the Bank is minimizing corruption by assessing corruption risk in projects upstream, by actively investigating allegations of fraud and corruption, and by strengthening project oversight and supervision. At the global level, the Bank is expanding partnerships with multilateral and bilateral development institutions, civil society, the private sector, and other actors in joint initiatives to address corruption.

The Bank's Poverty Reduction and Economic Management Department, the World Bank Institute, the Legal Department, and regional operations work with governments and businesses to open up to scrutiny in order to foster trust, credibility, and confidence in Bank operations; to increase accountability; and to put corruption control programs in place. The Office of Ethics and Business Conflict provides advice on internal ethical issues for Bank staff members.

In addition, a team of investigators in the World Bank Integrity Vice Presidency (INT) is in place to uncover fraud and corrupt practices in Bank projects and to investigate allegations of possible staff misconduct involving significant fraud and corruption. INT has an early-warning system in place so that information gathered during investigations can help operational Bank staff members make informed decisions about affected projects. The INT Preventive Services Unit helps raise awareness of fraud and corruption risks; provides practical tools, training, and advice to Bank staff members; and conducts research to distill lessons learned from investigations that are incorporated into future projects. For more information about INT and the fraud and corruption hotline it has established, go to http://www.worldbank.org/integrity/.

In 2008, the Bank began implementing the 18 recommendations of the Independent Review Panel (Volcker Panel). This effort has dramatically improved the Bank's ability to ensure that funds reach their intended beneficiaries.

The website for governance and anticorruption issues is at http://www.worldbank.org/; under "Topics," select "Anticorruption."

WBI supports in-country reform teams in creating and sustaining multistakeholder coalitions to help facilitate and manage the complex process of implementing governance reforms. It does so through the innovative use of capacity-building instruments that foster collaboration through problem solving and experiential learning. Partnerships with international, regional, and country-based organizations are critical to its work.

WBI focuses on three thematic areas—governance of extractive industries, public financial management (especially procurement), and strengthening of institutions of accountability (including access to information, parliamentary oversight, judicial accountability, and stolen asset recovery). In addition, WBI has three cross-cutting programs to support those (and future) thematic areas: the Leadership Capacity Development Program, the Skills Development and Advisory Services Program on Coalition Building, and the Multistakeholder for Reform program to strengthen the demand-side dimensions of reform. For more information, visit http://wbi.worldbank.org/wbi/, select "WBI Topics," and choose "Governance."

Debt Relief

A buildup of foreign debt owed by many low-income countries throughout the 1970s and 1980s left many nations with unsustainable debt burdens. Although the Paris Club and other bilateral creditors rescheduled and reduced many debts, a new initiative was called for to address the concern that debts were stifling poverty reduction efforts. In 1996, IDA and the IMF launched the Heavily Indebted Poor Countries (HIPC) Initiative to assist these countries. The initiative called for the voluntary provision of debt relief by all creditors and aimed to provide a fresh start to countries with a foreign debt that placed too great a burden on export earnings or fiscal revenues.

HIPC Initiative

The HIPC Initiative was enhanced in 1999 to provide deeper, more rapid relief to a wider group of countries and to increase the initiative's links with poverty reduction. By March 2011, 40 countries had benefited from HIPC debt relief, 32 had reached the completion point at which debt relief becomes irrevocable, and 4 more were receiving interim assistance. The debt-service payments of countries that have qualified for debt relief have declined as a result of the initiative. The decrease in debt service has led to increases in poverty-reducing expenditures in areas such as health, rural infrastructure, and education.

The Debt Reduction Facility (DRF), managed by IDA, provides grants to heavily indebted poor countries to buy back their public and publicly guaranteed external commercial debt at a deep discount, thereby extinguishing such debt obligations. Since its creation in 1989, the DRF has supported 25 buyback operations in 22 low-income countries, resulting in the extinguishing of over $10 billion of external commercial debt.

The Debt Management Facility for Low-Income Countries, launched in 2008, is a grant facility financed by a multidonor trust fund and managed by IDA. The facility works with low-income countries to manage their debt in a sustainable way.

The Economic Policy and Debt Department builds on the work of the HIPC Initiative. The department serves several purposes, including implementation of the debt sustainability framework for low-income countries and continued implementation of the HIPC Initiative. The department is also responsible for shaping the World Bank's position—when possible, in coordination with the debt policy community in general—on global debt issues facing developing countries. The e-mail address for comments on the HIPC Initiative is economicpolicyanddebt@worldbank.org.

For more information on the HIPC Initiative and the Multilateral Debt Relief Initiative, visit http://www.worldbank.org/debt/ and select "Debt Relief."

Paris Club

Many Bank Group countries also participate in the Paris Club, an informal group of official creditors—industrial countries, in most cases—that seek solutions for debtor nations facing payment difficulties. Paris Club creditors agree to reschedule debts due to them. Although the Paris Club has no legal basis, its members agree to a set of rules and principles designed to reach a coordinated agreement on debt rescheduling quickly and efficiently. This voluntary gathering dates back to 1956, when Argentina agreed to meet its public creditors in Paris. Since then, the Paris Club and related ad hoc groups have reached more than 415 agreements covering 87 debtor countries. Because the Paris Club normally requires countries to have an active IMF-supported program to qualify for a rescheduling agreement, it has extensive contact with the IMF and the Bank Group. The website is at http://www.clubdeparis.org/.

The Paris Club is paralleled by the London Club, an informal organization of commercial creditors. Officials of the Bank Group have been invited to meetings of the London Club in an effort to coordinate debt relief and repayment efforts with economic policy advice.

Education

The Bank Group recognizes that universal, high-quality education reduces poverty and inequality and sustains economic growth. Education is also fundamental for the construction of democratic societies and globally competitive economies. It improves people's skills, which, in turn, improve their incomes. Achieving universal primary education is one of the eight MDGs and is at the center of the World Bank's mission of poverty reduction.

The Bank Group pursues its work in education and training through the following units and programs.

Education Department of the World Bank

The Education Department is part of the Human Development Network. Education activities, programs, and projects at the region or country level can be accessed through the websites of the Bank's regions. Major education initiatives are described on the department's website (see http://www. worldbank.org/education/ and select "Topics"). These initiatives include the following:

- *Education for All (EFA).* EFA is a commitment by the international community to achieving education for every citizen in every society. The Bank supports the initiative with specific operations in almost 90 countries worldwide and through multidimensional efforts toward specific goals: to improve primary school access and equity, as well as educational quality and learning outcomes; to improve the dropout and retention rates of girls, as well as their learning outcomes; to assist educational systems in coping with HIV/AIDS; to promote early childhood development; and to protect EFA's prospects in fragile states.

■ *Education for the Knowledge Economy.* This initiative is an analytical program for understanding how education and training systems need to change to meet the challenges of the knowledge economy. The program offers practical and sustainable policy options for developing countries.

■ *Early Child Development.* This program is a knowledge source that assists policy makers, program managers, and practitioners in their efforts to promote the healthy growth and development of young children.

World Bank Institute

Capacity for development is the ability of individuals, institutions, and entire societies to solve problems, make informed choices, order their priorities, and plan their futures, as well as implement programs and projects and sustain them over time. However, technical solutions, political will, and financing—although necessary—are often insufficient conditions for sustainable development. Capacity is the key: the capacity of institutions, the people they support, and the people who make them work. And building that capacity depends heavily on society's ability to acquire and use knowledge.

WBI, the capacity development arm of the World Bank, partners with countries to share and apply global and local knowledge to meet development challenges. WBI's capacity development programs are designed not only to build skills among groups of individuals but also to strengthen the organizations in which they work and the sociopolitical environment in which they operate.

WBI conducts training sessions and policy consultations and creates and supports knowledge networks related to international economic and social development. The platforms for delivering these services include distance learning and other emerging technologies for education and training. WBI serves member countries, Bank Group staff members and clients, and other people working on poverty reduction and sustainable development. WBI programs address climate change, fragile and conflict-affected states, governance, growth and competitiveness, health systems, public-private partnerships, and urban services and management. Visit http://wbi.worldbank.org/.

IFC Investments in Private Education

IFC supports the development of private educational activities in its client countries and believes that such support can help improve access to and the quality of the education sector. To further this commitment, IFC's Health and Education Department invests in or advises on the start-up or expansion of initiatives in many subsectors of education. These subsectors include primary and secondary schools, universities, e-learning providers, student financing programs, online or information and communication technology service providers, and business institutes. For more information, see http://www.ifc.org/education.

Other Resources

The following resources are also useful:

- *Education Advisory Service.* The website is http://www.worldbank.org/education/; click "Contact us." The service can be contacted by e-mail at eservice@worldbank.org.
- *World Bank research.* To find out more about education research, go to http://econ.worldbank.org/, click on "Topics," and select "Education."

Energy Access and Renewable Energy

The Bank Group views energy as a fundamental driver of economic development and believes that countries must develop their own energy programs in careful and sustainable ways. Access to environmentally and socially sustainable energy is essential to poverty reduction. More than 1.4 billion people are still without access to electricity worldwide, almost all of whom live in developing countries. About 2.5 billion use solid fuels—wood, charcoal, and dung—for cooking and heating. Every year fumes and smoke from open cooking fires kill approximately 1.6 million people, mostly women and children, who die from emphysema and other respiratory diseases.

The World Bank supports developing countries' efforts to provide cleaner, more stable energy services to households and businesses and to reduce the impacts of climate change through its financing instruments, policy advice, technical assistance, partnerships, and knowledge transfer. The Bank supports governments in their efforts to rehabilitate and strengthen rural energy distribution networks, improve the capacity of regional and local governments to plan and manage electrification projects, promote energy investment opportunities to potential private investors, and strengthen the sector's overall governance and financial performance.

In addition, the Bank recognizes that energy efficiency and renewable energy hold vast potential to transform people's lives in the developing world. In the face of energy price volatility, supply uncertainties, and environmental concerns, the Bank is working with many countries to adopt renewable energy sources to enhance energy security, affordability, and reliability.

For more information on the World Bank's involvement in energy access and renewable energy sources, visit http://www.worldbank.org/, select "Topics," and click on "Energy Access and Renewables."

IFC and Energy

IFC works to maximize access to energy through private sector development of electricity generation and transmission, while minimizing greenhouse gas emissions to increase positive long-term development effects. Since 1961, IFC has financed more than 200 projects in 50 countries for $6 billion in cumulative commitments and has supported 30,000 megawatts of generation capacity. IFC investments are well diversified by technology and geography, with more than 150 million consumers reached through IFC's power projects.

As part of a wider program to help mitigate climate change, IFC is investing in and providing advisory services to private enterprises in the renewable energy sector throughout emerging markets. And because different technologies show promise in different parts of the world, IFC's activities support all proven renewable technologies, including biomass, geothermal, hydro, solar, and wind.

For more information on IFC's investments in clean energy and renewables, visit http://www.ifc.org/, go to the alphabetical listing of topics, and choose "Power," "Renewable Energy," or "Sustainable Energy."

Other Resources

Other resources include the following:

- *Energy Sector Management Assistance Program (ESMAP).* This global, multidonor technical assistance trust fund is administered by the World Bank and cosponsored by bilateral donors. ESMAP works with its clients—low- and middle-income countries—to increase their know-how and institutional capacity to achieve environmentally sustainable energy solutions for poverty reduction and economic growth. For more information, go to http://www.esmap.org/.

■ *Renewable Energy Toolkit.* This resource provides a broad set of tools to assist Bank staff members and country counterparts in improving the design and implementation of renewable energy projects and in incorporating best practices and lessons learned. It is intended to provide practical guidance for each stage in the renewable energy project cycle. For more information, go to http://www.worldbank.org/energy/, select "Topics," and click on the link for "Renewable Energy and Energy Efficiency."

Environment

Many view concern for the environment as a luxury for rich countries. It is not. Natural and engineered environmental resources—fresh water, clean air, forests, grasslands, marine resources, and agroecosystems—provide sustenance and a foundation for social and economic development. The World Bank is one of the key promoters and financiers of environmental upgrading in the developing world with its support for environmental protection and improvement. It conducts research and advocacy on environmental issues and ensures environmental protection in its own work through careful adherence to safeguards it has established.

The World Bank is a key member of a new global partnership called WAVES (Wealth Accounting and Valuation of Ecosystem Services). Launched at the Convention on Biological Diversity meeting in Nagoya, Japan, in 2010, WAVES aims to promote sustainable development through comprehensive wealth accounting that focuses on the value of natural capital and integration of "green accounting" into national accounts.

Part of SDN, the Environment Department is responsible for the World Bank's environment strategy for developing countries. This strategy has the following priorities: improving aspects of the quality of life (people's health, livelihoods, and vulnerability) that are affected by environmental conditions; improving the quality of growth by supporting policy, regulatory, and institutional frameworks for sustainable environmental management and by promoting sustainable private development; and protecting the quality of the regional and global commons, such as the climate, forests, water resources, and biodiversity. The department also maintains the Bank Group's website for environmental issues at http://www.worldbank.org/environment/.

Environmental and Social Sustainability Department of IFC

IFC helps private sector clients succeed in a challenging global environment by realizing their financial potential. It places a strong emphasis on environmental and social issues such as climate change, access to water, and the impact that business operations may have on local communities. The Environmental and Social Sustainability Department works to unite concerns about the environment with the needs of the private sector. The department's website is http://www.ifc.org/enviro.

In early 2006, IFC announced its strengthened environmental and social standards, which set forth requirements for its client companies. These performance standards are the basis of the Equator Principles—a benchmark for the financial industry to manage social and environmental issues in project financing—which approximately 40 of the world's leading commercial banks have adopted for their project finance lending.

IFC's specialists collaborate with clients to integrate risk management throughout the investment cycle to reduce environmental, social, and business risks and provide support for innovative products and business lines that contribute to the sustainability of private sector enterprises.

An IFC website on environmental and social standards provides information on the corporation's sustainability policy; environmental and social review procedure; performance standards; and environmental, health, and safety guidelines. It also lists those sectors in which IFC does not invest. Select "Environmental and Social Standards" at http://www.ifc.org/enviro.

Other Resources

For information on the Bank Group's environmental safeguards, see chapter 2 as well as the following resources:

- *MIGA environmental and disclosure policies.* MIGA's policies and other information are available at http://www.miga.org/; go to "Policies," and then select "Policy on Social and Environmental Sustainability."
- *World Bank Operational Manual.* The Bank's environmental and social safeguard policies can be found at http://www.worldbank.org/opmanual/.
- *Global Environment Facility (GEF).* The World Bank is a key partner in the GEF, which unites 182 member governments—along with international institutions, nongovernmental organizations, and the private sector—to address global environmental issues. The GEF secretariat is

located at Bank headquarters. For more information, see "Partnerships" in chapter 2 or go to http://www.worldbank.org/gef/.

■ *World Bank Carbon Finance Unit.* The carbon finance unit financially rewards, through carbon credits, the reduction of greenhouse gas emissions by emitters in developing countries. Activities of the World Bank Carbon Finance Unit are aligned with the Environment Department's mission to reduce poverty and improve living standards in the developing world. Since the first Prototype Carbon Fund in 2000, carbon finance operations at the World Bank have grown to $2.5 billion, managed through 11 funds and facilities, of which $1.9 billion is committed. See http://www.carbonfinance.org/.

■ *World Bank research.* For resources on environmental research, go to http://econ.worldbank.org/, select "Topics," and then choose "Environment."

Extractive Industries

Mineral resources can present opportunities for economic growth in many of the world's poorest regions. They help countries earn revenues, attract investment, and create jobs and economic opportunities for ordinary people. Mineral resources can also provide energy for millions of people around the globe. The Bank Group also works with countries to ensure environmentally and socially responsible development of their mineral resources. The Bank Group pursues its work in this area through the Oil, Gas, and Mining Unit of the Energy Department. The unit focuses on issues such as gas flaring and revenue management and transparency, and it works with an advisory group to identify best practices in the oil, gas, and mining industries. The Oil, Gas, and Mining Unit is the lead unit in implementing the Bank Group's response to the Extractive Industries Review, an independent stakeholder consultation process that concluded in 2004. Bank Group work in the extractive industries can be seen at http://www.worldbank.org/oilgasmining/.

IFC is developing new business models for investments involving renewable energy, energy efficiency, recovery and use of methane, and use of cleaner fuels. Through its internationally recognized Policy and Performance Standards on Social and Environmental Sustainability, IFC collaborates with clients to manage social and environmental risks as well as maximize development opportunities. In addition, it works with companies in emerging markets to increase their incomes while reducing environmental impacts by arranging for the purchase of carbon credits under the terms of the Kyoto

Protocol. IFC also works with the GEF and other donors to help commercialize climate-friendly investments. For more information, visit http://www.ifc.org/ogmc/.

The following resources are also useful:

- *Extractive Industries Transparency Initiative (EITI).* EITI works with about 30 countries to make revenues from extractive industries more transparent. To access the most recent report, visit http://www.ifc.org/eir/.
- *Global Gas Flaring Reduction (GGFR) Partnership.* The GGFR Partnership includes representatives of industry, government officials, and other stakeholders. Together they work to reduce harmful and wasteful gas flaring. See http://www.worldbank.org/ggfr/.
- *Community and Small-Scale Mining (CASM).* This initiative addresses the plight of millions of informal miners trying to make a living by digging for minerals. CASM's website is http://www.artisanalmining.org/.
- *Sustainable Community Development Fund (CommDev).* This IFC fund partners with other organizations to provide funding and knowledge to help ensure that communities benefit from their country's natural resources. CommDev also provides technical assistance, training, and tools for community development initiatives. See http://www.ifc.org/ifcext/commdev.nsf.

Financial Crisis

The global financial crisis that began in 2008 hit both developing and developed countries hard, but it was especially detrimental to the poorest countries. The World Bank Group responded quickly to the immediate needs of developing countries by stepping up its financing and technical assistance, supporting social programs, boosting trade, and creating special funding mechanisms for the private sector. These initiatives included the following, among others:

- IBRD financing and technical assistance to middle-income countries, where 70 percent of the world's poor live
- IDA low- or zero-interest loans and grants to the world's 79 poorest countries
- IFC initiatives to strengthen banks and boost trade liquidity, as well as to establish an infrastructure crisis facility and an equity fund

■ MIGA political risk guarantees to support banking systems and continued lending to the real economy in countries hardest hit by the crisis

■ A range of financing innovations to improve efficiency and flexibility to meet pressing development priorities

Although the most acute phase of the crisis has passed, recovery remains fragile and uncertain, and persistent risks to economic health remain, including high unemployment, low growth, and high indebtedness in developed countries and scarce international financing for developing countries.

As the world moves past the crisis to the recovery and beyond, developing countries are expected to lead global recovery, expanding almost twice as fast as high-income countries. Nevertheless, the poorest countries will need assistance to recover from the effects of the economic slide. The Bank will continue to sharpen its focus where it can add more value: targeting the poor and vulnerable, especially in Sub-Saharan Africa; creating opportunities for growth with a special emphasis on agriculture and infrastructure; promoting global collective action on issues ranging from climate change and trade to agriculture, food security, energy, water, and health; strengthening governance and anticorruption efforts; and preparing for future crises. For information on the crisis and the Bank's response, visit http://www.worldbank.org/financialcrisis/.

Other useful resources include the following:

■ *Interactive financial crisis timeline.* This interactive timeline shows the story of how the financial crisis unfolded and the Bank's response— in words, images, video, maps, and more. Users can click into individual dates and time spans for more in-depth coverage. Visit http://www.worldbank.org/financialcrisis/.

■ *Global Economic Prospects.* This website is a good source of information on the crisis and its aftermath; economic forecasts; and prospects for trade, financial markets, and inflation. The site also provides data sources for further study. See http://www.worldbank.org/prospects/.

■ *Regions and the impact of the crisis.* For information on how the global financial and economic crisis affected different regions, visit http://www.worldbank.org/financialcrisis/ and click on the links under "Regional Information."

Financial Sector

A healthy, trustworthy financial system is fundamental to economic development. The Bank Group works with countries to strengthen their financial systems, grow their economies, restructure and modernize institutions, and respond to the savings and financing needs of all people. Major initiatives are as follows.

Financial and Private Sector Development Vice Presidency of the World Bank Group

Government policies have a decisive effect on shaping the business environment for the private sector, and a healthy, trustworthy financial system is fundamental to economic development. The Financial and Private Sector Development (FPD) Vice Presidency, a joint World Bank and IFC vice presidency, focuses on several areas that help support the business environment for the private sector and that strengthen financial systems and access to a broad range of financial services. Here are some of these key areas:

- Support safe financial systems to sustainably expand financial intermediation
- Deepen financial markets to provide new financial options to support investment
- Broaden financial markets to create new opportunities and choices for the underserved
- Establish efficient regulations to stimulate private investment and productivity growth
- Help build competitive industries to create new opportunities for investment and jobs
- Create space for new business opportunities based on knowledge and entrepreneurship

The FPD Vice Presidency's website is http://www.worldbank.org/finance/.

IFC Investments and Advisory Services

IFC considers support for financial markets a cornerstone of its investment policies and a critical tool for private sector development. IFC's Global Financial Markets Department is the lead unit for investments in and technical support for banks and other financial institutions. The department includes investment and advisory services in a number of subsectors, including carbon finance, consumer finance, sustainability and climate change finance, housing finance, insurance, Islamic finance, leasing, banking for small and medium-size enterprises, and trade finance, as well as a global trade liquidity program. More information is available at http://www.ifc. org/gfm. IFC also seeks innovative ways to finance microentrepreneurs, who play a key role in the private sector of many economies in the developing world. See also the discussion of small and medium-size enterprises in the section on "Private Sector Development" later in this chapter.

In addition to providing core treasury services to the IFC, including funding and asset management, IFC's Finance Vice Presidency offers products and services to clients, including many in the financial sector. These products and services include structured finance transactions, derivative-based products, loan participations with commercial banks, and local currency financing. In some instances, the vice presidency has funded IFC's own operations through local currency bond issues that have helped develop domestic capital markets in developing countries. For more information, see http://www.ifc.org/finance.

Through its Private Equity and Investment Funds Department, IFC also invests in emerging market investment funds and fund management companies. IFC has become a center of expertise for this sector, developing best practices for the management of these funds and sponsoring conferences and industry organizations to make emerging market private equity more visible to investors. See http://www.ifc.org/funds.

Other Resources

Additional resources include the following:

- *Consultative Group to Assist the Poor (CGAP).* This global partnership program is dedicated to advancing access to financing for the world's poor. CGAP's secretariat is located at Bank headquarters. For more information, see "Partnerships" in chapter 2 or visit http://www.cgap.org/.
- *Stolen Assets Recovery (StAR) Initiative.* This partnership is jointly managed by the World Bank Group and the United Nations Office on Drugs and Crime. The StAR Initiative aims to trace assets that have been illegally diverted by government officials or their co-conspirators; assist law enforcement authorities, nongovernmental organizations, and the assets' rightful owners in freezing, claiming, and gaining control of the assets; and provide legal assistance for the assets' repatriation to the nations from which they were stolen. The initiative is administered by the FPD Vice Presidency of the World Bank Group. For more information, see http://www1.worldbank.org/publicsector/star_site/.

- *Knowledge Resources: Financial and Private Sector Development.* This website is an online knowledge resource specializing in policy for the private sector in developing countries. It aims to fill a gap in understanding about the relationship between successful business environments and financial sector reforms and about what makes reform processes successful in developing countries. Policy reformers and the business community can learn how to turn ideas into reform action with the information, tools, and access to critical data provided here. The website provides links to expert analysis, powerful databases, quick solutions, and comprehensive how-to guides; see http://rru.worldbank.org/.
- WBI has a financial sector learning program. For information, see http://www.worldbank.org/wbi/banking/financial sector/.
- *World Bank research.* For financial sector resources, click "Topics" at http://econ.worldbank.org/ and select "Finance and Financial Sector Development."

Food Crisis

Even before the food, fuel, and financial crises, 1.1 billion people were living on less than $1 a day and 923 million were undernourished. When food prices are high, poor people eat less; switch to cheaper, lower-quality foods; or forgo spending on health and education. Combined with the impact of the financial crisis, high volatility in food prices threatens to further increase food insecurity and exacerbate the hardships faced by the poor.

In response to the severity of the crisis and the need for prompt action, in 2008 the World Bank set up a $1.2 billion rapid financing facility under the Global Food Price Crisis Response Program (since increased to $2 billion) to provide immediate relief to countries hit hard by high food prices. The money is used to feed poor children and other vulnerable groups; provide for nutritional supplements to pregnant women, lactating mothers, infants, and small children; meet additional expenses of food imports; and buy seeds for the new season.

The Group of 20 Summit in September 2009 asked the World Bank to prepare a multilateral mechanism to help implement pledges to long-term food security made at the L'Aquila Summit in July 2009. This new mechanism, the Global Agriculture and Food Security Program, is intended to fill the financing gaps in national and regional agriculture and food security strategies. For more information, see http://www.gafspfund.org/gafsp/.

The Bank is also responding with strategies that address longer-term challenges. In 2009, it adopted a new action plan for agriculture, *Implementing Agriculture for Development: World Bank Group Agriculture Action Plan, 2010–2012.* This major analytical and strategic platform promotes "more and better" investment in agriculture and rural development by stakeholders in both developing countries and donor organizations, including the World Bank. The plan comprises five main areas: raising agricultural productivity, linking farmers to markets and strengthening value chains, reducing risk and vulnerability, facilitating agriculture entry and exit and rural nonfarm income, and enhancing environmental sustainability and services. Support to the sector by IDA, IBRD, and IFC is expected to increase significantly under the plan.

In developing countries, farmers, agroenterprises, and governments can employ a range of technical, managerial, and financial approaches to mitigate, transfer, and cope with risks. The World Bank supports the development and implementation of risk management strategies for the agricultural sector and supply chain in a growing number of developing countries through the provision of technical assistance. In addition, the World Bank provides capacity transfer and training in a number of risk-related areas.

The Consultative Group on International Agricultural Research mobilizes cutting-edge science to reduce hunger and poverty, improve human nutrition and health, and protect the environment. A key funder of CGIAR research, the Bank chairs the new CGIAR Fund Council and serves as trustee. Visit the website at http://www.cgiar.org/.

Fragile and Conflict-Affected Countries

The Bank Group works in countries afflicted by conflict by supporting international efforts to assist war-torn populations in resuming peaceful development. It also seeks to understand the causes of conflict and to determine ways that conflict can be prevented.

The Fragile and Conflict-Affected Countries Group serves as the Bank's corporate focal point on issues of fragility and conflict. It develops and implements the institution's policies on conflict and fragility across all different countries, regions, and sectors to increase the overall effectiveness of the World Bank's response to fragile and conflict-affected countries. It also manages the State and Peace-Building Fund, which addresses the governance and peace-building needs of fragile and conflicted-affected areas.

The group's work program has two key pillars:

- Working with the international community for greater effectiveness in addressing fragility through state building, rule of law, economic development, and understanding and generating of knowledge on fragility and conflict dynamics
- Improving the Bank's operational approaches and outcomes and its ability to capture and disseminate knowledge within the institution

The World Bank provides such state-building support to a large number of fragile and conflict-affected countries. This support involves all sectors, ranging from public administration, community development, and infrastructure to demobilization, health, education, and social services. The Bank also plays an important donor-coordinating role in administering multidonor trust funds in affected countries. The website is at http://www.worldbank.org/conflict/.

In addition, MIGA plays an important role in postconflict situations by providing coverage in countries where other insurers are often not willing to go. A report on MIGA activities is available at http://www.miga.org/documents/conflict09.pdf.

World Bank research that focuses on the economics of civil war, crime, and violence can be found under "Economics of Conflict" at http://econ.worldbank.org/programs. The *World Development Report 2011: Conflict, Security, and Development* and its related background research papers can be found at http://www.worldbank.org/wdr2011/.

Gender

Through its programs and projects, the Bank Group seeks to reduce gender disparities and to enhance women's participation in economic development. It summarizes knowledge and experience, provides gender statistics, and promotes discussion of issues of gender and development. The Gender and Development Group within the Poverty Reduction and Economic Management Network is the lead unit in this area. The key gender-related goal is the MDG to eliminate gender-related disparities at all levels of education by 2015; see the website at http://www.worldbank.org/gender/.

IFC assists women entrepreneurs through its Women in Business Program. For more information, visit http://www.ifc.org/GEM.

Other resources include the *PREM Advisory Service*, which deals with many issues, including gender. The service publishes *PREM Notes*, which summarizes good practice and key policy findings. The website is http://www.worldbank.org/prem/. The e-mail address is premadvisory@worldbank.org.

World Development Report 2012: Gender Equality and Development and its related background research papers can be found at http://www.worldbank.org/wdr2012/.

Governance

The Bank Group works to promote effective governance in the public sector and high standards of corporate governance in the private sector.

Public Sector Governance

A fundamental role of the Bank Group is to work with the governments of client countries to improve their functioning. Although this goal is simple to define, it is both complex and difficult to accomplish. The Bank Group has a number of initiatives dealing with governance issues, including its Public Sector Group activities, public services research, and WBI governance and knowledge-sharing programs.

The Public Sector Group is the lead unit in this area and is responsible for the World Bank's governance and public sector strategy. The unit focuses on building efficient and accountable public sector institutions rather than simply providing policy advice, and it also maintains the website on governance and public sector reform at http://www.worldbank.org/publicsector/.

Several units of IFC work with governments to strengthen institutions, laws, and regulations related to the private sector. The Foreign Investment Advisory Service, a joint unit of IFC, MIGA, and the World Bank, focuses specifically on working with governments of developing countries to attract and retain foreign direct investment. For more information, see http://www.wbginvestmentclimate.org/.

Corporate Governance

The joint IFC–World Bank Corporate Governance Group collaborates with companies and countries to improve standards of governance for corporations, focusing on shareholders' and stakeholders' rights, board members' duties, disclosure, and effective enforcement. The Bank Group provides technical assistance on such governance issues to a wide range of government and financial institutions. IFC has developed a methodology for assessing corporate governance, which it uses in its own risk analysis and investment decisions as well as to help client companies improve their practices. For more information, go to "Global Capital Markets Development" at http://www.ifc.org/economics.

Other Resources

Various resources are available on the Internet:

- *PREM Advisory Service.* The service deals with many issues, including governance and public sector reform. It publishes *PREM Notes*, which summarizes good practice and key policy findings. The website is at http://www.worldbank.org/prem/. The e-mail address is premadvisory@ worldbank.org.
- *World Bank Institute's governance program.* WBI works to develop the capacity of client countries to implement, support, and sustain governance reforms. For more information, see http://wbi.worldbank.org/wbi/ topic/governance.

Health, Nutrition, and Population

Ensuring adequate levels of basic health and nutrition lies at the heart of poverty reduction and economic development. In recent decades, improvements in income, education, hygiene, housing, water supply and sanitation, nutrition, and access to contraception have brought about notable health gains for much of the world. Yet the health, nutrition, and population challenges remain great for most developing countries.

The World Bank and Health

In recent years, the World Bank has committed more than $6 billion in new lending each year for health, nutrition, and population projects in the developing world. The Bank seeks to focus its assistance where the effects will be greatest—directly on people. The lead unit is Health, Nutrition, and Population, a sector unit of the Human Development Network. The unit organizes its work into the broad categories of health systems financing; the health, nutrition, and population MDGs; population and reproductive health; HIV/AIDS; nutrition; poverty and health; and public health. Public health is further broken down into categories that include avian flu, child heath, malaria, mental health, onchocerciasis, road safety, school health, tobacco, and tuberculosis. The unit's website is http://www.worldbank.org/hnp/.

IFC's Health and Education Department seeks to improve health care in developing countries by investing directly in health care companies, sharing industry knowledge and experience, and improving government policy that affects the private health sector. For more information, see http://www.ifc.org/ifcext/che.nsf.

Other Resources

Other health resources include the following:

- *Global Partnership to Eliminate River Blindness.* The partnership is discussed in chapter 3 of this book, under "Africa," and at http://www.worldbank.org/gper/.
- *Health and Population Advisory Service.* This World Bank service handles queries on health and population by e-mail at healthpop@worldbank.org; for information on nutrition, the e-mail address is nutrition@worldbank.org.
- *Health systems development.* The Health, Nutrition, and Population website examines all aspects of health systems, including market demand, financing, human resources, and service delivery. Go to http://www.worldbank.org/hnp/, select "Technical Focus," and choose "Health Systems."
- *HIV/AIDS.* HIV/AIDS is not only a health problem, but also a development problem that threatens human welfare, socioeconomic advances, productivity, social cohesion, and even national security. The World Bank is a key source of funding to combat HIV/AIDS. For information and resources, go to http://www.worldbank.org/hnp/ and select "HIV/AIDS."
- *HIV/AIDS Agenda for Action.* The Agenda for Action is described in chapter 3 of this book in the discussion of regional initiatives in the section on "Africa." See also http://www.worldbank.org/afr/aids/map.htm/.
- *Joint United Nations Programme on HIV/AIDS (UNAIDS).* UNAIDS has information on its website at http://www.unaids.org/.
- *Malaria.* One of the world's most important public health concerns, malaria causes more than a million deaths and up to 500 million clinical cases each year. Most of the 3,000 deaths each day—10 new cases every second—are in Africa, and more than a third of the world's population now lives in malaria-endemic areas. The Bank's approach combines an emphasis on monitoring results and outcomes with flexibility in approaches and lending instruments. For more information, go to http://www.worldbank.org/hnp/ and select "Malaria."
- *Nutrition Advisory Service.* Nearly half of child mortality in low-income countries can be linked to malnutrition. The World Bank's approach to

nutrition targets poor people, especially young children and their mothers, with an emphasis on community- and school-based nutrition programs, food fortification programs, and food policy reforms. To date, the World Bank has committed close to $2 billion to support nutrition programs. The Nutrition Advisory Service's website is at http://www.worldbank.org/nutrition/. Contact the service by phone at 1-202-473-2256, by fax at 1-202-614-0657, or by e-mail at nutrition@worldbank.org.

- *Population and reproductive health.* Problems such as early and unwanted childbearing, sexually transmitted infections, and pregnancy-related illness and death account for a significant part of the burden of disease in developing countries, especially among the poor, who often lack access to minimal health care. The Bank's action plan on reproductive health aims to work with country governments to ensure that core national health plans address maternal and neonatal health. For more information on Bank activities and resources, go to http://www.worldbank.org/population/.

- *Poverty and health.* This website focuses on how developments in health affect efforts to reduce poverty in developing countries. For more information, go to http://www.worldbank.org/hnp and select "Poverty."

- *Tobacco control.* This website provides information on tobacco policies and the economics of tobacco control measures. The World Bank has a formal policy of not lending for tobacco production or processing, directly or indirectly, and of encouraging tobacco control in developing countries. Visit http://www.worldbank.org/tobacco/.

- *Tuberculosis.* This website details the World Bank's efforts to fight tuberculosis. The Bank combats tuberculosis by providing policy dialogue and advice, by lending to countries to strengthen health systems and control the disease, by undertaking analysis, and by becoming involved in global partnerships. Go to http://www.worldbank.org/tuberculosis/.

- *WBI health systems.* For information on health systems and programs, visit http://wbi.worldbank.org/wbi/topics and click on "Health Systems."

- *World Bank research.* For research and data, go to http://econ.worldbank.org, select "Topics," and then choose "Health, Nutrition, and Population."

Information and Communication Technologies

Information and communication technologies (ICTs) are key components in the drive to speed development, improve governance and social services, and reduce poverty. ICTs are fueling a development revolution in which ordinary citizens can grasp the levers of their own economic growth. By

2010, the number of mobile phone subscriptions in developing nations had reached 3.7 billion, from 200 million just 10 years before, and the number of Internet users had grown more than 10-fold. Progress in the ICT Millennium Development Goal indicators has been remarkable: some 70 percent of people living in developing countries now have access to fixed or mobile telephones, and more than 20 percent are Internet users.

The World Bank directs its ICT operations through its Global Information and Communications Technology (GICT) Division, anchored in SDN. The GICT Division leads work related to ICT—operational (policy support and lending), analytical, capacity building, and knowledge sharing—and focuses on the best ways to support technology implementation by developing and promoting access to ICT in developing countries. The website is at http://www.worldbank.org/gict/.

Other resources include the following:

- The Bank also hosts infoDev, a multidonor partnership program that focuses primarily on promoting technology innovation (including clean technology) to small and medium-size enterprises. Visit http://www.infodev.org/.
- WBI is also active in ICT with a specific focus on governance and innovation. The Bank's Development Economics Department and WBI are encouraging development of ICT applications that make use of open-access World Bank data.
- *Development Gateway.* The mission of this international nonprofit organization is to enable change in developing nations through information technology. It provides Web-based platforms that make aid and development efforts more effective around the world by promoting broader access to critical information and greater reliance on local capabilities. The website is http://www.developmentgateway.org/.
- *Global Development Learning Network.* This network, discussed in the subsection "Capacity Development" under "Knowledge Sharing" in chapter 2, uses information technology in its effort to connect the world through learning. The website is at http://www.gdln.org/.

Infrastructure

Despite vast improvements in infrastructure over the past decade, 2.5 billion of the world's people still lack sanitation services, 1.5 billion live without electricity, 1 billion have no easy access to all-weather roads, and nearly 900 million have no choice but to use unsafe water. The global financial crisis has increased the enormous challenge of bridging this access gap by weakening countries' ability to fund infrastructure development.

Infrastructure development remains a fundamental focus of the Bank Group, and poor people are acutely aware that infrastructure can significantly improve the quality of their lives. At the same time, changes in the external environment are raising the stakes of infrastructure's contribution to sustainable development. Rapid urbanization and disaster risks (including climate-related risks) have created new demands on the quantity and type of infrastructure required. Technological advances offer opportunities to leapfrog.

The Bank Group's infrastructure work is a function of SDN and is organized by subject areas that focus on energy; ICT; oil, gas, and mining; transport; urban development; and water supply and sanitation. With the 2008 Sustainable Infrastructure Action Plan, the Bank Group committed to continue building and improving the infrastructure business, with an increased focus on leverage, sustainability, and governance risks in infrastructure projects.

The website for infrastructure issues is at http://www.worldbank.org/ sustainabledevelopment/; click "Topics" and select "Infrastructure."

IFC and Infrastructure

Infrastructure is a significant part of IFC's work of assisting the development of private sector business opportunities in emerging economies. IFC's Infrastructure Department offers expertise in helping private sector sponsors finance infrastructure projects in client countries. It focuses on investments in power, transport, and utilities. For information, visit http://www.ifc.org/ infrastructure. Other IFC departments handle some related sectors, including telecommunications and oil and gas.

In close partnership with the World Bank, IFC has also established the Subnational Finance Department to make direct investments in subsovereign governments and entities they control that bear much of the responsibility for infrastructure. For more information, see http://www.ifc.org/ municipalfund. In addition, IFC's advisory services assist national and municipal governments in implementing private sector participation projects in infrastructure, health, and education.

MIGA and Infrastructure

MIGA has extensive experience in the infrastructure sector. It supports infrastructure investments in water and sanitation, telecommunications, transport, and power. For information on MIGA's support to the infrastructure sector see http://www.miga.org/sectors/.

Public-Private Infrastructure Advisory Facility

■ A multidonor technical assistance facility, the Public-Private Infrastructure Advisory Facility (PPIAF) works with developing countries to improve the quality of their infrastructure through private sector involvement. PPIAF provides technical assistance to governments in the creation of sound enabling environments for private service provision. The website is at http://www.ppiaf.org/.

Other Resources

The following websites are also useful:

■ Energy: http://www.worldbank.org/energy/.
■ Global information and communication technologies: http://www. worldbank.org/gict/.
■ Oil, gas, and mining: http://www.worldbank.org/infrastructure/ under "Topics" and then "Oil, Gas, and Mining."
■ Transport: http://www.worldbank.org/infrastructure/ under "Topics" and then "Transport."
■ Urban development: http://www.worldbank.org/infrastructure/ under "Topics" and then "Urban Development"; contact by e-mail at urban-help@worldbank.org
■ Water supply and sanitation: http://www.worldbank.org/water/; contact by e-mail at whelpdesk@worldbank.org

Labor and Social Protection

The Bank Group studies and generally supports measures that seek to improve or protect human capital, such as labor market interventions, publicly mandated unemployment or old-age insurance, and targeted income support. Such measures allow individuals, households, and communities to better manage the income risks that leave people vulnerable, and they contribute to a country's solidarity, social cohesion, and social stability. Topics on which the Bank Group provides information and resources through its Human Development Network include disability, labor markets, pensions, safety nets and transfers, and social funds. The website for the Social Protection Unit is http://www.worldbank.org/sp/. The World Bank also maintains the Social Protection and Labor Advisory Service. Fax queries to 1-202-614-0471 or e-mail socialprotection@worldbank.org.

IFC and Social Protection

IFC will not support projects that use forced or harmful child labor. Projects should comply with the national laws of host countries, including laws that protect core labor standards, and with related treaties ratified by host countries.

Forced labor consists of all work or service not voluntarily performed that is exacted from an individual under threat of force or penalty. Harmful child labor consists of the employment of children that is economically exploitative; likely to be hazardous to the child or to interfere with the child's education; or likely to be harmful to the child's health or physical, mental, spiritual, moral, or social development. IFC's Policy and Performance Standards on Social and Environmental Sustainability address labor and working conditions. Learn more from http://www.ifc.org/ifcext/enviro.nsf/Content/PerformanceStandards/.

Other Resources

Other resources include the following:

- *Social Protection Help Desk.* Contact the help desk by e-mail at socialprotection@worldbank.org.
- *World Bank research.* Go to http://econ.worldbank.org/; select "Topics" and then select "Social Protection and Labor."

Law and Development

The Bank Group is an active supporter of legal and judicial reforms that address the needs of the poor and the most vulnerable in developing countries. The lead unit in this area, the Legal and Judicial Reform Practice Group of the World Bank, works with governments, judges, lawyers, scholars, civil society representatives, and other organizations to build better legal institutions and judicial systems. Other areas of activity for the Bank include environmental and international law and the role of legal systems in private sector development, finance, and infrastructure. For information on all these activities and links to several legal databases, type "Law and Justice" in the search box on http://www.worldbank.org/, or visit http://www.worldbank.org/legal/.

The Bank Group is working with governments to make laws and regulations more conducive to private sector development. Efforts include the products of the Financial and Private Sector Development Network such as the Doing Business project, a joint World Bank–IFC effort that compares administrative barriers facing private sector enterprises in more than 150 countries. The project is now being extended to the subnational level in selected countries and regions. Many of IFC's regional advisory services facilities and the joint World Bank–IFC–MIGA Investment Climate Advisory Services work with governments to assess administrative barriers and develop legislative or judicial solutions. IFC has worked to establish alternative dispute resolution in several countries in an effort to ensure that conflicts among private enterprises are addressed more quickly and at lower cost than through court proceedings.

Other resources on law and development are as follows:

- *Law Resource Center.* Links to key Bank Group documents, including articles of agreement, manuals and guidelines, and other materials, can be found at http://www.worldbank.org/lawlibrary/.
- *Legal Help Desk.* At the Law and Development website, http://www.worldbank.org/legal/, select "Legal Help Desk," or e-mail legalhelp-desk@worldbank.org.

Migration and Remittances

Migration of people across international borders affects economic growth and social welfare in both sending and receiving countries. Across the world, the money that migrants send home (remittances) is more than twice as large as foreign aid. For many countries, remittances are the largest source of foreign exchange. The World Bank has placed new emphasis on understanding the importance of migration and remittances to both economic and human development.

Research shows that migration brings strong economic gains. In developing countries, remittances frequently lead to more investment in education and greater entrepreneurship; they have a positive effect on learning and health, savings, and macroeconomic stability; and they also appear to contribute to reducing poverty and social inequality. But migration can also have disruptive effects, such as the "brain drain"—the massive migration of highly skilled professionals, especially from small, low-income countries. Issues also arise in rich countries because of illegal immigration, social welfare of migrants, and security concerns.

The semiannual Bank publication, the *Migration and Remittances Factbook*, provides a snapshot of migration and remittance data for all countries, regions, and income groups of the world, compiled from various sources. For more information, go to http://www.worldbank.org/migration/.

Other resources are as follows:

- *Global Migration Group.* This interagency organization brings together heads of agencies to promote the wider application of all relevant international and regional instruments and norms relating to migration. The group is particularly concerned with improving the effectiveness of its members and other stakeholders in capitalizing on the opportunities and responding to the challenges presented by international migration. Information on the group is available at http://www.globalmigrationgroup.org/.
- *Data and research.* The interactive data tool on the Bank's main data site, http://econ.worldbank.org/, offers additional sources of information on migration and remittances. Go to the "Research Programs" tab, and select "International Migration and Development." Also see "Migration and Remittances" at http://www.worldbank.org/prospects/.

Poverty

Fighting poverty is central to the Bank Group's mission. The Bank Group considers a comprehensive understanding of poverty and its possible solutions to be fundamental for everyone involved in development. This understanding involves defining poverty, studying trends over time, setting goals to reduce poverty, and measuring results. The Bank Group's website on this topic is PovertyNet at http://povertynet.org/. See also http://www.worldbank.org/poverty/, which introduces key issues and provides in-depth information on poverty measurement, monitoring, and analysis and on poverty reduction strategies for researchers and practitioners.

IFC and Poverty

IFC assists in the fight against poverty by focusing many of its investments on sectors that have the most direct effect on living standards. Sectors include the financial sector, infrastructure, ICT, small and medium-size enterprises, microfinance, health, and education.

Other Resources

Other resources include the following:

- *PREM Advisory Service.* The service's focus includes poverty. It publishes *PREM Notes,* which summarizes good practice and key policy findings.

The website is http://www.worldbank.org/prem/; the e-mail address is premadvisory@worldbank.org.

- *WBI growth and competitiveness practice.* At the WBI website, http:// wbi.worldbank.org/wbi/, select "WBI Topics" and then "Growth and Competitiveness."
- *World Bank research.* Data and research on poverty reduction are at http://econ.worldbank.org/. Go to "Browse by Topic" and select "Poverty Reduction."

Private Sector Development

The Bank Group places major emphasis on the role of the private sector in spurring economic growth and reducing poverty, with two of its institutions, IFC and MIGA, focusing specifically on private enterprises. In addition, a joint World Bank–IFC vice presidency takes the lead on many aspects of private sector development. The Bank Group institutions provide research and advisory services on corporate governance, corporate social responsibility, investment climate diagnostics and reform, private participation in infrastructure, privatization transactions, and microenterprise and small business development.

Financial and Private Sector Development Vice Presidency

This joint World Bank–IFC vice presidency takes the lead on many aspects of private sector development, such as small and medium-size enterprises; corporate governance and capital markets; and the investment climate, including the Doing Business project and the Foreign Investment Advisory Service.

The activities of the Corporate Governance Department are aimed at collaborating with companies and countries to improve standards of governance for corporations. The focus is on shareholders' and stakeholders' rights, board members' duties, disclosure, and effective enforcement. The department promotes the spirit of enterprise and accountability, encouraging fairness, transparency, and responsibility. The website is at http://worldbank.org/corporategovernance/.

IFC Investments and Advisory Services

IFC's Global Industries Vice Presidency includes departments responsible for its investment portfolio across a wide range of industry sectors, including agribusiness, global financial markets, global manufacturing and services, health and education, infrastructure, private equity and investment funds, and subnational finance. Departments dealing with global information and communication technologies and with oil, gas, mining, and chemicals report both to this group and to the World Bank's Infrastructure Vice Presidency.

IFC's Business Advisory Services Vice Presidency includes environmental and social development; partnerships; knowledge management; the sustainability business line; and dedicated advisory services on corporate issues, infrastructure, and access to finance. Increasingly, IFC is working to integrate its investments with related advisory services to improve the sustainability, competitiveness, governance, and development effect of private enterprises.

Private sector development is the focus of many Bank Group partnerships with other organizations, including IFC's donor-funded operations, which encompass trust funds and a network of facilities that serve developing regions or promote specific aspects of development. For information on advisory services, including links to facilities, see http://www.ifc.org/ifcext/about.nsf/Content/TAAS.

Small and Medium Enterprises

Units across the World Bank Group focus on ways to develop and sustain small and medium enterprises (SMEs), which are the growth engines of developing economies. The Bank promotes institutional innovations and encourages policy reforms that improve access to finance and reduce obstacles to economic growth.

IFC fosters SME development mainly through investments in financial institutions that provide financing to SMEs. Leasing companies, banks, venture capital funds, and business service providers are just a few examples. IFC also supports SMEs through technical assistance programs, such as its regional facilities and linkage programs. IFC's Partnerships and Advisory Services Operations manages and coordinates these activities. For more information, see http://www.ifc.org/sme.

The Doing Business Report and Database

In 2003, the World Bank and IFC launched the Doing Business project, which measures the ease of doing business around the world. The project's reports are widely read and foster dialogue on business environment reforms at the local, regional, and global levels. *Doing Business* allows policy makers to compare their countries' regulatory performance with that of other countries, learn from best practices globally, and prioritize reforms.

A public database on the Doing Business website shares the data collected for the reports. These data provide objective measures of business regulations and their enforcement, with indicators comparable across 183 economies, as of 2011. They indicate the regulatory costs of business and can be used to analyze specific regulations that enhance or constrain investment, productivity, and growth. See http://www.doingbusiness.org/.

Other Resources

Other resources include the following:

- *MIGA's Small Investment Program.* This program is designed to increase MIGA's support for investors in SMEs. For more information on the program, see http://www.miga.org/guarantees/ and select "Small Investment Program."
- *Donor Committee for Enterprise Development.* This committee works to share information and coordinate the efforts of agencies in this field. Visit http://www.sedonors.org/.
- *Foreign Investment Advisory Service.* This service advises governments of developing and transition countries on how to improve their investment climate for domestic and foreign investors. Visit https://www.wbginvestmentclimate.org/.
- *Private Sector Development Blog.* This informal network gathers news, resources, and ideas about the role of private enterprise in fighting poverty. The blog represents the quirks and opinions of the bloggers, not of the World Bank Group. Visit http://psdblog.worldbank.org/.
- *World Bank Group journals.* Two journals are available on these topics. *Crisis Response* assesses the policy responses to the financial crisis, shedding light on financial reforms currently under debate. *Viewpoint* focuses on public policy innovations for private sector–led and market-based solutions for development. Articles can be viewed and downloaded at http://rru.worldbank.org/PublicPolicyJournal/.
- *Public-Private Infrastructure Advisory Facility.* This multidonor technical assistance facility collaborates with developing countries to improve the quality of their infrastructure through private sector involvement. It provides technical assistance to governments to support the creation of a sound enabling environment for private service provision. The website is at http://www.ppiaf.org/.
- *World Bank research.* For more information in this area, go to http://econ.worldbank.org/, choose "Topics," and select "Private Sector Development."

Social Development

The World Bank has consolidated its approach to social development in a single Bank-wide strategy and implementation plan titled *Empowering People by Transforming Institutions: Social Development in World Bank Operations*, which was produced after extensive stock taking, research, and consultation. The plan focuses on efforts to empower the poor through enhanced Bank support for social inclusion, cohesive societies, and accountable institutions. *Social development* is defined as the transformation of institutions and, as such, promotes enhanced growth, improved projects, and a better quality of life. The plan sets a vision, objectives, and a course of action for the long term and suggests specific actions, targets, and institutional measures.

The Sustainable Development Network of the World Bank coordinates several thematic work programs. These programs are on conflict, crime, and violence; gender; social analysis and social policy; social sustainability and safeguards; governance and accountability; and the social dimensions of climate change. The website is at http://www.worldbank.org/socialdevelopment/ or can be found under "Topics" on the SDN website, http://www.worldbank.org/sustainabledevelopment/. More information can be found in the "Environment" section of this chapter, in the subsection "Environmental and Social Sustainability Department of IFC." That IFC website is at http://www.ifc.org/enviro.

More information about social development can be obtained from World Bank research. At the website http://econ.worldbank.org/, select "Topics" and then choose "Social Development."

Sustainable Development

Much of the World Bank's work in sustainable development is piloted through an internal group of departments, the Sustainable Development Network, which supports its clients, directly or through the Bank's regional units, in the complex agenda of sustainable development. The network's work covers a wide range of economic sectors: agriculture and rural development; energy; environment; global ICT; infrastructure; oil, gas, and mining; social development; transport; urban development; and water, as well as subnational activities.

The aim of SDN is to make sustainability a comparative advantage by enhancing the quality of growth experienced by developing countries. Such countries can then move to a development path that reduces poverty and meets the needs of people today without reducing the ability of future generations to meet their own goals.

The concept of sustainability has been incorporated into all the work carried out under the auspices of the network. Its agenda embraces the "triple bottom line" of sustainability—economic, environmental, and social—as well as anticipates and addresses major trends such as climate change, natural resource depletion, food scarcity, and urban expansion.

The website for the Bank's sustainable development work and related information is http://www.worldbank.org/sustainabledevelopment/.

IFC and Sustainability

Growing public awareness of environmental and social issues is driving changes in the products consumers buy, how companies do business, and how investment decisions are made. IFC focuses on financially, environmentally, and socially sustainable business so that private sector clients can succeed amid global challenges and realize their financial potential. IFC works with its client companies to identify, reduce, and manage the environmental and social risks associated with their services, products, and business operations; provides technical assistance on climate change, labor and social assets, and biodiversity; and maintains its rigorous Policy and Performance Standards on Social and Environmental Sustainability. The website for IFC sustainability resources is at http://www.ifc.org/sustainability.

MIGA and Sustainability

MIGA strives for positive development outcomes in the private sector projects for which it provides guarantee support. An important component of positive development outcomes is the social and environmental sustainability of projects, which MIGA expects to achieve by applying a comprehensive set of social and environmental performance standards. See http://www.miga.org/projects/ and select the key link "Environmental and Social Sustainability."

Trade

The World Bank promotes the expansion of trade in developing countries as a way of contributing to economic growth and reducing poverty. However, although international economic integration creates new opportunities, it also introduces new sources of vulnerabilities. To address both the promises and the challenges of more intensive trade relationships, the Bank is stepping up its work through expanded country programs on trade and competitiveness, as well as increased lending for trade infrastructure, trade finance services, assistance in trade facilitation and logistics, training and technical assistance in strategic areas, provision of benchmarking indicators, and research into globalization and poverty. The Bank Group's website on trade issues is at http://www.worldbank.org/trade/.

IFC and Trade

Through investments and advisory services, IFC supports banking institutions that provide trade enhancement facilities to local companies. Its Global Trade Finance Program maintains a worldwide network of bank partnerships that finance trade under risk coverage provided by IFC. The program extends and complements the capacity of banks to deliver trade financing by providing risk mitigation in new or challenging markets where trade lines may be constrained. The program aims to increase the developing countries' share of global trade and to promote flows of goods and services between developing countries. For more information, go to http://www.ifc.org/gtfp.

Other Resources

The following websites provide more information on trade:

- *International trade.* The website for the World Bank's program on trade and international integration is http://www.worldbank.org/research/trade/.
- *World Bank research.* At http://econ.worldbank.org/, select "Topics" and then "International Economics and Trade."

Transport

Transport is crucial for economic growth and trade, both of which depend highly on the conveyance of people and goods. Virtually no production can take place unless inputs such as raw materials, labor, and fuel are moved from different locations. Also, manufactured products cannot be delivered to consumers, nor can a wide variety of services be carried out. Transport, therefore, is the key infrastructure asset for the movement of goods, people, and resources; it encompasses roads, rail, seaports, airports, and all manner of vehicles and management systems. This sector focuses on access, the role of the public and private sectors, and institutional and financial development.

The transport sector constitutes a significant part of the World Bank's portfolio, with lending of $46 billion since 2000. Areas of activity include economics and policy, ports and logistics, railways, roads and highways, road safety, and rural and urban transport. Special concerns include globalization of trade, congestion and pollution, safety, budget constraints, rapid urbanization, and institutional capacity to maintain and modernize transport infrastructure. The website for transport issues is at http://www.worldbank.org/transport/. The Transport Help Desk can be found at "Contact Us" at that site. The e-mail address is transport@worldbank.org.

IFC also considers sound transport infrastructure and services to be crucial to private sector development. The private sector is playing a larger role in financing projects, as well as in providing managerial and technical expertise. Through its Infrastructure Department, IFC invests in ports, airlines and airports, roads, railroads, shipping, and trucking; visit http://www.ifc.org/infrastructure. IFC's Infrastructure Advisory Services advises governments on private sector participation in transportation infrastructure and services; visit http://www.ifc.org/ifcext/psa.nsf.

Urban Development

More than half of the world's population lives in urban areas. Today's global urban population of about 3.3 billion is projected to reach 5 billion by 2030. Ninety percent of this growth is taking place in developing countries. Urban populations of Africa and South Asia are expected to double over the next 20 years. The World Bank is acutely aware that, with most of the world's gross domestic product generated in cities, the economic future of most developing countries, and therefore much of the poverty reduction agenda, will hinge on the productivity of their urban populations.

The World Bank's Urban and Local Government Strategy, launched in 2009, will allow governments at all levels to make cities more equitable, efficient, sustainable, and environmentally friendly. The strategy draws on two principles. First, density, agglomeration, and proximity are fundamental to human advancement, economic productivity, and social equity. Second, cities need to be well managed and sustainable. The strategy unfolds along five business lines: (a) city management, governance, and finance; (b) urban poverty; (c) cities and economic growth; (d) city planning, land, and housing; and (e) urban environment and climate change. These business lines set out the objectives and benchmarks for the Bank to monitor its financing and policy advice. Many inhabitants of the cities in developing countries face an immense lack of resources, and it will take some time until all the poor will be fully integrated in the city infrastructure network. For this reason, the new strategy calls for a broader-based, scaled-up approach to urban poverty, focusing more than ever on policies and actions that can create livable cities. The main website for urban issues is http://www.worldbank.org/urban/.

A joint effort of the World Bank and IFC, the Subnational Finance Department, provides capital investment to municipalities and other local public entities in the developing world without central government guarantees. Its offerings provide states, municipalities, and municipally controlled institutions new financial products and access to capital markets. The objective is to strengthen their ability to deliver key infrastructure services such as water, wastewater management, transportation, electricity, and power and to improve efficiency and accountability. More information is available at http://www.ifc.org/municipalfund.

Other urban development resources include the following:

- *Cities Alliance*. This global alliance of cities and their development partners is committed to improving the living conditions of the urban poor. The secretariat is housed at the World Bank. Visit http://www.citiesalliance.org/.
- *Eco² Cities*. This initiative aims to work with cities in developing countries to achieve greater ecological and economic sustainability. For more information, see http://www.worldbank.org/eco2/.
- *Urban Help Desk*. Advice is available through e-mail to urbanhelp@worldbank.org.
- *WBI urban government program*. For more information, visit the website at http://wbi.worldbank.org/wbi/topic/urban-development.
- *World Bank research*. For information on research and data, go to http://econ.worldbank.org/; select "Topics" and then "Urban Development."

Water

The livelihoods of the poorest are critically associated with access to water services. Properly managed water resources are a vital component of growth, poverty reduction, and equity. The sustainable management of water resources has acquired a new urgency in the face of a growing population and as economic development spurs demand for more and better food. The need is further exacerbated by hydrological variability caused by climate change. Countries in Africa, the Middle East, and South Asia are under severe water stress. By 2025, an estimated 4 billion people—about half of the world's population—will live in countries vulnerable to flooding and drought. The challenge is to harness the productive potential of water, limit its destructive impacts, and achieve basic water security. By 2050, there will be an estimated 2.3 billion more people to feed (one-third more than today). Meeting future food needs will require more efficient water use and additional sources of supply to support the increasing demand for water for agriculture. Moreover, demand for energy will more than double in poor and emerging markets, and much of the response to this demand will tap hydropower.

The Bank Group is the largest external financier in water supply and sanitation, irrigation and drainage, river basin management, transboundary water programs, and other water-related sectors. It provides strong advisory and analytical support to developing countries. Water is the focus of Bank Group efforts in two broad areas: water resources management and water supply and sanitation. Specific issues include coastal and marine management, dams and reservoirs, hydropower, groundwater, irrigation and drainage, river basin and watershed management, water management across national boundaries, water and the environment, and water economics. Water is also the focus of one of the MDGs: the objective for 2015 is to reduce by half the proportion of people without sustainable access to safe drinking water. The World Bank's website on water issues is at http://www.worldbank.org/water/. The Water Help Desk offers e-mail advice at whelpdesk@worldbank.org.

IFC is represented on the World Bank Group's Water and Urban Sector Board and contributes to the development of ideas and policies in this sector. IFC draws on its experience to provide inputs from an investor perspective. It often works in collaboration with the World Bank; however, IFC's main role is to support investors that undertake private sector water projects. IFC has invested in water projects in a wide range of countries; see http://www.ifc.org/infrastructure and click on "Water and Utilities." IFC has also advised on the privatization of several water companies; learn more at http://www.ifc.org/about and click on "Investment and Advisory Services."

MIGA's projects in the water sector are located at http://www.miga.org/sectors/.

World Bank Reform

The World Bank Group is advancing multiple reforms to promote inclusiveness, innovation, efficiency, effectiveness, accountability, and results. It is expanding cooperation with the United Nations, the IMF, other multilateral development banks, donors, civil society, and foundations. The goal of these reforms is to realize a World Bank Group that represents the international economic realities of the 21st century, recognizes the role and responsibility of a growing number of stakeholders, and provides a larger voice for developing countries. The reforms center on five themes:

- *Reforming the lending model.* The Bank is modernizing its financial services and lending model to provide more tailored responses to borrowers' needs. The approach calls for closer attention to results and for streamlined processes, improved supervision, and higher-risk investments.
- *Increasing voice and participation.* The Bank is seeking to elevate the influence and representation of developing and transition countries in the Bank Group, with an additional seat on the Board of Executive Directors for Sub-Saharan Africa and an increase in the voting power of developing countries.
- *Promoting accountability and good governance.* Governance and anticorruption are key concerns of Bank operations across sectors and countries. The Bank's focus on governance and anticorruption is based on the mandate to reduce poverty: a capable and accountable state creates opportunities for the poor.
- *Increasing transparency, accountability, and access to information.* The Bank's Access to Information Policy offers opportunities for the Bank to share its global knowledge and experience with a wide audience and to enhance the quality of its operations by providing more information about projects and programs than ever before.
- *Modernizing the organization.* The Bank is undergoing a series of reforms to make it a better development partner. First, it is modernizing its lending and knowledge products and services to better serve its clients and better support their efforts to reduce poverty. Second, the Bank is improving the way the institution shares and accesses knowledge and expertise from inside and outside the institution. Third, it is modernizing the processes and systems underpinning the Bank's work.

For more information on World Bank reforms, visit http://www.worldbank.org/worldbankreform/. For more information on the individual reform themes, see the related websites, reports, policy statements, videos, speeches, and press releases.

Growing demographic and economic pressures are forcing both developing and developed countries to undertake pension reforms. The Bank has been involved in pension reform in more than 80 developing countries.

Appendixes

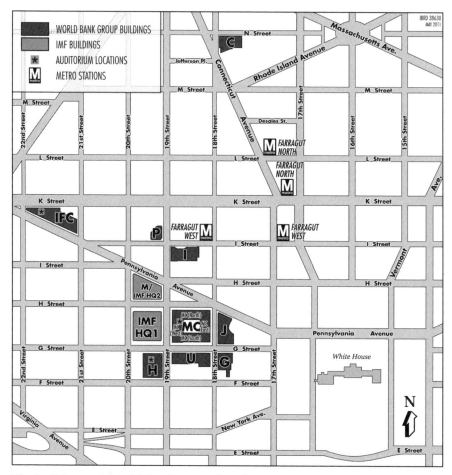

The buildings of World Bank Group headquarters.

CONTACTING THE WORLD BANK GROUP

Headquarters and General Inquiries

The offices and websites listed here are good sources of general information about the five World Bank Group institutions: the International Bank for Reconstruction and Development (IBRD), the International Development Association (IDA), the International Finance Corporation (IFC), the Multilateral Investment Guarantee Agency (MIGA), and the International Centre for Settlement of Investment Disputes (ICSID).

General Contact Information

World Bank Group
1818 H Street NW
Washington DC 20433 USA
Tel: 1-202-473-1000
Fax: 1-202-477-6391
Web: http://www.worldbankgroup.org or
   http://www.worldbank.org

IBRD and IDA Contact Information

Same as for the World Bank Group
Contact page: http://www.worldbank.org/
   contacts

IFC Contact Information

International Finance Corporation
2121 Pennsylvania Avenue NW
Washington DC 20433 USA
Tel: 1-202-473-1000
Web: http://www.ifc.org
General Inquiries, IFC Corporate Relations:
   Tel: 1-202-473-3800

Fax: 1-202-974-4384
Contact page: http://www.ifc.org/contacts

MIGA Contact Information

Mail: Same as for the World Bank Group
Location:
Multilateral Investment Guarantee Agency
1818 H Street NW
Washington DC 20433 USA
Tel: 1-202-473-1000
Web: http://www.miga.org
Business Inquiries:
Tel: 1-202-458-2538
Fax: 1-202-522-2630
E-mail: migainquiry@worldbank.org
Contact page: see "Contacts" at http://
   www.miga.org

ICSID Contact Information

Same address as for the World Bank Group
Tel: 1-202-458-1534
Fax: 1-202-522-2615
Web: http://www.worldbank.org/icsid
Contact page: see "Contact Us" at http://
   www.worldbank.org/icsid

Media Relations, News, and Public Affairs

The External Affairs Department of the World Bank and the Corporate Relations units of IFC and MIGA are the key resources for media relations, news, press contacts, public affairs, and access to World Bank Group experts and the Speakers' Bureau. Generally, the Bank Group organizations also feature news stories and major events on their home pages.

IBRD and IDA

The following are links to various World Bank media resources:

- The DevNews Media Center provides press releases, feature stories, reviews of press coverage, speeches and transcripts, issue briefs, and an events calendar. It also provides access to World Bank experts and to media contacts.
  Web: http://www.worldbank.org/mediacontacts.
- Electronic newsletters offer a wide range of material by free e-mail subscription, including the daily press review; the World Bank weekly update; and many newsletters from specific sectors, regions, and partnerships of the Bank.
  Web: http://www.worldbank.org/subscriptions.
- The Online Media Briefing Center is a password-protected site available only to accredited journalists.
  Web: http://media.worldbank.org.

IFC

The IFC "News" site provides media tools and links to press releases, feature stories, the latest news, IFC resources, and media contacts. See "News" at http://www.ifc.org.

MIGA

MIGA posts press releases, feature stories, news briefs, and an events calendar on its news page at http://www.miga.org.

ICSID

ICSID posts news releases and announcements on its home page. See http://www.worldbank.org/icsid.

Public Information

Various offices within the World Bank provide public information.

Public Information Centers

InfoShop/Public Information Center
1818 H Street NW, Room J1-060
Washington DC 20433 USA
Tel: 1-202-458-4500
Fax: 1-202-522-1500
E-mail: pic@worldbank.org
(For public information centers in other countries, go to http://www.worldbank.org/reference/ and click on "Public Information Centers" in the "Finding Publications" box.)

World Bank Publications

To order publications:
Tel: 1-800-645-7247 or 1-703-661-1580
Fax: 1-703-661-1501
Web: http://www.worldbank.org/publications

Projects, Policies, Strategies, and Research

These database portals provide access to information on World Bank Group projects, policies, and strategies. They are searchable by sector, region, country, or development theme.

- Documents and reports: http://www-wds.worldbank.org.
- Projects and operations: http://www.worldbank.org/projects.
- IFC projects: http://www.ifc.org/projects.
- World Bank *Operational Manual:* http://go.worldbank.org/DZDZ9038D0
- World Bank data and research: http://econ.worldbank.org.
- World Bank Group articles of agreement and other basic documents: http://www.worldbank.org/articles.

Annual Reports

Annual reports of World Bank Group organizations and programs are available online. The reports are published in multiple languages and the websites include past editions.

- World Bank annual report: http://www.worldbank.org/annualreport.
- IFC annual report: go to "About IFC" and click on "Annual Report" under "IFC Reports" at http://www.ifc.org/.
- MIGA annual report: go to "Publications" and click on "Reports" at http://www.miga.org.
- ICSID annual report: go to "About ICSID" and click on "Annual Reports" at http://www.worldbank.org/icsid.

Libraries

The Library Network consists of multiple libraries and resource centers that serve the World Bank Group and the International Monetary Fund:

- Joint Bank-Fund Library
- Board Resource Center
- Consultative Group on International Agricultural Research
- Law Library (IMF)
- Staff Development Center (IMF)
- World Bank Group Library
- World Bank Law Resource Center

The libraries offer the following services, which span the full spectrum of Bank Group and International Monetary Fund business: research, consultation, procurement of information products, content organization, and document delivery. All of the libraries are located in Washington, DC, with the exception of World Bank country office libraries and the public information centers. Some libraries admit visitors by appointment only.

The list of libraries, including locations, contact information, and hours of operation, can be found at http://jolis.worldbankimflib.org/e-nldirect.htm. The Library Network external website is http://jolis.worldbankimflib.org/external.htm.

TIMELINE OF WORLD BANK GROUP HISTORY

1944 The United Nations (UN) Monetary and Financial Conference draws up the World Bank (International Bank for Reconstruction and Development [IBRD]) Articles of Agreement at Bretton Woods, New Hampshire, with 44 countries represented.

1945 Twenty-eight governments sign the Articles of Agreement in Washington, DC.

1946 The World Bank formally begins operations on June 25.

The first loan applications are received (from Chile, Czechoslovakia, Denmark, France, Luxembourg, and Poland).

1947 The Bank makes its first bond offering—$250 million—in New York City.

The Bank makes its first loan—$250 million—to France.

1948 The Bank makes its first development loan—$13.5 million—to Chile.

1950 The Bank makes its first loan to a national development bank—$2 million—to Ethiopia.

1951 Finland and Yugoslavia are the first countries to repay their Bank loans in full.

1952 Japan and the Federal Republic of Germany become members.

1953 The first three loans to Japan, totaling $40.2 million, are approved.

1955 The Economic Development Institute (now the World Bank Institute) is established to serve as the Bank's staff college.

1956 The International Finance Corporation (IFC) is established as a private sector affiliate of the Bank, with 31 members and authorized capital of $100 million.

1957 IFC makes its first investment—$2 million—in Siemens in Brazil to expand manufacturing.

1958 In the wake of deterioration in India's balance of payments, the first meeting of the India Aid Consortium takes place in Washington, DC.

1960 India, Pakistan, and the World Bank sign the Indus Water Treaty.

The International Development Association (IDA) is established as part of the World Bank with initial subscriptions of $912.7 million.

1961   The Bank loans $80 million to Japan to finance the bullet train.

IDA extends its first development credit—$9 million—to Honduras for highway development.

1962   IFC establishes an advisory panel of investment bankers.

The Bank makes its first education loan, a $5 million IDA credit to Tunisia for school construction.

IFC makes its first equity investment in Fabrica Española Magentos S.A. of Spain.

1963   The Bank launches the Junior Professional Recruitment and Training Program (now the Young Professionals Program).

Eighteen newly independent African countries join the Bank.

1966   The International Centre for Settlement of Investment Disputes (ICSID) is established.

1967   Developing countries form the Group of 77 as a convention and a negotiation arm.

France, the Federal Republic of Germany, Japan, the United Kingdom, and the United States form the Group of Five to convene meetings of finance ministers and governors of central banks. (The group became the Group of Seven in 1976 with the addition of Canada and Italy. This group, with the addition of the Russian Federation, is now known as the Group of Eight.)

1970   The Bank makes its first loan for population planning—$2 million—to Jamaica.

The Bank's new commitments exceed $2 billion for the first time.

1971   Japan becomes one of the Bank's five largest shareholders.

The Bank makes its first loan for pollution control—$15 million—to Brazil.

1972   The Bank redeploys project and program staff members into regional departments to enable the institution to function more effectively.

The World Bank Group Staff Association comes into existence.

1974   The Interim Committee of the International Monetary Fund (IMF) and the Development Committee are established to advise the Boards of Governors.

The position of director general of operations evaluation is established to ensure independent evaluation of projects and programs.

President Robert S. McNamara delivers a speech at the Annual Meetings at which, for the first time, poverty is placed at the top of the Bank's agenda.

1975   IBRD and IDA commit nearly $1 billion in one fiscal year for rural development projects.

Shirley Boskey is appointed as the Bank's first female manager at the director level (International Relations Department). (The diversity strategy is extended in 1998 to include gender, nationality, race, sexual orientation, culture, and disability.)

IFC's first major commercial loans are syndicated for projects in Brazil and the Republic of Korea.

1978   The executive directors endorse a Bank policy to assess the environmental impact of Bank-assisted projects.

The first *World Development Report* team, led by Ernest Stern, publishes a report on the theme of accelerating growth and alleviating poverty.

1979   The Bank's new commitments exceed $10 billion for the first time.

The Bank begins lending for health projects.

The Bank Group suspends operations in Afghanistan after the invasion by the former Soviet Union. (Normal operations resume in 2002.)

1980   IBRD's authorized capital stock increases by $44 billion to $85 billion.

The first structural adjustment loan is approved—$200 million—for Turkey.

The People's Republic of China assumes representation for China and quickly becomes one of the largest borrowers.

1981   The position of World Bank ombudsman is established.

IFC coins the term "emerging markets." The Emerging Markets Database is developed.

1982   Anne Krueger is appointed as the first female vice president (Economics and Research).

A Bank loan for the Polonoroeste Program in Brazil finances a 90-mile highway across the Amazon rain forest, unintentionally attracting a large influx of settlers and spurring deforestation and international outcry.

1983   The Bank establishes a small grants program to fund activities to promote cooperation among nongovernmental organizations (NGOs), governments, academics, and the media.

1984   IFC establishes a $20 billion special fund to stimulate private sector development.

IFC undertakes its first direct borrowings in international capital markets.

1986   The Foreign Investment Advisory Service (FIAS)—a multidonor service of the International Finance Corporation that advises governments of developing and transition countries on how to improve their investment climate for domestic and foreign investors—is formed.

1987   In a major reorganization, all staff members are reselected into positions. New country departments combine functions formerly divided between programs and projects staff. Regional and central environment departments are created.

The Emerging Markets Database is launched commercially.

1988   The Multilateral Investment Guarantee Agency is established.

1989   The Bank's Board of Executive Directors endorses a directive on disclosure of information.

1990   The Global Environment Facility is launched.

1991   China replaces India as the largest IDA borrower.

1992   An independent review of the Sardar Sarovar Project in India (Narmada Dam) is conducted. (Bank participation in the project is canceled in 1995.)

Excellence through Equality recommends an increase in the proportion of women at higher grade levels.

Russia and 12 other republics of the former Soviet Union become members of IBRD and IDA.

1993   The Institutional Development Fund is established to support innovative capacity-building initiatives.

The independent Inspection Panel is established to investigate external complaints from individual groups negatively affected by Bank-funded projects.

IFC initiates the first environmental training for financial intermediaries.

1994   The first Public Information Center is opened.

The Bank unveils a three-year, $1.2 billion program to assist Palestinians in the West Bank and Gaza in transition to autonomous rule.

"Dollar budgeting" is introduced.

The World Bank celebrates its 50th anniversary while being widely criticized by NGOs and member governments.

1995   The Bank Group emphasizes the importance of girls' education.

1996   A trust fund for Bosnia and Herzegovina is created.

The Quality Assurance Group is established to provide real-time information on the quality of the Bank's work.

Knowledge management is launched to connect those who need to know with those who do know, to collect know-how, and to make knowledge accessible.

The IMF, the World Bank, and donors launch the Heavily Indebted Poor Countries Initiative to alleviate debt. (The framework is significantly enhanced in 1999.)

1997   The Governance Action Plan is introduced. After just two years, more than 600 specific governance and clean government initiatives are started in almost 100 borrower countries.

Bank operations are reorganized into a matrix structure (country departments and networks of related sector families) and begin to decentralize.

The Bank approves a loan of $3 billion to the Republic of Korea and approves other loans to economies affected by the Korean financial crisis to restore investor confidence and minimize the social costs of the crisis.

The Board of Executive Directors approves the Strategic Compact, a fundamental organizational renewal program.

1998   The Knowledge Bank Initiative is launched.

The Bank approves the Kosovo Special Fund.

The Bank holds the first Development Marketplace to reward innovation in development.

IFC strengthens its environmental and social policies.

1999   The Bank's vision for the new millennium is articulated: "Our dream is a world free of poverty."

The Bank Group adopts the Comprehensive Development Framework, and at their Annual Meetings, the Bank Group and the IMF agree to implement country-owned poverty reduction strategies.

IFC and MIGA appoint a compliance adviser/ombudsman to improve accountability to locally affected communities.

2000   The Bank and IMF Spring Meetings in Washington, DC, and the Annual Meetings in Prague draw large protests.

The Bank commits an additional $500 million to fight HIV/AIDS.

The Inspection Panel reviews the China Western Poverty Project. Chinese authorities decide to use their own resources to implement the controversial component.

The Bank and its partners create the Global Development Gateway, a portal on development where users can find and contribute information, resources, and tools.

The Heavily Indebted Poor Countries Initiative delivers on its promise made in 2000: 22 countries receive more than $34 billion in debt service relief.

Completed Bank projects with satisfactory outcome ratings reach 75 percent for the first time in nearly 20 years (up from 60 percent in 1996).

IFC reaches a record for new investment approvals in Sub-Saharan Africa—$1.2 billion.

The United Nations Millennium Summit establishes the Millennium Development Goals for achievement by 2015.

2001   The IMF and the Bank Group cancel their Annual Meetings following the attacks of September 11.

The Bank and its partners establish the Global Development Learning Network, a distance-learning initiative in developing countries.

Partners in the Global Partnership to Eliminate River Blindness pledge $39 million to eliminate the disease in Africa by 2010.

The Bank Group participates in calls for decreasing agricultural subsidies in developed countries.

The Bank revises its disclosure policy to promote better transparency and accountability in its development work.

2002   The Bank Group participates in the first UN International Conference on Financing for Development, held in Monterrey, Mexico.

With its partners, the World Bank establishes the Education for All Fast-Track Initiative to help ensure that developing countries provide every child with a complete primary school education by 2015.

2003	The Bank lends $505 million to support Brazil's accelerated program of human development reforms.

The Bank Group participates in the World Water Forum in Kyoto, Japan, asserting that water is a key driver of growth and poverty reduction.

IFC and its partners launch a program to help local businesses in Azerbaijan benefit from investments in the oil industry.

Ten leading commercial banks adopt the Equator Principles, choosing to follow World Bank and IFC environmental and social guidelines for all their investment work in developing countries.

A major conference with youth organizations is held in Paris to discuss the role of young people in peace and development.

The Council of the Global Environment Facility approves $224 million in grants for 19 new projects in developing countries and countries with economies in transition.

The first annual *Doing Business* report is published.

2004	The Bank establishes the Low-Income Countries Under Stress Trust Fund.

The Bank's Board of Executive Directors authorizes the Bank to act as an administrator for the Iraq Trust Fund to finance a program of emergency projects and technical assistance.

The Bank and the IMF adopt a more comprehensive and integrated approach to fighting money laundering and terrorist financing in member countries.

The Bank and the IMF launch the Quarterly External Debt Database, an online database that offers access to external debt statistics for 41 countries.

The first issue of the *Global Monitoring Report* is published, warning that, based on current trends, most developing countries would fail to meet most of the Millennium Development Goals.

The World Bank issues a wide-ranging reform proposal for the World Bank Group's activities in the extractive industries—oil, gas, and mining.

2005	The Bank publishes *Focus on Sustainability 2004,* its first report on sustainability.

Donor countries agree to the IDA-14 replenishment of $34 billion, which represents a 25 percent increase over the previous replenishment and the largest expansion of IDA resources in two decades.

The Bank publishes its first annual report investigating fraud and corruption both internally and in Bank-financed projects.

The Bank approves a $20 million grant to step up the fight against HIV/AIDS in the six countries of the Great Lakes region—Burundi, the Democratic Republic of Congo, Kenya, Rwanda, Tanzania, and Uganda.

The Bank launches a new global approach to help developing countries make faster progress in their fight against malaria.

The Bank issues a revised policy on indigenous peoples that reflects a strategic shift toward a broader and direct engagement with indigenous peoples' communities.

The World Bank makes its first loan to Iraq in three decades.

2006   An avian flu pledging conference—cosponsored by the European Commission, the government of China, and the Bank—is held in Beijing, with pledges amounting to almost $1.9 billion.

Wolfowitz outlines a comprehensive strategy for tackling corruption, a serious impediment to development and effective governance.

The Bank announces the creation of the independent, high-level Commission on Growth and Development comprising leading practitioners from government, business, and the policy-making arena.

To mobilize more resources for the very poorest countries, IBRD and IFC make a record transfer of $950 million to IDA, substantially more than the $500 million to be transferred under the IDA-14 replenishment agreement.

The Board of Executive Directors approves the Multilateral Debt Relief Initiative, an extension of debt relief available under the enhanced Highly Indebted Poor Countries Initiative.

The Bank announces the Bank Gender Action Plan, a four-year, $24.5 million plan to enhance women's economic power in key economic sectors in the developing world.

2007   IFC donates $150 million to IDA, the first such contribution by the private sector arm of the World Bank Group.

The Board of Executive Directors approves a new health, nutrition, and population strategy.

2008   The Bank develops six strategic themes to support inclusive and sustainable globalization: focus on the poorest countries, fragile and postconflict states, middle-income countries, global public goods, expanding opportunity for the Arab world, and knowledge and learning.

Donor countries agree to the IDA-15 replenishment of $41.7 billion, which represents a 30 percent increase over the previous replenishment.

The Bank achieves its first reduction on loan prices in over a decade, along with simplification of processes, extension of maturities, and improved access to risk management tools.

The Bank Group creates a $1.2 billion Global Food Crisis Response Program to respond quickly to the needs of its clients during the crisis brought on by high food prices.

The Bank launches its governance and anticorruption strategy.

The Board approves the establishment of a State- and Peace-Building Fund to assist postconflict and fragile states.

2009   The World Bank Group initiates a number of measures to address the global financial crisis.

Bank support to IBRD borrowers triples, reaching $100 billion through fiscal 2011.

The Bank establishes the Vulnerability Financing Facility to streamline crisis support to the poor and vulnerable.

IFC launches its Asset Management Company, which lays the foundation for the future mobilization of private capital for development.

The Bank triples support for safety net programs, including school feeding, nutrition, conditional cash transfer projects, and cash for work, with particular emphasis on women and girls.

IFC sets up the IFC Capitalization Fund to strengthen banks in smaller emerging markets, and the Mircofinance Enhancement Facility, which will support lending to as many as 60 million borrowers .

The Bank establishes the Infrastructure Recovery and Assets Platform to help partner countries respond to the global crisis through increased investment in infrastructure and support for public-private partnerships in infrastructure.

IFC and German development bank KfW create the Microfinance Enhancement Facility to support microfinance institutions in the world's poorest countries.

2010   In response to the devastating January 12 earthquake, the Bank provides an initial $100 million in grants and cancels Haiti's remaining debt. Assistance to Haiti continues throughout the year, culminating in a recovery package of $479 million.

Bank Group shareholders endorse the World Bank's first major capital increase—$86 billion—in more than 20 years.

Shareholders increase the voting power at IBRD for developing and transition countries to 47.19.

MIGA changes its procedures and modifies its Convention to be more flexible and to expand its range of services.

Sustained flooding in Pakistan affects more than 20 million people and 1.4 million acres of cropland. The World Bank commits $1 billion in support of the country's recovery.

A new agreement allows IFC to market MIGA products, a deal that will give businesses added comfort as they move into riskier markets.

A first-ever Open Forum invites participation in the Bank-IMF Annual Meetings.

In October, the World Bank extends its Global Food Crisis Response Program through June 2011 to fast-track disbursement of $760 million to countries in need.

In the first gathering of its kinds, more than 200 members of the International Corruption Hunters Alliance—representing 134 countries—meet at World Bank headquarters in Washington, D.C., to create an international enforcement regime to track and resolve bribery and fraud cases.

The International Development Association receives a record replenishment of $49.3 billion.

2011   The World Bank approves a US$4.9 million grant from the Global Environment Facility (GEF) for the Save our Species (SOS) program, which aims to tackle the challenge of biodiversity loss by matching financial support from private business with international conservation expertise and countries facing species extinction. The approved GEF funding is complemented by an additional $5 million from the World Bank's Development Grant Facility.

The World Bank announces the winners of its first ever Apps for Development competition. The event brought together the best ideas from both the software developer and the development practitioner communities to create innovative apps using World Bank data.

The World Bank and IMF hold a Food Crisis Open Forum as part of the Bank-IMF Annual Meetings.

The World Bank, along with six other development banks, announces a joint initiative to improve road safety and stem rising road deaths and injuries in developing countries.

PRESIDENTS OF THE WORLD BANK GROUP

Eugene Meyer (1875–1959). Term: June 1946 to December 1946. Head of a banking house, Eugene Meyer & Company, and owner of the *Washington Post.*

John J. McCloy (1896–1989). Term: March 1947 to April 1949. A lawyer whose firm was counsel to Chase National Bank. Held positions in the U.S. government, including assistant secretary of war. Resigned from the World Bank to become the U.S. high commissioner to Germany.

Eugene Black (1898–1992). Term: July 1949 to December 1962. Investment banker and senior vice president of Chase Manhattan Bank. Had previously been the U.S. executive director to the World Bank and assistant secretary at the U.S. Treasury. Served the longest of any World Bank president.

George Woods (1901–1982). Term: January 1963 to March 1968. Investment banker and chair of the First Boston Corporation.

Robert S. McNamara (1916–2009). Term: April 1968 to June 1981. Was previously director and president of the Ford Motor Company and served as secretary of defense in the Kennedy and Johnson administrations.

A. W. Clausen (b. 1923). Term: July 1981 to June 1986. Held positions at the Bank of America and Bank America Corporation before and after his World Bank tenure. These positions included president, chief executive officer, and chair.

Barber B. Conable (1922–2003). Term: July 1986 to August 1991. Member of the U.S. House of Representatives from 1965 to 1985, where his committee memberships included the House Ways and Means Committee, the Joint Economic Committee, and the House Budget and Ethics committees.

Lewis T. Preston (1926–1995). Term: September 1991 to May 1995. Held positions at J. P. Morgan & Company, including president, board chair, chief executive officer, and chair of the Executive Committee.

James D. Wolfensohn (b. 1933). Term: June 1995 to May 2005. Established his career as an international investment banker with a parallel involvement in development issues. Currently holds the position of senior adviser to Citigroup.

Paul D. Wolfowitz (b. 1943). Term: June 2005 to June 2007. Served as a public servant, ambassador, and educator, including 24 years in government service. He is currently a visiting scholar at the American Enterprise Institute and chairman of the US-Taiwan Business Council.

Robert B. Zoellick (b. 1953). Term: July 2007 to present. For biography, see box 2.1.

COUNTRY MEMBERSHIP IN WORLD BANK GROUP INSTITUTIONS

Once a country has joined the IMF, it may apply for membership in IBRD. Only countries belonging to IBRD may apply for membership in the other Bank Group institutions. More information on regions and countries is available in chapter 3, including specific ways that IFC regions differ from those used by IBRD and IDA.

Table D.1 Country Memberships and Voting Shares in Each Institution

Country	IBRD/ IDA region	IBRD (founded 1945)			IDA (founded 1960)			IFC (founded 1956)			MIGA (founded 1988)			ICSID (founded 1966)
		Year joined	Votes	Share of total	Year joined	Votes	Share of total	Year joined	Votes	Share of total	Year joined	Votes	Share of total	Year joined
Afghanistan	SA	1955	550	0.03	1961	54,983	0.27	1957	361	0.01	2003	359	0.16	1968
Albania	ECA	1991	1,080	0.06	1991	45,667	0.22	1991	1,552	0.06	1991	343	0.16	1991
Algeria	MENA	1963	9,502	0.57	1963	83,313	0.41	1990	5,871	0.24	1996	1,385	0.63	1996
Angola	AFR	1989	2,926	0.18	1989	66,866	0.33	1989	1,731	0.07	1989	428	0.20	nm
Antigua and Barbuda	LAC	1983	770	0.05	nm	nm	nm	1987	263	0.01	2005	291	0.13	nm
Argentina	LAC	1956	18,161	1.10	1962	134,439	0.65	1959	38,379	1.59	1992	2,451	1.12	1994
Armenia	ECA	1992	1,389	0.08	1993	47,981	0.23	1995	1,242	0.05	1995	321	0.15	1992
Australia	n.a.	1947	24,714	1.50	1960	235,560	1.15	1956	47,579	1.97	1999	3,260	1.50	1991
Austria	n.a.	1948	11,313	0.68	1961	151,598	0.74	1956	19,991	0.83	1997	1,607	0.74	1971
Azerbaijan	ECA	1992	1,896	0.11	1995	51,627	0.25	1995	2,617	0.11	1992	356	0.16	1992
Bahamas, The	LAC	1973	1,321	0.08	2008	46,228	0.22	1986	585	0.02	1994	417	0.19	1995
Bahrain	n.a.	1972	1,353	0.08	nm	nm	nm	1995	1,996	0.08	1988	377	0.17	1996
Bangladesh	SA	1972	5,104	0.31	1972	107,859	0.53	1976	9,287	0.38	1988	840	0.38	1980
Barbados	LAC	1974	1,198	0.07	1999	46,340	0.23	1980	611	0.03	1988	361	0.16	1983
Belarus	ECA	1992	3,573	0.22	nm	nm	nm	1992	5,412	0.22	1992	474	0.22	1992
Belgium	n.a.	1945	29,233	1.77	1964	219,294	1.07	1956	50,860	2.11	1992	3,818	1.75	1970
Belize	LAC	1982	836	0.05	1982	13,653	0.07	1982	351	0.01	1992	329	0.15	nm
Benin	AFR	1963	1,118	0.07	1963	48,911	0.24	1987	369	0.02	1994	349	0.16	1966
Bhutan	SA	1981	729	0.04	1981	43,467	0.21	2003	970	0.04	nm	nm	nm	nm
Bolivia	LAC	1945	2,035	0.12	1961	55,614	0.27	1956	2,152	0.09	1991	461	0.21	nm

Bosnia and Herzegovina	ECA	1993	799	0.05	1993	51,994	0.25	1993	870	0.04	1993	321	0.15	1997
Botswana	AFR	1968	865	0.05	1968	44,980	0.22	1979	363	0.02	1990	329	0.15	1970
Brazil	LAC	1946	33,537	2.03	1963	306,709	1.49	1956	39,729	1.65	1993	2,847	1.30	nm
Brunei Darussalam	n.a.	1995	2,623	0.16	nm		nm	nm	nm	nm	nm	nm	nm	2002
Bulgaria	ECA	1990	5,465	0.33	nm	nm	nm	1991	5,117	0.21	1992	884	0.40	2001
Burkina Faso	AFR	1963	1,118	0.07	1963	48,910	0.24	1975	1,086	0.04	1988	302	0.14	1966
Burundi	AFR	1963	966	0.06	1963	52,038	0.25	1979	350	0.01	1998	315	0.14	1969
Cambodia	EAP	1970	464	0.03	1970	55,249	0.27	1997	589	0.02	1999	405	0.18	2005
Cameroon	AFR	1963	1,777	0.11	1964	54,982	0.27	1974	1,135	0.05	1988	348	0.16	1967
Canada	n.a.	1945	45,045	2.73	1960	524,963	2.56	1956	81,592	3.38	1988	5,466	2.51	nm
Cape Verde	AFR	1978	758	0.05	1978	43,840	0.21	1990	265	0.01	1993	291	0.13	2011
Central African Republic	AFR	1963	1,112	0.07	1963	48,910	0.24	1991	369	0.02	2000	301	0.14	1966
Chad	AFR	1963	1,112	0.07	1963	48,910	0.24	1998	1,614	0.07	2002	301	0.14	1966
Chile	LAC	1945	7,181	0.43	1960	31,782	0.15	1957	11,960	0.50	1988	1,096	0.50	1991
China	EAP	1945	45,049	2.73	1960	421,071	2.05	1969	24,750	1.02	1988	5,771	2.64	1993
Colombia	LAC	1946	6,602	0.40	1961	92,384	0.45	1956	12,856	0.53	1995	1,011	0.46	1997
Comoros	AFR	1976	532	0.03	1977	43,840	0.21	1992	264	0.01	nm	nm	nm	1978
Congo, Dem. Rep.	AFR	1963	2,893	0.18	1963	79,399	0.39	1970	2,409	0.10	1989	837	0.38	1970
Congo, Rep.	AFR	1963	1,177	0.07	1963	48,910	0.24	1980	381	0.02	1991	356	0.16	1966
Costa Rica	LAC	1946	483	0.03	1961	12,480	0.06	1956	1,202	0.05	1994	447	0.20	1993
Côte d'Ivoire	AFR	1963	2,766	0.17	1963	54,982	0.27	1963	3,794	0.16	1988	551	0.25	1966
Croatia	ECA	1993	2,543	0.15	1993	64,324	0.31	1993	3,132	0.13	1993	571	0.26	1998
Cyprus	n.a.	1961	1,711	0.10	1962	52,405	0.26	1962	2,389	0.10	1988	424	0.19	1966

(continued)

223

Table D.1 continued

Country	IBRD (founded 1945)				IDA (founded 1960)			IFC (founded 1956)			MIGA (founded 1988)			ICSID (founded 1966)
	IBRD/ IDA region	Year joined	Votes	Share of total	Year joined	Votes	Share of total	Year joined	Votes	Share of total	Year joined	Votes	Share of total	Year joined
Czech Republic	ECA	1993	6,558	0.40	1993	89,272	0.43	1993	9,163	0.38	1993	1,025	0.48	1993
Denmark	n.a.	1946	13,701	0.83	1960	187,722	0.91	1956	18,804	0.78	1988	1,506	0.69	1968
Djibouti	MENA	1980	809	0.05	1980	44,816	0.22	1980	271	0.01	2007	291	0.13	nm
Dominica	LAC	1980	754	0.05	1980	43,840	0.21	1980	292	0.01	1991	291	0.13	nm
Dominican Republic	LAC	1961	2,342	0.14	1962	27,780	0.14	1961	1,437	0.06	1997	388	0.18	nm
Ecuador	LAC	1945	3,021	0.18	1961	50,151	0.24	1956	2,411	0.10	1988	562	0.26	nm
Egypt, Arab Rep. of	MENA	1945	7,358	0.45	1960	92,365	0.45	1956	12,610	0.52	1988	1,050	0.48	1972
El Salvador	LAC	1946	391	0.02	1962	46,464	0.23	1956	279	0.01	1991	363	0.17	1984
Equatorial Guinea	AFR	1970	965	0.06	1972	6,167	0.03	1992	293	0.01	1994	291	0.13	nm
Eritrea	AFR	1994	843	0.05	1994	43,969	0.21	1995	1,185	0.05	1996	291	0.13	nm
Estonia	ECA	1992	1,173	0.07	2008	36,150	0.18	1993	1,684	0.07	1992	356	0.16	1992
Ethiopia	AFR	1945	1,228	0.07	1961	48,923	0.24	1956	377	0.02	1991	364	0.17	nm
Fiji	EAP	1971	1,237	0.07	1972	19,462	0.09	1979	537	0.02	1990	312	0.14	1977
Finland	n.a.	1948	8,810	0.53	1960	120,274	0.59	1956	15,947	0.66	1988	1,298	0.59	1969
France	n.a.	1945	69,647	4.22	1960	790,360	3.85	1956	121,265	5.02	1989	8,806	4.02	1967
Gabon	AFR	1963	1,237	0.07	1963	2,093	0.01	1970	1,518	0.06	2003	410	0.19	1966
Gambia, The	AFR	1967	793	0.05	1967	46,108	0.22	1983	344	0.01	1992	291	0.13	1975
Georgia	ECA	1992	1,834	0.11	1993	51,259	0.25	1995	1,630	0.07	1992	352	0.16	1992

Country													
Germany	n.a.	1952	72,649	4.40	1960	1,163,980	5.67	1956	129,158	5.35	1988	9,177	4.19	1969
Ghana	AFR	1957	1,775	0.11	1960	71,336	0.35	1958	5,321	0.22	1988	673	0.31	1966
Greece	n.a.	1945	1,934	0.12	1962	53,139	0.26	1957	7,148	0.30	1993	734	0.34	1969
Grenada	LAC	1975	781	0.05	1975	20,627	0.10	1975	324	0.01	1988	291	0.13	1991
Guatemala	LAC	1945	2,251	0.14	1961	37,396	0.18	1956	1,334	0.06	1996	381	0.17	2003
Guinea	AFR	1963	1,542	0.09	1969	33,987	0.17	1982	589	0.02	1995	332	0.15	1968
Guinea-Bissau	AFR	1977	790	0.05	1977	44,500	0.22	1977	268	0.01	2006	291	0.13	nm
Guyana	LAC	1966	1,308	0.08	1967	52,674	0.26	1967	1,642	0.07	1989	325	0.15	1969
Haiti	LAC	1953	1,317	0.08	1961	52,038	0.25	1956	1,072	0.04	1996	316	0.14	2009
Honduras	LAC	1945	891	0.05	1960	46,457	0.23	1956	745	0.03	1992	419	0.19	1989
Hungary	ECA	1982	8,300	0.50	1985	139,921	0.68	1985	11,182	0.46	1988	1,235	0.56	1987
Iceland	n.a.	1945	1,508	0.09	1961	46,379	0.23	1956	292	0.01	1998	331	0.15	1966
India	SA	1945	45,045	2.73	1960	573,783	2.80	1956	81,592	3.38	1994	5,612	2.56	nm
Indonesia	EAP	1967	15,231	0.92	1968	176,979	0.86	1968	28,789	1.19	1988	2,090	0.95	1968
Iran, Islamic Rep.	MENA	1945	23,936	1.45	1960	15,455	0.08	1956	1,694	0.07	2003	1,900	0.87	nm
Iraq	MENA	1945	3,058	0.18	1960	15,207	0.07	1956	397	0.02	2008	591	0.27	nm
Ireland	n.a.	1957	5,521	0.33	1960	72,255	0.35	1958	1,540	0.06	1989	891	0.41	1981
Israel	n.a.	1954	5,000	0.30	1960	67,473	0.33	1956	2,385	0.10	1992	1,076	0.49	1983
Italy	n.a.	1947	45,045	2.73	1960	484,642	2.36	1956	81,592	3.38	1988	5,211	2.38	1971
Jamaica	LAC	1963	2,828	0.17	nm	nm	nm	1964	4,532	0.19	1988	560	0.26	1966
Japan	n.a.	1952	157,569	9.54	1960	1,790,495	8.72	1956	141,424	5.86	1988	9,220	4.21	1967
Jordan	MENA	1952	1,638	0.10	1960	24,865	0.12	1956	1,191	0.05	1988	412	0.19	1972
Kazakhstan	ECA	1992	3,235	0.20	1992	5,685	0.03	1993	4,887	0.20	1993	609	0.28	2000
Kenya	AFR	1964	2,711	0.16	1964	63,143	0.31	1964	4,291	0.18	1988	544	0.25	1967
Kiribati	EAP	1986	715	0.04	1986	43,592	0.21	1986	262	0.01	nm	nm	Nm	nm
Korea, Rep.	EAP	1955	16,067	0.97	1961	142,740	0.70	1964	16,196	0.67	1988	1,032	0.47	1967

(continued)

Table D.1 continued

Country	IBRD/IDA region	IBRD (founded 1945)			IDA (founded 1960)			IFC (founded 1956)			MIGA (founded 1988)			ICSID (founded 1966)
		Year joined	Votes	Share of total	Year joined	Votes	Share of total	Year joined	Votes	Share of total	Year joined	Votes	Share of total	Year joined
Kosovo	ECA	2009	1,216	0.07	2009	48,357	0.24	2009	1,704	0.07	2009	337	0.15	2009
Kuwait	MENA	1962	13,530	0.82	1962	93,478	0.46	1962	10,197	0.42	1988	1,880	0.86	1979
Kyrgyz Republic	ECA	1992	1,357	0.08	1992	47,718	0.23	1993	1,970	0.08	1993	318	0.15	nm
Lao PDR	EAP	1961	428	0.03	1963	48,910	0.24	1992	528	0.02	2000	301	0.14	nm
Latvia	ECA	1992	1,634	0.10	1992	33,956	0.17	1993	2,400	0.10	1998	412	0.19	1997
Lebanon	MENA	1947	590	0.04	1962	8,562	0.04	1956	385	0.02	1994	491	0.22	2003
Lesotho	AFR	1968	913	0.05	1968	44,816	0.22	1972	321	0.01	1988	329	0.15	1969
Liberia	AFR	1962	713	0.04	1962	52,038	0.25	1962	333	0.01	2007	325	0.15	1970
Libya	AFR	1958	8,090	0.49	1961	53,337	0.26	1958	305	0.01	1993	790	0.36	nm
Lithuania	ECA	1992	1,757	0.11	nm	nm	nm	1993	2,591	0.11	1993	428	0.20	1992
Luxembourg	n.a.	1945	1,902	0.11	1964	53,581	0.26	1956	2,389	0.10	1991	445	0.20	1970
Macedonia, FYR	ECA	1993	677	0.04	1993	46,885	0.23	1993	786	0.03	1993	329	0.15	1998
Madagascar	AFR	1963	1,672	0.10	1963	54,982	0.27	1963	682	0.03	1988	417	0.19	1966
Malawi	AFR	1965	1,344	0.08	1965	52,038	0.25	1965	2,072	0.09	1988	318	0.15	1966
Malaysia	EAP	1958	8,494	0.51	1960	73,397	0.36	1958	15,472	0.64	1991	1,261	0.58	1966
Maldives	SA	1978	719	0.04	1978	43,229	0.21	1983	266	0.01	2005	291	0.13	nm
Mali	AFR	1963	1,412	0.09	1963	53,345	0.26	1978	701	0.03	1992	384	0.18	1978
Malta	MENA	1983	1,324	0.08	nm	nm	nm	2005	1,865	0.08	1990	373	0.17	2003
Marshall Islands	EAP	1992	719	0.04	1993	4,902	0.02	1992	913	0.04	nm	nm	nm	nm
Mauritania	AFR	1963	1,150	0.07	1963	48,910	0.24	1967	464	0.02	1992	352	0.16	1966
Mauritius	AFR	1968	1,492	0.09	1968	53,320	0.26	1968	1,915	0.08	1990	394	0.18	1969

Country	Region														
Mexico	LAC	1945	19,054	1.15	1961	142,236	0.69	1956	27,839	1.15	2009	1,433	0.65	1993	nm
Micronesia, Federated States of	EAP	1993	729	0.04	1993	18,424	0.09	1993	994	0.04	1993	291	0.13	1993	
Moldova	ECA	1992	1,618	0.10	1994	49,684	0.24	1995	1,442	0.06	1993	337	0.15	2011	
Mongolia	ECA	1991	716	0.04	1991	45,667	0.22	1991	394	0.02	1999	299	0.14	1991	
Montenegro	ECA	2007	938	0.06	2007	47,096	0.23	2007	1,285	0.05	2007	302	0.14	nm	
Morocco	MENA	1958	5,223	0.32	1960	85,559	0.42	1962	9,287	0.38	1992	854	0.39	1967	
Mozambique	AFR	1984	1,180	0.07	1984	59,370	0.29	1984	572	0.02	1994	412	0.19	1995	
Myanmar	EAP	1952	2,734	0.17	1962	67,326	0.33	1956	916	0.04	nm	nm	nm	nm	
Namibia	AFR	1990	1,773	0.11	nm	nm	nm	1990	654	0.03	1990	348	0.16	nm	
Nepal	SA	1961	1,218	0.07	1963	48,910	0.24	1966	1,072	0.04	1994	363	0.17	1969	
Netherlands	n.a.	1945	35,753	2.16	1961	392,488	1.91	1956	56,381	2.33	1988	4,063	1.86	1966	
New Zealand	n.a.	1961	7,486	0.45	1974	56,431	0.27	1961	3,833	0.16	2008	754	0.34	1980	
Nicaragua	LAC	1946	858	0.05	1960	46,457	0.23	1956	965	0.04	1992	421	0.19	1995	
Niger	AFR	1963	1,102	0.07	1963	48,910	0.24	1980	397	0.02	nm	nm	nm	1966	
Nigeria	AFR	1961	12,905	0.78	1961	83,411	0.41	1961	21,893	0.91	1988	1,728	0.79	1966	
Norway	n.a.	1945	10,232	0.62	1960	200,226	0.98	1956	17,849	0.74	1989	1,473	0.67	1967	
Oman	MENA	1971	1,811	0.11	1973	46,580	0.23	1973	1,437	0.06	1989	407	0.19	1995	
Pakistan	SA	1950	9,589	0.58	1960	168,679	0.82	1956	19,630	0.81	1988	1,404	0.64	1966	
Palau	EAP	1997	266	0.02	1997	3,804	0.02	1997	275	0.01	1997	291	0.13	nm	
Panama	LAC	1946	635	0.04	1961	10,185	0.05	1956	1,257	0.05	1997	472	0.22	1996	
Papua New Guinea	EAP	1975	1,544	0.09	1975	48,346	0.24	1975	1,397	0.06	1991	337	0.15	1978	
Paraguay	LAC	1945	1,479	0.09	1961	29,968	0.15	1956	686	0.03	1992	382	0.17	1983	
Peru	LAC	1945	5,581	0.34	1961	64,322	0.31	1956	7,148	0.30	1991	898	0.41	1993	
Philippines	EAP	1945	7,094	0.43	1960	103,963	0.51	1957	12,856	0.53	1994	1,094	0.50	1978	

(continued)

Table D.1 *continued*

Country	IBRD/IDA region	IBRD (founded 1945) Year joined	IBRD Votes	IBRD Share of total	IDA (founded 1960) Year joined	IDA Votes	IDA Share of total	IFC (founded 1956) Year joined	IFC Votes	IFC Share of total	MIGA (founded 1988) Year joined	MIGA Votes	MIGA Share of total	ICSID (founded 1966) Year joined
Poland	ECA	1986	11,158	0.68	1988	405,835	1.98	1987	7,486	0.31	1990	1,005	0.46	nm
Portugal	n.a.	1961	5,710	0.35	1992	54,554	0.27	1966	8,574	0.36	1988	914	0.42	1984
Qatar	MENA	1972	1,346	0.08	nm	nm	nm	2008	1,900	0.08	1996	482	0.22	2011
Romania	ECA	1972	4,261	0.26	nm	nm	nm	1990	2,911	0.12	1992	1,219	0.56	1975
Russian Federation	ECA	1992	45,045	2.73	1992	60,937	0.30	1993	81,592	3.38	1992	5,769	2.63	nm
Rwanda	AFR	1963	1,296	0.08	1963	52,038	0.25	1975	556	0.02	2002	373	0.17	1979
Samoa	EAP	1974	781	0.05	1974	43,901	0.21	1974	285	0.01	1988	291	0.13	1978
San Marino	n.a.	2000	845	0.05	nm	nm	nm	nm	nm	nm	nm	nm	nm	nm
São Tomé and Príncipe	AFR	1977	745	0.04	1977	43,719	0.21	2008	689	0.03	nm	nm	nm	nm
Saudi Arabia	MENA	1957	45,045	2.73	1960	652,965	3.18	1962	30,312	1.26	1988	5,769	2.63	1980
Senegal	AFR	1962	2,322	0.14	1962	63,143	0.31	1962	2,549	0.11	1988	497	0.23	1967
Serbia	ECA	1993	3,096	0.19	1993	69,507	0.34	1993	2,053	0.09	1993	648	0.30	2007
Seychelles	AFR	1980	513	0.03	nm	nm	nm	1981	277	0.01	1992	291	0.13	1978
Sierra Leone	AFR	1962	968	0.06	1962	52,038	0.25	1962	473	0.02	1996	373	0.17	1966
Singapore	n.a.	1966	570	0.03	2002	14,933	0.07	1968	427	0.02	1998	513	0.23	1968
Slovak Republic	ECA	1993	3,466	0.21	1993	65,977	0.32	1993	4,707	0.19	1993	632	0.29	1994
Slovenia	ECA	1993	1,511	0.09	1993	44,339	0.22	1993	1,835	0.08	1993	421	0.19	1994
Solomon Islands	EAP	1978	763	0.05	1980	43,901	0.21	1980	287	0.01	2005	291	0.13	1981
Somalia	AFR	1962	802	0.05	1962	10,506	0.05	1962	333	0.01	nm	nm	nm	1968

		1945	13,712	0.83	1960	55,503	0.27	1957	16,198	0.67	1994	1,903	0.87	nm
South Africa	AFR	1945	13,712	0.83	1960	55,503	0.27	1957	16,198	0.67	1994	1,903	0.87	nm
Spain	n.a.	1958	28,247	1.71	1960	191,688	0.93	1960	37,276	1.54	1988	2,506	1.14	1994
Sri Lanka	SA	1950	4,067	0.25	1961	79,436	0.39	1956	7,385	0.31	1988	719	0.33	1967
St. Kitts and Nevis	LAC	1984	525	0.03	1987	13,778	0.07	1996	888	0.04	1999	291	0.13	1995
St. Lucia	LAC	1980	802	0.05	1982	30,532	0.15	1982	324	0.01	1988	329	0.15	1984
St. Vincent and the Grenadines	LAC	1982	528	0.03	1982	34,787	0.17	nm	nm	nm	1990	329	0.15	2003
Sudan	AFR	1957	1,100	0.07	1960	54,982	0.27	1960	361	0.01	1991	447	0.20	1973
Suriname	LAC	1978	662	0.04	nm	nm	nm	nm	nm	nm	2003	323	0.15	nm
Swaziland	AFR	1969	690	0.04	1969	19,022	0.09	1969	934	0.04	1990	299	0.14	1971
Sweden	n.a.	1951	15,224	0.92	1960	392,816	1.91	1956	27,126	1.12	1988	2,090	0.95	1967
Switzerland	n.a.	1992	26,856	1.63	1992	228,751	1.11	1992	41,830	1.73	1988	2,884	1.32	1968
Syrian Arab Rep.	MENA	1947	2,452	0.15	1962	11,027	0.05	1962	444	0.02	2002	537	0.25	2006
Tajikistan	ECA	1993	1,310	0.08	1993	47,378	0.23	1994	1,462	0.06	2002	371	0.17	nm
Tanzania	AFR	1962	1,545	0.09	1962	63,143	0.31	1962	1,253	0.05	1992	489	0.22	1992
Thailand	EAP	1949	6,599	0.40	1960	79,436	0.39	1956	11,191	0.46	2000	983	0.45	nm
Timor-Leste	EAP	2002	767	0.05	2002	45,123	0.22	2004	1,027	0.04	2002	291	0.13	2002
Togo	AFR	1962	1,355	0.08	1962	52,038	0.25	1962	1,058	0.04	1988	318	0.15	1967
Tonga	EAP	1985	744	0.04	1985	43,714	0.21	1985	284	0.01	nm	nm	nm	1990
Trinidad and Tobago	LAC	1963	2,914	0.18	1972	59,184	0.29	1971	4,362	0.18	1992	599	0.27	1967
Tunisia	MENA	1958	969	0.06	1960	2,793	0.01	1962	3,816	0.16	1988	516	0.24	1966
Turkey	ECA	1947	8,578	0.52	1960	119,975	0.58	1956	14,795	0.61	1988	1,055	0.48	1989
Turkmenistan	ECA	1992	776	0.05	nm	nm	nm	1997	1,060	0.04	1993	307	0.14	1992

(continued)

Table D.1 *continued*

Country	IBRD/IDA region	IBRD (founded 1945)			IDA (founded 1960)			IFC (founded 1956)			MIGA (founded 1988)			ICSID (founded 1966)
		Year joined	Votes	Share of total	Year joined	Votes	Share of total	Year joined	Votes	Share of total	Year joined	Votes	Share of total	Year joined
Tuvalu	EAP	2010	461	0.03	2010	504	0.00	nm	nm	nm	nm	nm	nm	nm
Uganda	AFR	1963	867	0.05	1963	47,092	0.23	1963	985	0.04	1992	474	0.22	1966
Ukraine	ECA	1992	11,158	0.68	2004	1,762	0.01	1993	9,755	0.40	1994	1,587	0.72	2000
United Arab Emirates	MENA	1972	2,635	0.16	1981	1,367	0.01	1977	4,283	0.18	1993	897	0.41	1982
United Kingdom	n.a.	1945	69,647	4.22	1960	1,117,538	5.44	1956	121,265	5.02	1988	8,806	4.02	1967
United States	n.a.	1945	265,219	16.06	1960	2,252,973	10.98	1956	569,629	23.59	1988	32,805	14.98	1966
Uruguay	LAC	1946	3,062	0.19	nm	nm	nm	1968	3,819	0.16	1993	443	0.20	2000
Uzbekistan	ECA	1992	2,743	0.17	1992	57,807	0.28	1993	4,123	0.17	1993	416	0.19	1995
Vanuatu	EAP	1981	836	0.05	1981	45,152	0.22	1981	305	0.01	1988	291	0.13	nm
Venezuela, RB	LAC	1946	20,611	1.25	nm	nm	nm	1956	27,838	1.15	1994	1,668	0.76	1995
Vietnam	EAP	1956	1,218	0.07	1960	61,168	0.30	1967	696	0.03	1994	629	0.29	nm
Yemen, Rep.	MENA	1969	2,462	0.15	1970	60,415	0.29	1970	965	0.04	1996	396	0.18	2004
Zambia	AFR	1965	3,060	0.19	1965	75,427	0.37	1965	1,536	0.06	1988	559	0.26	1970
Zimbabwe	AFR	1980	3,575	0.22	1980	92,455	0.45	1980	2,370	0.10	1992	477	0.22	1994
TOTAL		187	1,619,595	100	170	20,524,247	100	182	2,414,896	100	175	218,384	100	147

Source: World Bank Group Corporate Secretariat.

Note: Membership information is as of June 25, 2010, for IBRD and IDA; July 18, 2009, for IFC and MIGA; and January 26, 2011, for ICSID. Votes and voting share data are as of April 28, 2011, for IBRD and IDA; March 31, 2011, for IFC and MIGA; and March 15, 2011, for IFC and MIGA. Totals may not add to 100 because of rounding; 0.00 signifies less than 0.005 percent. AFR = Africa, EAP = East Asia and Pacific, ECA = Europe and Central Asia, LAC = Latin America and the Caribbean, MENA = Middle East and North Africa, SA = South Asia, n.a. = high-income country that does not currently borrow or receive financing from the World Bank or IFC (these countries are not necessarily classified as Part I relative to IDA), nm = nonmember.

CONSTITUENCIES OF THE EXECUTIVE DIRECTORS

IBRD's general operations are delegated to the Board of Executive Directors. Under IBRD's Articles of Agreement, the five member countries holding the largest number of shares each appoint one executive director, and the remaining member countries elect the other executive directors. At present, IBRD's Board consists of 25 executive directors. Of these, five were appointed by the largest shareholders—the United States, Japan, Germany, France, and the United Kingdom, and 19 were elected by other country constituencies. (See chapter 1 for more information.)

Under the Articles of Agreement for IDA and IFC, respectively, the executive directors of IBRD serve ex officio on IDA's Board of Executive Directors and on IFC's Board of Directors. Members of MIGA's Board of Directors are elected separately, but it is customary for the directors of MIGA to be the same individuals as the executive directors of IBRD. (See chapter 1 for more information.)

Regular elections of executive directors are held every two years, normally at the time of the Annual Meetings. Elections are coordinated by the Bank Group's Corporate Secretariat, which anticipates changes in constituency groupings resulting from new memberships or political events, as well as increases in members' capital subscriptions and the corresponding changes in voting power. The Corporate Secretariat also verifies the credentials of governors who are entitled to vote.

In the event that an executive director elected during the regular election terminates his or her service before the next regular election, the constituency affected by the vacancy holds an interim election for a successor. The interim election is conducted either by mail vote or during an Annual Meetings session that does not fall on a regular election year.

Table E.1 Voting Shares of Executive Directors of IBRD as of April 2011

Nationality of executive director	Constituency	Number of votes	Percentage of total votes
Appointed directors			
1 United States	United States	265,219	16.10
2 Japan	Japan	157,569	9.56
3 Germany	Germany	72,649	4.41
4 France	France	69,647	4.23
5 United Kingdom	United Kingdom	69,647	4.23
Elected directors			
6 Austria, casting the votes of	Austria, Belarus, Belgium, Czech Republic, Hungary, Kosovo, Luxembourg, Slovak Republic, Slovenia, and Turkey	75,650	4.59
7 Netherlands, casting the votes of	Armenia, Bosnia and Herzegovina, Bulgaria, Croatia, Cyprus, Georgia, Israel, former Yugoslav Republic of Macedonia, Moldova, Montenegro, Netherlands, Romania, and Ukraine	73,146	4.44
8 Spain, casting the votes of	Costa Rica, El Salvador, Guatemala, Honduras, Mexico, Nicaragua, Spain, and República Bolivariana de Venezuela	72,786	4.42
9 Canada, casting the votes of	Antigua and Barbuda, The Bahamas, Barbados, Belize, Canada, Dominica, Grenada, Guyana, Ireland, Jamaica, St. Kitts and Nevis, St. Lucia, and St. Vincent and the Grenadines	62,217	3.78
10 Brazil, casting the votes of	Brazil, Colombia, Dominican Republic, Ecuador, Haiti, Panama, Philippines, Suriname, and Trinidad and Tobago	58,124	3.53
11 Italy, casting the votes of	Albania, Greece, Italy, Malta, Portugal, San Marino, and Timor-Leste	56,705	3.44
12 Australia, casting the votes of	Australia, Cambodia, Kiribati, Republic of Korea, Marshall Islands, Federated States of Micronesia, Mongolia, New Zealand, Palau, Papua New Guinea, Samoa, Solomon Islands, Tuvalu, and Vanuatu	56,261	3.41
13 India, casting the votes of	Bangladesh, Bhutan, India, and Sri Lanka	54,945	3.33
14 Sweden, casting the votes of	Denmark, Estonia, Finland, Iceland, Latvia, Lithuania, Norway, and Sweden	54,039	3.28
15 Switzerland, casting the votes of	Azerbaijan, Kazakhstan, Kyrgyz Republic, Poland, Serbia, Switzerland, Tajikistan, Turkmenistan, and Uzbekistan	52,427	3.18
16 Pakistan, casting the votes of	Afghanistan, Algeria, Ghana, Islamic Republic of Iran, Morocco, Pakistan, and Tunisia	51,544	3.13

	Nationality of executive director	Constituency	Number of votes	Percentage of total votes
17	Kuwait, casting the votes of	Bahrain, Arab Republic of Egypt, Iraq, Jordan, Kuwait, Lebanon, Libya, Maldives, Oman, Qatar, Syrian Arab Republic, United Arab Emirates, and Republic of Yemen	47,042	2.86
18	China, casting the votes of	China	45,049	2.73
19	Russian Federation, casting the votes of	Russian Federation	45,045	2.73
20	Saudi Arabia, casting the votes of	Saudi Arabia	45,045	2.73
21	Indonesia, casting the votes of	Brunei Darussalam, Fiji, Indonesia, Lao People's Democratic Republic, Malaysia, Myanmar, Nepal, Singapore, Thailand, Tonga, and Vietnam	41,096	2.49
22	Argentina, casting the votes of	Argentina, Bolivia, Chile, Paraguay, Peru, and Uruguay	37,499	2.28
23	South Africa, casting the votes of	Angola, Nigeria, and South Africa	29,543	1.79
24	São Tomé and Principe, casting the votes of	Benin, Burkina Faso, Cameroon, Cape Verde, Central African Republic, Chad, Comoros, Democratic Republic of Congo, Republic of Congo, Côte d'Ivoire, Djibouti, Equatorial Guinea, Gabon, Guinea-Bissau, Mali, Mauritania, Mauritius, Niger, São Tomé and Principe, Senegal, and Togo	27,742	1.68
25	Sudan, casting the votes of	Botswana, Burundi, Eritrea, Ethiopia, The Gambia, Kenya, Lesotho, Liberia, Malawi, Mozambique, Namibia, Rwanda, Seychelles, Sierra Leone, Sudan, Swaziland, Tanzania, Uganda, Zambia, and Zimbabwe	26,943	1.64
			1,616,804	100.00

Source: World Bank Group Corporate Secretariat.
Note: Individual percentages may not total 100 because of rounding. Guinea, Madagascar, and Somalia did not participate in the 2010 regular election of executive directors.

Table E.2 Voting Shares of Executive Directors of IDA as of March 2011

Nationality of executive director	Constituency	Number of votes	Percentage of total votes
Appointed directors			
1 United States	United States	2,252,973	11.03
2 Japan	Japan	1,790,495	8.77
3 Germany	Germany	1,163,980	5.70
4 United Kingdom	United Kingdom	1,117,538	5.47
5 France	France	790,360	3.87
Elected directors			
6 Sweden, casting the votes of	Denmark, Estonia, Finland, Iceland, Latvia, Norway, and Sweden	1,017,523	4.98
7 São Tomé and Principe, casting the votes of	Benin, Burkina Faso, Cameroon, Cape Verde, Central African Republic, Chad, Comoros, Democratic Republic of Congo, Republic of Congo, Côte d'Ivoire, Djibouti, Equatorial Guinea, Gabon, Guinea-Bissau, Mali, Mauritania, Mauritius, Niger, São Tomé and Principe, Senegal, and Togo	982,555	4.81
8 Sudan, casting the votes of	Botswana, Burundi, Eritrea, Ethiopia, The Gambia, Kenya, Lesotho, Liberia, Malawi, Mozambique, Rwanda, Sierra Leone, Sudan, Swaziland, Tanzania, Uganda, Zambia, and Zimbabwe	963,620	4.72
9 Austria, casting the votes of	Austria, Belgium, Czech Republic, Hungary, Kosovo, Luxembourg, Slovak Republic, Slovenia, and Turkey	932,314	4.56
10 Switzerland, casting the votes of	Azerbaijan, Kazakhstan, Kyrgyz Republic, Poland, Serbia, Switzerland, Tajikistan, and Uzbekistan	914,308	4.48
11 Canada, casting the votes of	The Bahamas, Barbados, Belize, Canada, Dominica, Grenada, Guyana, Ireland, St. Kitts and Nevis, St. Lucia, and St. Vincent and the Grenadines	899,677	4.40
12 Netherlands, casting the votes of	Armenia, Bosnia and Herzegovina, Croatia, Cyprus, Georgia, Israel, former Yugoslav Republic of Macedonia, Moldova, Montenegro, Netherlands, and Ukraine	873,351	4.28
13 India, casting the votes of	Bangladesh, Bhutan, India, and Sri Lanka	804,545	3.94

	Nationality of executive director	Constituency	Number of votes	Percentage of total votes
14	Australia, casting the votes of	Australia, Cambodia, Kiribati, Republic of Korea, Marshall Islands, Federated States of Micronesia, Mongolia, New Zealand, Palau, Papua New Guinea, Samoa, Solomon Islands, and Vanuatu	788,173	3.86
15	Brazil, casting the votes of	Brazil, Colombia, Dominican Republic, Ecuador, Haiti, Panama, Philippines, and Trinidad and Tobago	702,394	3.44
16	Italy, casting the votes of	Albania, Greece, Italy, Portugal, and Timor-Leste	684,125	3.35
17	Saudi Arabia, casting the votes of	Saudi Arabia	652,965	3.20
18	Indonesia, casting the votes of	Fiji, Indonesia, Lao People's Democratic Republic, Malaysia, Myanmar, Nepal, Singapore, Thailand, Tonga, and Vietnam	634,235	3.11
19	Spain, casting the votes of	Costa Rica, El Salvador, Guatemala, Honduras, Mexico, Nicaragua, and Spain	523,178	2.56
20	Pakistan, casting the votes of	Afghanistan, Algeria, Ghana, Islamic Republic of Iran, Morocco, Pakistan, and Tunisia	482,118	2.36
21	Kuwait, casting the votes of	Arab Republic of Egypt, Iraq, Jordan, Kuwait, Lebanon, Libya, Maldives, Oman, Syrian Arab Republic, United Arab Emirates, and Republic of Yemen	450,432	2.21
22	China, casting the votes of	China	421,071	2.06
23	Argentina, casting the votes of	Argentina, Bolivia, Chile, Paraguay, and Peru	316,125	1.55
24	South Africa	Angola, Nigeria, and South Africa	205,780	1.01
25	Russian Federation, casting the votes of	Russian Federation	60,937	0.30
			20,424,772	100.00

Source: World Bank Group Corporate Secretariat.
Note: Individual percentages may not total 100 because of rounding. Guinea, Madagascar, and Somalia did not participate in the 2010 regular election of executive directors.

Table E.3 Voting Shares of Directors of IFC as of March 2011

Nationality of executive director	Constituency	Number of votes	Percentage of total votes
Appointed directors			
1 United States	United States	569,629	23.60
2 Japan	Japan	141,424	5.86
3 Germany	Germany	129,158	5.35
4 France	France	121,265	5.02
5 United Kingdom	United Kingdom	121,265	5.02
Elected directors			
6 Austria, casting the votes of	Austria, Belarus, Belgium, Czech Republic, Hungary, Kosovo, Luxembourg, Slovak Republic, Slovenia, and Turkey	122,038	5.06
7 Italy, casting the votes of	Albania, Greece, Italy, Malta, Portugal, and Timor-Leste	101,758	4.22
8 India, casting the votes of	Bangladesh, Bhutan, India, and Sri Lanka	99,234	4.11
9 Spain, casting the votes of	Costa Rica, El Salvador, Guatemala, Honduras, Mexico, Nicaragua, Spain, and República Bolivariana de Venezuela	97,478	4.04
10 Canada, casting the votes of	Antigua and Barbuda, The Bahamas, Barbados, Belize, Canada, Dominica, Grenada, Guyana, Ireland, Jamaica, St. Kitts and Nevis, and St. Lucia	92,944	3.85
11 Netherlands, casting the votes of	Armenia, Bosnia and Herzegovina, Bulgaria, Croatia, Cyprus, Georgia, Israel, former Yugoslav Republic of Macedonia, Moldova, Montenegro, Netherlands, Romania, and Ukraine	89,325	3.70
12 Sweden, casting the votes of	Denmark, Estonia, Finland, Iceland, Latvia, Lithuania, Norway, and Sweden	86,693	3.59
13 Russian Federation, casting the votes of	Russian Federation	81,592	3.38
14 Brazil, casting the votes of	Brazil, Colombia, Dominican Republic, Ecuador, Haiti, Panama, Philippines, and Trinidad and Tobago	75,980	3.15
15 Australia, casting the votes of	Australia, Cambodia, Kiribati, Republic of Korea, Marshall Islands, Federated States of Micronesia, Mongolia, New Zealand, Palau, Papua New Guinea, Samoa, Solomon Islands, and Vanuatu	73,309	3.04
16 Switzerland, casting the votes of	Azerbaijan, Kazakhstan, Kyrgyz Republic, Poland, Serbia, Switzerland, Tajikistan, Turkmenistan, and Uzbekistan	67,488	2.80

	Nationality of executive director	Constituency	Number of votes	Percentage of total votes
17	Argentina, casting the votes of	Argentina, Bolivia, Chile, Paraguay, Peru, and Uruguay	64,144	2.66
18	Indonesia, casting the votes of	Fiji, Indonesia, Lao People's Democratic Republic, Malaysia, Myanmar, Nepal, Singapore, Thailand, Tonga, and Vietnam	59,912	2.48
19	Pakistan, casting the votes of	Afghanistan, Algeria, Ghana, Islamic Republic of Iran, Morocco, Pakistan, and Tunisia	45,980	1.91
20	South Africa, casting the votes of	Angola, Nigeria, and South Africa	39,822	1.65
21	Kuwait, casting the votes of	Bahrain, Arab Republic of Egypt, Iraq, Jordan, Kuwait, Lebanon, Libya, Maldives, Oman, Qatar, Syrian Arab Republic, United Arab Emirates, and Republic of Yemen	36,376	1.51
22	Saudi Arabia, casting the votes of	Saudi Arabia	30,312	1.26
23	China, casting the votes of	China	24,750	1.03
24	São Tomé and Principe, casting the votes of	Benin, Burkina Faso, Cameroon, Cape Verde, Central African Republic, Chad, Comoros, Democratic Republic of Congo, Republic of Congo, Côte d'Ivoire, Djibouti, Equatorial Guinea, Gabon, Guinea-Bissau, Mali, Mauritania, Mauritius, Niger, São Tomé and Principe, Senegal, and Togo	21,809	0.90
25	Sudan, casting the votes of	Botswana, Burundi, Eritrea, Ethiopia, The Gambia, Kenya, Lesotho, Liberia, Malawi, Mozambique, Namibia, Rwanda, Seychelles, Sierra Leone, Sudan, Swaziland, Tanzania, Uganda, Zambia, and Zimbabwe	19,607	0.81
			2,413,292	100.00

Source: World Bank Group Corporate Secretariat.
Note: Individual percentages may not total 100 because of rounding. Guinea, Madagascar, and Somalia did not participate in the 2010 regular election of directors.

Table E.4 Voting Shares of Directors of MIGA as of March 2011

	Nationality of executive director	Constituency	Number of votes	Percentage of total votes
Directors elected by 6 largest shareholders				
1	United States	United States	32,805	15.03
2	Japan	Japan	9,220	4.23
3	Germany	Germany	9,177	4.21
4	France	France	8,086	4.04
5	United Kingdom	United Kingdom	8,086	4.04
6	China	China	5,771	2.64
Directors elected by other shareholders				
7	Netherlands, casting the votes of	Armenia, Bosnia and Herzegovina, Bulgaria, Croatia, Cyprus, Georgia, Israel, former Yugoslav Republic of Macedonia, Moldova, Montenegro, Netherlands, Romania, and Ukraine	11,786	5.40
8	Belgium, casting the votes of	Austria, Belarus, Belgium, Czech Republic, Hungary, Kosovo, Luxembourg, Slovak Republic, Slovenia, and Turkey	11,049	5.06
9	Canada, casting the votes of	Antigua and Barbuda, The Bahamas, Barbados, Belize, Canada, Dominica, Grenada, Guyana, Ireland, Jamaica, St. Kitts and Nevis, St. Lucia, and St. Vincent and the Grenadines	10,171	4.66
10	Kuwait, casting the votes of	Bahrain, Arab Republic of Egypt, Iraq, Jordan, Kuwait, Lebanon, Libya, Maldives, Oman, Qatar, Syrian Arab Republic, United Arab Emirates, and Republic of Yemen	8,601	3.94
11	Sweden, casting the votes of	Denmark, Estonia, Finland, Iceland, Latvia, Lithuania, Norway, and Sweden	7,894	3.62
12	Italy, casting the votes of	Albania, Greece, Italy, Malta, Portugal, and Timor-Leste	7,866	3.60
13	Sudan, casting the votes of	Botswana, Burundi, Eritrea, Ethiopia, The Gambia, Kenya, Lesotho, Liberia, Malawi, Mozambique, Namibia, Rwanda, Seychelles, Sierra Leone, Sudan, Swaziland, Tanzania, Uganda, Zambia, and Zimbabwe	7,648	3.50
14	Spain, casting the votes of	Costa Rica, El Salvador, Guatemala, Honduras, Mexico, Nicaragua, Spain, and República Bolivariana de Venezuela	7,638	3.50
15	Brazil, casting the votes of	Brazil, Colombia, Dominican Republic, Ecuador, Haiti, Panama, Philippines, Suriname, and Trinidad and Tobago	7,612	3.49

	Nationality of executive director	Constituency	Number of votes	Percentage of total votes
16	Australia, casting the votes of	Australia, Cambodia, Republic of Korea, Federated States of Micronesia, Mongolia, New Zealand, Palau, Papua New Guinea, Samoa, Solomon Islands, and Vanuatu	7,542	3.46
17	India, casting the votes of	Bangladesh, India, and Sri Lanka	7,171	3.29
18	Pakistan, casting the votes of	Afghanistan, Algeria, Ghana, Islamic Republic of Iran, Morocco, Pakistan, and Tunisia	7,091	3.25
19	Switzerland, casting the votes of	Azerbaijan, Kazakhstan, Kyrgyz Republic, Poland, Serbia, Switzerland, Tajikistan, Turkmenistan, and Uzbekistan	6,914	3.17
20	São Tomé and Principe, casting the votes of	Benin, Burkina Faso, Cameroon, Cape Verde, Central African Republic, Chad, Democratic Republic of Congo, Republic of Congo, Côte d'Ivoire, Djibouti, Equatorial Guinea, Gabon, Guinea-Bissau, Mali, Mauritania, Mauritius, Senegal, and Togo	6,864	3.15
21	Indonesia, casting the votes of	Fiji, Indonesia, Lao People's Democratic Republic, Malaysia, Nepal, Singapore, Thailand, and Vietnam	6,452	2.96
22	Russian Federation, casting the votes of	Russian Federation	5,769	2.64
23	Saudi Arabia, casting the votes of	Saudi Arabia	5,769	2.64
24	Argentina, casting the votes of	Argentina, Bolivia, Chile, Paraguay, Peru, and Uruguay	5,731	2.63
25	South Africa	Angola, Nigeria, and South Africa	4,059	1.86
			218,212	100.00

Source: World Bank Group Corporate Secretariat.
Note: Individual percentages may not total 100 because of rounding. Guinea and Madagascar did not participate in the 2010 regular election of directors.

ADDITIONAL RESOURCES

World Bank and IFC regional websites serve as portals to country-specific websites or pages (box F.1). Those country-specific Web pages typically provide a brief summary of activities and issues in the country, with links to specific projects, economic data and statistics, publications, websites of the country's government, and related news.

The World Bank Group produces a number of free electronic products—including online collections of data and research tools; thematically focused, interactive electronic atlases; and mobile phone applications covering a range of topics (box F.2).

Additionally, the following resources are available:

- *Bank Group Offices.* For links to country office websites, go to http://www.worldbank.org/ and select the "Countries" tab.
- *Public Information Centers (PICs).* These centers disseminate information on the Bank Group's work. They are hosted in either the World Bank offices or in external organizations that work closely with the Bank. Most PICs have project documents and publications specific to the country in which the office is located and will generally have access to World Bank online databases. PIC Europe in Paris and PIC Tokyo offer the complete range of Bank operational documents for all member countries and maintain libraries of recent World Bank publications. For more information go to http://www.worldbank.org/reference/ and select "Public Information Centers" in the "Finding Publications" box.
- *World Bank Depository Libraries.* Each member country of the World Bank is entitled to at least one depository library. Additional depositories may be designated in developing countries. There are currently some 500 Depository Libraries in more than 100 countries, which provide public access to Bank publications, either in print or e-book, form free of charge. Download the World Bank InfoFinder iPad or iPhone app from iTunes, which contains a locator map of Depository Libraries and Public Information Centers http://itunes.apple.com/us/app/world-bank-infofinder/id387949223?mt=8 or go to http://www.worldbank.org/reference/ and select "Worldwide Depository Libraries" in the "Finding Publications" box.

■ *Distributors of World Bank Group Publications.* The Bank Group encourages customers outside the United States to order through local distributors. For a list of distributors go to http://www.worldbank.org/reference/ and select "Book Distibutors" in the "Finding Publications" box. The Bank Group also sells direct to all member countries.

Box F.1 Regional Websites

Sub-Saharan Africa
World Bank vice presidency: http://www.worldbank.org/afr
IFC regional department: http://www.ifc.org/africa

East Asia and the Pacific
World Bank vice presidency: http://www.worldbank.org/eap
IFC regional department: http://www.ifc.org/eastasia

South Asia
World Bank vice presidency: http://www.worldbank.org/sar
IFC regional department: http://www.ifc.org/southasia

Europe and Central Asia
World Bank vice presidency: http://www.worldbank.org/eca
IFC regional department: http://www.ifc.org/europe

Latin America and the Caribbean
World Bank vice presidency: http://www.worldbank.org/lac
IFC regional department: http://www.ifc.org/lac

Middle East and North Africa
World Bank vice presidency: http://www.worldbank.org/mena
IFC regional department: http://www.ifc.org/mena

Western Europe
World Bank Europe External Affairs: http://www.worldbank.org/europe

Box F.2 Electronic Products: Online Resources and Mobile Applications

ONLINE RESOURCES
World Bank eLibrary
http://elibrary.worldbank.org

The Complete World Development Report Online
http://wdronline.worldbank.org

World Bank Open Data
http://data.worldbank.org

WORLD BANK eATLASES
World Bank eAtlas of Global Development
http://data.worldbank.org/atlas-global

World Bank eAtlas of Millennium Development Goals
http://data.worldbank.org/mdg-atlas

WORLD BANK GROUP MOBILE APPS
The following mobile apps can be downloaded from the iTunes App Store.
Visit **bit.ly/WBmobile** for more information.

World Bank Results at a Glance
Available for iPhone.

World Bank InfoFinder
Available for iPad and iPhone.

World Bank DataFinder
Available for iPad and iPhone

Doing Business at a Glance
Available for iPhone
doingbusiness.org/iphone or download from the iTunes App Store

World Bank at a Glance
Available for iPhone

INDEX

Boxes, figures, maps, and tables are indicated by b, f, m, and t, respectively.

France (*continued*)
  KNA (Knowledge Networks Agency), 149
  voting power in IBRD, 10*f,* 231
fraud and corruption, 65*b,* 165–66
FTF (Financial Crisis Response Fast-Track Facility), IDA, 21
funding, 67–74
  of IBRD, 13–14, 67–68
  of ICSID, 73
  of IDA, 18–20, 19–20*t,* 67–68
  of IFC, 22, 68–73
  of MIGA, 68–73
  reporting requirements, 73–74

G

G-7 (Group of Seven), 20
G-20 (Group of 20), 17, 21, 179
GAFSP (Global Agriculture and Food Security Program), 161, 179
GAVI Alliance (formerly Global Alliance for Vaccines and Immunisation), 101–2
GDLN (Global Development Learning Network), 82, 186
GEF (Global Environment Facility), 77, 102, 134, 164, 173–74, 175
Gender and Development Group, 156
gender equality issues, 156, 181–82
GEO-CAN, 138
Germany
  IBRD board of executive directors and, 9
  as IDA donor, 68
  voting power in IBRD, 10*f,* 231
GGFR (Global Gas Flaring Reduction) Partnership, 175
GICT (Global Information and Communications Technology), 186
girls, education of, in South Asia, 156
Global Agriculture and Food Security Program (GAFSP), 161, 179
Global Alliance for Vaccines and Immunisation (now GAVI Alliance), 101–2
Global and regional partnership programs (GRPPs), 100
Global Development Finance, 87
Global Development Horizons, 87
Global Development Learning Network (GDLN), 82, 186

Global Environment Facility (GEF), 77, 102, 134, 164, 173–74, 175
Global Facility for Disaster Reduction and Recovery, 164
global financial crisis of 2008-09, 14–17, 21, 175–76
Global Financial Markets Department, IFC, 177
Global Food Price Crisis Response Program, 179
Global Fund to Fight AIDS, Tuberculosis, and Malaria, 77
Global Gas Flaring Reduction (GGFR) Partnership, 175
Global Industries Vice Presidency, IFC, 192–93
Global Information and Communications Technology (GICT), 186
Global Migration Group, 191
Global Monitoring Report, 54, 87
Global Partnership to Eliminate River Blindness, 184
Global Secondment Program, 104
Global Trade Finance Program, IFC, 121, 197
Google, World Bank Group collaboration with, 87
governance, 182–83
  corporate, 182–83
  East Asian and Pacific Regional Governance Hub, 129
  forest law enforcement and governance in Europe and North Asia, 134
  Initiative on Governing Development and Developing Governance in the Middle East and North Africa, 148–49
  public sector, 182
  in Sub-Saharan Africa, 119
  of World Bank Group, 7–10
governors, boards and councils of, 7–8
grants, 76–77
greenhouse gas emissions, reduction of, 138
GreenMachine, 154
Group of Seven (G-7), 20
Group of 20 (G-20), 17, 21, 179
GRPPs (Global and regional partnership programs), 100
guarantees, as financial service, 78, 80. *See also* Multilateral Investment Guarantee Agency

Eco-Audit

Environmental Benefits Statement

The World Bank is committed to preserving endangered forests and natural resources. The Office of the Publisher has chosen to print *A Guide to the World Bank* on recycled paper with 30 percent post-consumer waste, in accordance with the recommended standards for paper usage set by the Green Press Initiative, a nonprofit program supporting publishers in using fiber that is not sourced from endangered forests. For more information, visit www.greenpressinitiative.org.

Trees	Solid Waste	Water	Net Greenhouse Gases	Total Energy
20	564	8.885	1,970	8
	Pounds	Gallons	Pounds	Btu